National Key Publication Planning Project of the 14th Five-Year Plan
Hubei Special Funds for Academic and Public-interest Publications
Book Series on the Belt and Road Initiative and Issues Concerning China's National Rights and Interests
Editor-in-Chief: Yang Zewei

A Study on the Application of Law for the Joint Development of Offshore Oil and Gas Resources

By Zhang Sheng

Translated by Ma Bo, Tan Yusheng

CHICAGO ACADEMIC PRESS

A Study on the Application of Law for the Joint Development of Offshore Oil and Gas Resources
Author: Zhang Sheng
Translator: Ma Bo, Tan Yusheng
Language: English
Word Count: Approximately 622,000 words
Publisher: Chicago Academic Press
Number of Pages: 498
ISBN: 978-1-965890-78-3

Publishing	Chicago Academic Press
	5923 N Artesian Ave
	Chicago IL 60659
Email	contact@chicagoacademicpress.com
Website	http://chicagoacademicpress.com/
Book Size	6X9 inches
First Edition	

Author Profile

Zhang Sheng holds a Master of Philosophy from the University of Cambridge and a Doctor of Laws from Wuhan University. He previously served in the Ministry of Foreign Affairs, working successively in the Department of West European Affairs, the Chinese Embassy in Finland, the Department of European Affairs, and the General Office. He later joined the China National Offshore Oil Corporation (CNOOC), where he has long been engaged in foreign affairs management and international cooperation. His positions have included Senior Supervisor for Neighboring Affairs, Director of the Division of Neighboring Affairs, and Deputy Director of the Office of Neighboring Affairs and concurrently Director of the Division of Neighboring Affairs. He has led and participated in numerous special research projects commissioned by central government bodies such as the Office of the Central Commission for Foreign Affairs (Office of the Central Commission for Maritime Rights Protection) and the Ministry of Foreign Affairs. His project, An Empirical Study on the Joint Development in China's Neighboring Maritime Areas, received the National Energy Administration's Award for Excellence in Energy Soft Science Research. He has published numerous articles in journals such as the *Pacific Journal* and the *Journal of Boundary and Ocean Studies*, with his work being reprinted by the *Chinese Social Science Digest*. Furthermore, his research reports have been adopted and endorsed by institutions including the Standing Committee of the National People's Congress.

Book Series on the Belt and Road Initiative and Issues Concerning China's National Rights and Interests

01. A Study on the International Law Issues of the High-Quality Development of the Belt and Road Initiative

02. A Study on the Legal Issues Concerning Oil and Gas Pipeline Transit under the Belt and Road Initiative

03. A Study on the Belt and Road Initiative and China's Discourse Power in the International Rule of Law

04. A Study on the Coordination between China's Evolving National Identity and the Protection of Its Interests

05. A Study on the Rule of Effective Control in International Law

06. A Study on the Legal Issues in Global Ocean Governance

07. A Study on International Legal Issues Concerning Dispute Settlement Mechanisms for Joint Maritime Development

08. A Study on the Implementation of the United Nations Convention on the Law of the Sea in France

09. A Study on the International Legal Institutionalization of a Maritime Community with a Shared Future and Its Realization Path

10. A Study on the Legal Issues Concerning the Application of Straight Baselines

11. A Study on the International Legal Issues in the Maritime Delimitation of the Gulf of Thailand

12. A Study on the Application of Law for the Joint Development of Offshore Oil and Gas Resources

Yang Zewei, born in 1968 in Xinning, Hunan, is a Specially-Appointed Professor of a Major National Talent Program of the Ministry of Education, a Luojia Distinguished Scholar at Wuhan University, a Doctor of Laws, and a doctoral supervisor at the Wuhan University Institute of International Law. He is also the Chief Expert for the research team at the Wuhan University Academy of International Law and Global Governance (a national high-end think tank), and serves as the Chief Expert for several major state-funded projects, including Major Bidding Projects and Major Research Programs of the National Social Science Fund of China, and Major Research Projects in Philosophy and Social Sciences of the Ministry of Education. Recognized as a Young and Middle-aged Expert with Outstanding Contributions of Hubei Province, he has been a visiting scholar at the Max Planck Institute for Comparative Public Law and International Law in Germany and a visiting professor at the University of Dundee, UK. He was selected for the Ministry of Education's "New Century Excellent Talents" Support Program and has received funding from the Fok Ying Tung Education Foundation's Fund for Young Teachers in Higher Education. He concurrently serves as a member of the National Expert Committee on the Implementation of the Chemical

Weapons Convention. He is the Editor-in-Chief of the Book Series on New Energy Law and Policy Research (thirteen volumes) and the Book Series on International Cases and Practices in Joint Maritime Development (nine volumes). His sole-authored works include *Analysis of International Law* (Fifth Edition), *Study on the History of International Law* (Second Edition), *On Sovereignty*, *International Law* (Fourth Edition), and *On Legal Safeguard of China's Energy Security*. He has published dozens of academic papers in Chinese and English in journals such as the *Chinese Journal of Law*, *China Legal Science*, *World History*, the *Journal of East Asia & International Law* (SSCI), the *Hong Kong Law Journal* (SSCI), and the *Journal of the History of International Law*.

This book is one of the phased achievements of the 2022 Major Project of the Ministry of Education for Philosophy and Social Science Research, titled "The Regional Turn in Global Governance and the Practice of China's Participation in Asian Regional Organizations" (Project Approval No.: 22JZD040), led by Professor Yang Zewei.

General Preface to the "Book Series on the Belt and Road Initiative and Issues Concerning China's National Rights and Interests"

Since its proposal in 2013, the Belt and Road Initiative (BRI) has made globally recognized achievements and has had a widespread international impact. By February 2022, China had signed more than 200 intergovernmental cooperation agreements with 148 countries and 32 international organizations to jointly build the Belt and Road. Arguably, the BRI aligns with the new trend of international cooperation that has emerged in the 21st century, signals a new phase in the transformation of the international political order, and is a constructive effort to enhance China's voice in global affairs. The joint construction of the Belt and Road is becoming China's framework for participating in open global cooperation, improving the global economic governance system, promoting common development and prosperity worldwide, and building a community with a shared future for mankind. Moreover, as a new form of international cooperation under modern international law, a new platform for global governance, and a new dimension of trans-regional collaboration, the BRI has had a multifaceted impact on the development of modern international law.[1]

Meanwhile, China has become the world's second-largest economy, the largest manufacturer, the largest holder of foreign exchange reserves, the largest creditor nation, the largest trading nation in goods, the largest oil importer, the largest shipbuilding nation, and the largest global investor, with its economic dependence on foreign trade consistently remaining at around 60%. Furthermore, over 30,000 Chinese enterprises are spread across the globe, millions of Chinese citizens work, study, and live in every corner of the world, and in 2019, the number of outbound Chinese tourists reached 155 million, a figure that continues to rise annually. It is clear that the scope of China's national rights and interests is ever-expanding, and its overseas interests, in particular, have become a vital component of its overall national interests. Therefore, against this backdrop, the publication of the "Book Series on the Belt and Road Initiative and Issues Concerning China's National Rights and Interests" is of great significance.

First, it will provide theoretical support for implementing the 14th Five-Year Plan and realizing the Long-Range Objectives Through the Year 2035. General Secretary Xi Jinping emphasized at the Central Conference on Work Related to Overall Law-Based Governance in November 2020 that "we must coordinate the advancement of domestic rule of law and foreign-related rule

---

① Yang Zewei et al., *A Study on the Belt and Road Initiative and the International Rules System*, Law Press China, 2020, p. 22.

of law." The Outline of the 14th Five-Year Plan for National Economic and Social Development of the People's Republic of China and the Long-Range Objectives Through the Year 2035 proposes to "strengthen the construction of the foreign-related legal system and the cultivation of foreign-related legal talent." China's Long-Range Objectives Through the Year 2035 include "basically realizing the modernization of the national governance system and governance capacity" and "basically building a country, government, and society under the rule of law." The foreign-related legal system is a vital aspect of modernizing the national governance system and capacity and of building a country, government, and society based on the rule of law. This book series, by focusing on topics such as "Legal Issues in Global Ocean Governance," "International Law Issues of Dispute Settlement Mechanisms for Joint Maritime Development," and "Legal Issues Concerning the Application of Straight Baselines," will contribute to improving China's foreign-related legislative system through the coordinated application of international law. This will in turn form a well-functioning system that is complementary to domestic rule of law, thereby helping to achieve the goals of the 14th Five-Year Plan and the Long-Range Objectives Through the Year 2035.

Secondly, it will provide intellectual support in the field of international law for promoting the high-quality development of the Belt and Road. The Fifth Plenary Session of the 19th Central Committee of the Communist Party of China explicitly proposed to continue expanding opening-up, uphold multilateralism and the principle of extensive consultation, joint contribution, and shared benefits, advance the reform of global governance, and promote the building of a community with a shared future for humankind. This book series covers topics such as "The Belt and Road Initiative and the Issue of China's Discursive Power in the International Rule of Law" and "Legal Issues Concerning the Transit of Oil and Gas Pipelines in the Context of the Belt and Road Initiative." In-depth research on these issues not only responds to the major concerns of the Chinese international law academia but will also provide intellectual support from an international law perspective for advancing the high-quality development of the Belt and Road.

Thirdly, it will provide international legal safeguards for the protection of China's national rights and interests. Effectively safeguarding China's national sovereignty, security, and development interests, substantially protecting its national rights and interests, and jointly addressing global risks and challenges are among the key tasks of the 14th Five-Year Plan. General Secretary Xi Jinping has specifically pointed out: "We must strengthen our rule-of-law thinking, employ rule-of-law methods to effectively respond to challenges and guard against risks, and comprehensively utilize legislative, law enforcement, and judicial means to carry out struggles and resolutely safeguard national sovereignty, dignity, and core interests."② In view of this,

---

② Xi Jinping, Steadfastly Follow the Path of Socialist Rule of Law with Chines

this book series covers topics such as "The Coordination Between China's Changing National Identity and Interest Protection" and "A Study on the Rule of Effective Control in International Law," offering answers for how to actively apply international law to effectively respond to external challenges and safeguard China's national rights and interests.

Finally, it will also help to further improve the foreign relations legal system with Chinese characteristics. The law on foreign relations is an important component of the socialist legal system with Chinese characteristics and serves as the legal basis for handling various foreign-related disputes. Foreign-related rule of law is a key aspect of overall law-based governance and the "smart power" for safeguarding China's national rights and interests. However, since the founding of the People's Republic of China, while China's foreign relations legal system has continuously developed, it is not without its shortcomings. As the Belt and Road Initiative continues to advance, this system is in need of further improvement. This book series, by exploring topics such as "The Belt and Road Initiative and the Issue of China's Discursive Power in the International Rule of Law," "Legal Issues in Global Ocean Governance," "Legal Issues Concerning the Transit of Oil and Gas Pipelines in the Context of the Belt and Road Initiative," and "International Law Issues of Dispute Settlement Mechanisms for Joint

---

e Characteristics and Provide a Strong Legal Guarantee for Building a Modern S ocialist Country in All Respects: Speech at the Central Conference on Work Rela ted to Overall Law-Based Governance, *Qiushi*, Issue 5, 2021.

Maritime Development," is not only conducive to the improvement of China's foreign relations legal system but will also provide international legal safeguards for China's active participation in the reform of the global governance system and the promotion of building a community with a shared future for humankind.

In summary, the publication of the "Book Series on the Belt and Road Initiative and Issues Concerning China's National Rights and Interests" will help to deepen research on related theoretical issues in international law, enhance China's discursive power in the development and improvement of the international legal order, and better safeguard and protect China's national rights and interests.

As a publisher renowned at home and abroad, Wuhan University Press has always offered its full support for the publication of academic works. Zhang Xin is a commissioning editor with a true passion for scholarship. These unique advantages have ensured the smooth publication of this book series. On this occasion, all authors of this series would like to express their sincere gratitude to the leadership of the Press and to Zhang Xin. Furthermore, as the series covers novel and wide-ranging topics, and most of its authors are emerging scholars, it may inevitably contain shortcomings or errors. We sincerely welcome any corrections from our readers.

Yang Zewei③

February 19, 2022

Wuhan University Institute of International Law

③ Yang Zewei is a Specially-Appointed Professor of the Ministry of Education's National Major Talent Program, a Luojia Distinguished Scholar, a Professor (Level II), and a doctoral supervisor at the Wuhan University Institute of International Law. He holds a Ph.D. in Law. He serves as the Chief Expert at the Wuhan University Academy of International Law and Global Governance, a national high-end think tank. He is also the Chief Expert for Major Tendered Projects and Special Major Research Projects of the National Social Science Fund of China, as well as for Major Projects of Philosophy and Social Sciences Research of the Ministry of Education.

Table of Contents

Introduction

I. Statement of the Problem

On January 5, 2023, the Joint Statement of the People's Republic of China and the Republic of the Philippines explicitly stated: "In the area of oil and gas cooperation, both sides agreed to bear in mind the spirit of the Memorandum of Understanding on Cooperation on Oil and Gas Development between the Government of the People's Republic of China and the Government of the Republic of the Philippines signed in 2018, and, based on the outcomes already achieved, to resume negotiations on maritime oil and gas development at an early date for the benefit of both countries and their peoples."① Clearly, the governments of China and the Philippines hold a positive attitude toward the joint development of offshore oil and gas resources. Therefore, this issue has once again garnered public attention.

In fact, as early as the late 1970s, the Chinese government put forward the initiative of "sovereignty belongs to China, shelving disputes and pursuing joint development." This was an attempt to find a practical and feasible way to maintain regional peace and stability, meet practical needs, achieve mutual benefit, and safeguard national sovereignty, all before the disputes over islands and maritime rights and interests with its maritime neighbors could be resolved. In 2005, the governments of China and North Korea signed the Sino-North Korean Agreement on the Joint Development

① Joint Statement of the People's Republic of China and the Republic of the Philippines (January 5, 2023), from the website of the Ministry of Foreign Affairs https://www.fmprc.gov.cn/zyxw/202301/t20230105_11001029.shtml.

of Maritime Petroleum. This was the first agreement on the joint development of offshore oil and gas resources that China concluded with one of its maritime neighbors. That same year, the China National Offshore Oil Corporation (CNOOC) and the Vietnam Oil and Gas Group (PetroVietnam) also signed the Framework Agreement on Oil and Gas Cooperation in the Beibu Gulf in Hanoi, Vietnam. In June 2008, China and Japan reached the Principled Consensus on the East China Sea Issue.② In October 2013, China and Brunei issued the Joint Statement of the People's Republic of China and Brunei Darussalam, in which the two countries decided to further deepen their relations and agreed to support their relevant enterprises in carrying out joint maritime development for the exploration and exploitation of offshore oil and gas resources. Shortly thereafter, China and Vietnam issued the Joint Statement on Deepening the China-Vietnam Comprehensive Strategic Cooperative Partnership in the New Era. In it, both sides agreed to actively study and negotiate the issue of joint development and to establish a working group for consultations on joint maritime development under the framework of their government-level delegation for boundary negotiations. In line with the principle of tackling easier issues before difficult ones and proceeding in

② The main points of the Principled Consensus on the East China Sea Issue inc lude: First, cooperation in the East China Sea shall not prejudice the respective l egal positions of either side. Second, the two sides will engage in joint developm ent in a designated block in the central-northern part of the East China Sea and will continue consultations on joint development in other parts of the East China Sea. Third, Japanese corporations will participate in the development of the Chun xiao oil and gas field in accordance with relevant Chinese laws on foreign coope ration in the exploitation of offshore petroleum resources. See "China and Japan Reach Principled Consensus on East China Sea Issue" (Xinhua News Agency, Be ijing, June 18, 2008), published in *People's Daily*, June 19, 2008, p. 4.

a step-by-step manner, they would steadily advance the delimitation negotiations for the waters outside the mouth of the Beibu Gulf and actively promote joint development in that maritime area. In November 2014, during separate meetings with Sultan Hassanal Bolkiah of Brunei and Prime Minister Najib Razak of Malaysia, who were attending the 22nd APEC Economic Leaders' Meeting, Chinese President Xi Jinping also noted that "China is willing to strengthen maritime cooperation with Brunei and push for substantive progress on joint development in the South China Sea at an early date," and that China and Malaysia "should advance maritime cooperation and joint development to promote regional peace, stability, and prosperity." In November 2015, the China-Vietnam Joint Statement again emphasized: "The two sides will steadily advance the negotiations on the delimitation of the maritime area outside the mouth of the Beibu Gulf and actively promote joint development in this maritime area; they agree to intensify the negotiations of the working group for the area outside the mouth of the Beibu Gulf, continue to advance the work of the working group for consultation on joint maritime development, and strengthen cooperation in less sensitive areas." From October 30 to November 1, 2022, Nguyen Phu Trong, General Secretary of the Central Committee of the Communist Party of Vietnam, paid an official visit to China. The subsequently issued Joint Statement on Further Strengthening and Deepening the China-Vietnam Comprehensive Strategic Cooperative Partnership clearly stated: "The two sides agreed to continue to abide by the important consensus reached by the leaders of the two Parties and two countries and the Agreement on Basic Principles Guiding the Settlement of Maritime Issues between China and Vietnam... actively consult on transitional and temporary solutions that do not affect the respective positions and propositions of either side... actively advance consultations on joint maritime development and consultations on the delimitation of the waters outside the mouth of the Beibu Gulf, and work to achieve substantive progress in these two tasks at an early date; the two sides are willing to continue to actively carry out cooperation in less sensitive maritime areas."③

However, viewing China's surrounding maritime areas as a whole, the joint development of offshore oil and gas resources has struggled to advance and has yet to be truly realized.④ While the reasons for this are certainly multifaceted, legal obstacles—including the issue of applicable law for joint development—are one of the significant contributing factors. Therefore, studying the issues of the application of law for the joint development of offshore oil and gas resources undoubtedly holds great theoretical value and practical significance.

---

③ See the Joint Statement on Further Strengthening and Deepening the China-Vietnam Comprehensive Strategic Cooperative Partnership (November 1, 2022), from the website of the Ministry of Foreign Affairs https://www.fmprc.gov.cn/zyxw/202211/t20221102_10795594.shtml.

④ See Yang Zewei, General Preface to the Book Series on International Cases and Practice of Joint Maritime Development, in Dong Shijie, *A Study on the Legal Issues of Existing Petroleum Contracts in Disputed Maritime Areas*, Wuhan University Press, 2019, p. 2.

II. Significance of the Research

This study possesses significant theoretical value and practical importance, as outlined below.

(I) Theoretical Value

1. The research findings of this book will help to further deepen the study of theoretical issues related to the joint development of offshore oil and gas resources. From the perspective of international law, the question of whether the joint development of offshore oil and gas resources constitutes customary international law will affect the policies of the relevant countries and the direction of their actual maritime activities; the principles of international law that must be followed for joint development serve as the basis and frame of reference for the negotiations and practices of the countries involved; and after a joint development agreement for offshore oil and gas resources is reached, the domestic laws of the relevant countries must be adjusted according to the agreement. Therefore, this book attempts to systematically review the formation and development of the concept of joint development of offshore oil and gas resources and related practices. On this basis, it delves into theoretical issues, such as whether the joint development of offshore oil and gas resources is evolving toward customary international law, as well as the issues of the application of law for such development. This will undoubtedly help to advance the current level of research on theoretical issues concerning the joint development of offshore oil and gas resources.

2. The research findings of this book will also help to broaden perspectives on fundamental theoretical issues in international law, such as the relationship between international law and domestic law and the domestic application of the former. The interplay between international and domestic law, along with the question of how international law is applied domestically, has always been one of the most foundational and critical theoretical problems in the field of international law and a subject of considerable debate within China's legal academia and among its practitioners.⑤ Therefore, studying the issues of the application of law for the joint development of offshore oil and gas resources not only involves questions regarding the application of international treaties, international petroleum development contracts, and special laws, but also offers new approaches and broadens our perspectives on how to properly manage the relationship between international and domestic law.

(II) Practical Significance

1. The research findings of this book will provide policy recommendations on the issue of law application for the future joint

---

⑤ For example, regarding the application of international treaties in China, Artic le 142, Paragraph 2 of the *General Principles of the Civil Law* stipulated: "If an international treaty concluded or acceded to by the People's Republic of China c ontains provisions different from those in the civil laws of the People's Republic of China, the provisions of the international treaty shall apply, except for the cla uses on which the People's Republic of China has declared a reservation." This provision in the *General Principles of the Civil Law* was, in effect, a standard a pproach in China's domestic law concerning the application of international treatie s. However, the *Civil Code of the People's Republic of China*, which came into effect on January 1, 2021, lacks specific provisions on the validity and applicatio n of international treaties in China.

development of offshore oil and gas resources between China and its neighboring countries. To date, China has engaged in contacts, attempts, and discussions regarding the joint development of offshore oil and gas resources with maritime neighbors such as Vietnam, the Philippines, and Japan, while other pairs of countries, like Vietnam and Malaysia, and Japan and South Korea, have practical experience in joint development with each other. Therefore, by systematically summarizing existing international practices of joint development of offshore oil and gas resources and identifying the commonalities and patterns in issues of law application, this book can offer important reference and inspiration for future joint development of offshore oil and gas resources between China and its neighboring countries.

2. The research findings of this book will provide intellectual support for a breakthrough in the joint development of offshore oil and gas resources between China and its neighboring countries. Based on a systematic review of the relevant issues of law application, this book will focus on discussing strategic choices for China's joint development of offshore oil and gas resources: how to design negotiation plans on this issue; how to accurately determine the bottom lines that must be upheld and the boundaries where concessions can be made; key issues to be considered when designing cooperation models; and how to resolve the challenges concerning law application that may be encountered during the implementation process. It is self-evident that in-depth research on these issues will provide the intellectual support needed for a breakthrough in the joint development of offshore oil

and gas resources between China and its neighboring countries.

III. Current State of Domestic and International Research

Since Bahrain and Saudi Arabia signed the Agreement Concerning the Delimitation of the Continental Shelf in the Persian Gulf in February 1958, establishing the world's first regime for the joint development of offshore oil and gas resources, a considerable body of scholarly work on the theory and practice of the subject has emerged in academia, both in China and internationally.

(I) On the Origin of Joint Development of Offshore Oil and Gas Resources

Current studies in international law on the origin and development of the joint development of offshore oil and gas resources typically take the 1958 joint development case between Bahrain and Saudi Arabia as their starting point.[⑥] However, in reality, no concept emerges or finds its practical application in a vacuum. The foundation for the joint development of offshore oil and gas resources lies in the prior evolution of the oil and gas industry and the practices established within it. Nonetheless, while research and discussion in this area by scholars in China and abroad have been

⑥ See Yang Zewei (ed.), *A Study on the Theory and Practice of International Law on Joint Maritime Development*, Wuhan University Press, 2018, p. 2.

relatively cursory, it is fortunate that some have already noted the relationship between the "rule of capture" and the origins of joint development for offshore oil and gas resources.

The application of the "rule of capture" as a principle of property rights for oil and gas resources emerged alongside the development of the modern oil and gas industry in the United States. As one scholar notes: "The rule of capture appears at the very beginning of the chain of events that has brought us to where we are today, and it has given rise, directly or indirectly, to the characteristic patterns of behavior of oil companies large and small, which in turn have shaped the corrective responses made by government. Like it or not, the rule of capture stands at the starting point of the path of development that the oil industry has in fact taken."[⑦] Initially, this principle stimulated the rapid development of the oil and gas industry[⑧], but it ultimately led to disorderly and irrational development, causing severe resource waste, environmental degradation, and economic losses for developers. This, in turn, drove developers of adjacent tracts to seek cooperation, and the concept of unitized or cooperative development gradually emerged.[⑨] The 1958 joint development case between Bahrain and Saudi Arabia represented a successful attempt to transplant this form of cooperation on transboundary

---

⑦ See [UK] Aileen McHarg et al. (eds.), *Property and Law in Energy and Natu ral Resources*, trans. by Hu Desheng, Wei Tiejun, et al. Peking University Press, 2014, p. 195.

⑧ See Zhen Xingbiao, A Study on the Rule of Capture in the U.S. Oil and Ga s System, Master's thesis of Shanxi University, 2016, pp. 6-7.

⑨ See Vasco Becker-Weinberg, *Joint Development of Hydrocarbon Deposits in th e Law of the Sea*, Springer-Verlag Berlin Heidelberg 2014, pp. 10-18.

deposits from domestic practice to the interstate level. This drew the attention of international law scholars ⑩ and was subsequently noted by the International Court of Justice, being cited by Judge Jessup in the North Sea Continental Shelf Cases (Federal Republic of Germany/Denmark, Federal Republic of Germany/the Netherlands).[11] Thereafter, more instances of joint development of offshore oil and gas resources appeared, leading to the evolution of new concepts and practices in international law: namely, the unitization of transboundary deposits and the joint development of disputed maritime areas. While most scholars believe that the rule of capture does not exist in international law[12], some still argue that the rule of capture is applicable within the framework of international law[13]; or, at the very least, that the underlying logic behind the actions of certain states—seeking to maximize their own interests and intensify exploration and development efforts in matters involving the joint development of transboundary oil and gas resources and resources in disputed maritime areas—is still based on the rule of capture[14].

---

⑩ See William T. Onorato, Apportionment of an International Common Petroleum Deposit, *International and Comparative Law Quarterly*, Vol. 17, 1968, pp. 85-102.

11 See Separate Opinion of Judge Jessup, in "the North Sea Continental Shelf Cases (Federal Republic of Germany/Denmark, Federal Republic of Germany/the Netherlands)", available at https://www.icj-cij.org/public/files/case-related/51/051-19690220-JUD-01-03-EN.pdf.

12 See Masahiro Miyoshi, The Basic Concept of Joint Development of Hydrocarbon Resources on the Continental Shelf: With Special Reference to the Discussions at the East-West Centre Workshops on the South-East Asian Seas, *International Journal of Estuarine and Coastal Law*, Vol. 3, No.1, 1988, p.6.

13 See Joseph W. Morris, the North Sea Continental shelf: Oil and Gas Legal Problems, *International Lawyer*. Vol. 2, 1967, p. 206.

14 See Youri van Logchem, The Status of a Rule of Capture Under International

(II) On the Definition of Joint Development of Offshore Oil and Gas Resources

Defining the concept of the joint development of offshore oil and gas resources is a prerequisite for any research into the related legal issues. Therefore, the definition of "joint development of offshore oil and gas resources" has been a subject of extensive discussion in academia, both in China and internationally.

Scholars in China and abroad have distinguished between broad and narrow definitions of the joint development of offshore oil and gas resources. As for the broad definition, the view of the Chinese scholar Pan Shiying is quite representative. He argues that joint development, in its broad sense, refers to exploration and development activities for the natural resources of a region by two or more administrative units. In this context, "administrative units" can refer to sovereign states, as well as transnational or domestic enterprises or corporate groups; "the region" can be either disputed or undisputed, and can be on land or at sea; and "natural resources" can be biological, non-biological, or both.[15] However, this definition is clearly too broad, as it encompasses all forms of resource cooperation among states and enterprises, and is therefore generally not adopted by researchers.

Law of the Sea with regard to Offshore Oil and Gas Resource Related Activities, *Michigan State International Law Review*, Vol. 26.2, 2018, p. 203.

15 Quoted in Xiao Jianguo, *Joint Development of Petroleum on International Maritime Boundaries*, China Ocean Press, 2006, pp. 15-16.

In its narrow sense, the concept of the joint development of offshore oil and gas resources is a highly strict definition, referring exclusively to joint development conducted by states on the basis of an agreement in disputed maritime areas that have not yet been delimited or are subject to overlapping claims. For example, the Chinese scholar Gao Zhiguo, a former judge of the International Tribunal for the Law of the Sea, states: "Joint development refers to an intergovernmental agreement between two or more states to jointly exercise sovereignty and jurisdiction in an area of overlapping territorial dispute that has not been delimited, for the purpose of developing and apportioning its potential natural resources." [16] Japanese scholar Masahiro Miyoshi emphasizes: "Joint development is a provisional intergovernmental arrangement of a functional nature, which aims at the joint exploration and/or exploitation of hydrocarbon resources of the seabed beyond the territorial sea."[17] German professor Rainer Lagoni considers offshore joint development to be a form of interstate economic cooperation, based on an agreement, for the purpose of exploiting the non-living resources of a disputed maritime area.[18] British scholar Hazel Fox and others argue that: "Joint development is an agreement between two states to develop and

16 See Gao Zhiguo, The Legal Concept and Aspects of Joint Development in International Law, in *Ocean Yearbook*, Vol. 13, the University of Chicago Press, 1998, p.112.
17 See Masahiro Miyoshi, The Joint Development of Offshore Oil and Gas in Relation to Maritime Boundary Delimitation, Maritime Briefing (International Boundaries Research Unit), Vol. 2, No. 5, 1999, p.3.
18 See Rainer Lagoni, Oil and Gas Deposits Across National Frontiers, *American Journal of International Law*, Vol. 73, 1979, p.215.

share the offshore oil and gas resources of the continental shelf seabed and subsoil over which one or both of them hold sovereign rights under international law, to be achieved through interstate cooperation and domestic measures, with these resources being shared in a specified area according to an agreed-upon proportion; if the parties agree to extend the concept to the exclusive economic zone (EEZ), the aforementioned cooperation may also be implemented in overlapping areas of their EEZs."[19]

In addition, there is a definition slightly broader than the narrow concept, which defines joint development as "the exploration or development by sovereign states, based on an agreement and through some form of cooperation, of a common mineral deposit that either straddles their mutual maritime boundary or is located in a disputed area." The core of this definition lies in its inclusion of both the exploration and development of disputed areas prior to delimitation and the unitization of single transboundary deposits after delimitation. This view is held by scholars such as Dutch professor Bernard Taverne, and Chinese scholars Ambassador Xiao Jianguo and Professor Yang Zewei.[20] Because the provisional arrangements for disputed areas before delimitation and the unitization of transboundary deposits after delimitation—two scenarios that arise in international

19 See Hazel Fox etc. ed., Joint Development of Offshore Oil and Gas: A Mode l Agreement for States for Joint Development with Explanatory Commentary, Brit ish Institute of International and Comparative Law 1989, pp. 43-45.

20 See Xiao Jianguo, *Joint Development of Petroleum on International Maritime Boundaries*, China Ocean Press, 2006, pp. 14, 16; Yang Zewei (ed.), *Research on International Law Issues of Joint Maritime Development*, Social Sciences Acade mic Press (China), 2016, p. 1.

practice—share considerable commonalities, and because the joint development of a disputed area can transform into the unitization of a transboundary deposit once a boundary is set, researching, discussing, and summarizing the issues of offshore joint development under this slightly broader definition holds significant academic value and practical relevance. The research in this book on the legal issues applicable to the joint development of offshore oil and gas resources also proceeds from this definition.

Additionally, some domestic scholars have specifically explored from an international law perspective issues such as the concept, objectives, and characteristics of the joint development regime for offshore petroleum resources, as seen in works like "The Joint Development Regime for Disputed Maritime Areas—An Exposition Starting from Comrade Deng Xiaoping's Diplomatic Thought on the Peaceful Settlement of International Disputes" by Wan Xia and Song Dong.[21]

(III) On the Scope of Joint Development of Offshore Oil and Gas Resources

The general consensus in both Chinese and international academia is that the scope of joint maritime development—whether considered from the evolution of the concept itself or from an analysis of relevant international

21 See Wan Xia and Song Dong, The Joint Development Regime for Disputed Maritime Areas—An Exposition Starting from Comrade Deng Xiaoping's Diplomatic Thought on the Peaceful Settlement of International Disputes, *Pacific Journal*, 2007, Issue 6, pp. 34-40.

practices—primarily pertains to the joint development of offshore oil and gas resources. However, some scholars have pointed out that, based on recent international practice, the scope of joint maritime development is gradually extending from oil and gas resources to other fields, such as living resources and maritime tourism.[22] In practice, relevant national decision-making bodies have also proposed that the scope of joint maritime development should be expanded to a broader range of activities, including tourism and fisheries, and not be confined merely to oil and gas resources.

In my view, joint maritime development originated from the development of offshore oil and gas resources. By virtue of their fluidity, these resources are distinct from typical solid mineral resources.[23] The development of transboundary offshore oil and gas, in particular directly affects the rights and interests of neighboring countries, and the issues involved in its resolution are more numerous and complex. Fishery resources, due to their migratory nature, can also give rise to transboundary development issues. Maritime tourism resources, which can be defined as secondary economic resources derived from marine resources, differ from

22 See Yang Zewei, On the Developing Trends of Joint Maritime Development, *Oriental Law*, 2014, Issue 3, pp. 71-79; Yang Zewei (ed.), *A Study on the Theor y and Practice of International Law on Joint Maritime Development*, Wuhan Uni versity Press, 2018, pp. 15-17.

23 Some scholars point out that for solid resources such as coal, even if they ex ist in a transboundary formation, each state can fully develop the resource within its own jurisdiction in accordance with its own laws, generally without harming t he rights and interests of a neighboring state. See Masahiro Miyoshi, The Basic Concept of Joint Development of Hydrocarbon Resources on the Continental Shel f: With Special Reference to the Discussions at the East-West Centre Workshops on the South-East Asian Seas, *International Journal of Estuarine and Coastal La w*, Vol. 3, No.1, 1988, p.6.

natural resources that are directly exploitable. The joint development of these two distinct types of resources can, to a certain extent, be considered transboundary in nature, or as involving resources that are difficult to confine within even clear boundaries during their actual development and utilization. In this respect, their development is comparable to that of oil and gas. Therefore, as far as current international practice is concerned, oil and gas resources remain the primary subject of joint maritime development and are the central topic discussed in this book.

(IV) On the Issue of International Law Applicable to the Joint Development of Offshore Oil and Gas Resources

Regarding the international law applicable to the joint development of offshore oil and gas resources, the most fiercely debated question in both Chinese and international academia is whether this practice has become customary international law. [24] Many scholars maintain that the joint development of offshore oil and gas resources has indeed become a rule of customary international law. [25] For example, William T. Onorato, an American petroleum law expert and senior consultant to the World Bank, was one of the earliest scholars to address the issue of joint development and is also the one with the most radical views on the subject. He argues that the

24 See Yang Zewei, On the Developing Trends of Joint Maritime Development, *Oriental Law*, 2014, Issue 3, p. 77.
25 See David M. Ong, Joint Development of Common Offshore Oil and Gas De posits: "Mere" State Practice or Customary International Law? *The American Jour nal of International Law*, Vol. 93, No. 4, 1999, p. 800.

joint exploration and development of oil and gas resources within a common deposit constitutes customary international law and is mandatory.[26] The Chinese scholar Gao Zhiguo holds a similar view, having pointed out that "joint maritime development is an emerging rule of customary international law."[27]

Other scholars, however, hold the opposite view.[28] For example, Rainer Lagoni, a German professor of international law at the Kiel University, and the Japanese scholar Masahiro Miyoshi maintain that active cooperation to jointly develop a common deposit is not a principle of customary international law; rather, joint development is an action driven by considerations of practical interest, not by legal compulsion. They argue that what international law does establish as legal obligations or responsibilities for the states concerned are the duties to adopt a cooperative approach, to avoid unilateral actions regarding resource development in transboundary deposits or areas of overlapping claims, and to negotiate in good faith.[29]

26 See William T. Onorato, Apportionment of an International Common Petroleu m Deposit, *International and Comparative Law Quarterly*, Vol. 17, 1968, p. 85; William T. Onorato, Apportionment of an International Common Petroleum Depos it, *International and Comparative Law Quarterly*, Vol. 26, 1977, pp. 324-337.

27 Gao Zhiguo, The Legal Concept and Aspects of Joint Development in Interna tional Law, Nonliving Resources, 1998, p.123.

28 See Rainer Lagoni, Oil and Deposit Across National Frontiers, *American Jour nal of International Law*, Vol. 73, No.2, 1979, p.215; Masahiro Miyoshi, The Bas ic Concept of Joint Development of Hydrocarbon Resources on the Continental S helf: With Special Reference to the Discussions at the East-West Centre Worksho ps on the South-East Asian Seas, *International Journal of Estuarine and Coastal Law*, Vol. 3, No.1, 1988, pp. 8-18; Beckman etc. ed., *Beyond Territorial Disputes in the South China Sea: Legal Framework for the Joint Development of Hydroc arbon Resources*, Edward Elgar Publishing Limited 2013, p. 111.

29 See Masahiro Miyoshi, The Basic Concept of Joint Development of Hydrocar bon Resources on the Continental Shelf: With Special Reference to the Discussio

Professor Zhang Hui of Wuhan University holds a similar view, arguing that joint development does not constitute customary international law and that its legal basis can only derive from treaty agreements among the states concerned—that is, from a coordinated consensus of the parties' wills.[30]

Furthermore, some scholars argue that the joint development of offshore oil and gas resources is evolving into a rule of customary international law.[31] For example, Professor Yang Zewei of Wuhan University contends that "although it is still premature to conclude that the joint development of offshore oil and gas resources has fully become a rule of customary international law, the trend of its evolution in this direction is indeed clear."[32] Other scholars abroad hold similar views.[33]

(V) On Issues of Domestic Law Applicable to the Joint Development of Offshore Oil and Gas Resources

In existing cases of joint development of offshore oil and gas resources, the management models can be classified from the perspective of oil and gas

ns at the East-West Centre Workshops on the South-East Asian Seas, *International Journal of Estuarine and Coastal Law*, Vol. 3, No.1, 1988, pp. 9-10.

30 See Zhang Hui, A Study on the Fundamental Issues of Joint Development in China's Surrounding Disputed Maritime Areas, *Wuhan University International Law Review*, Vol. 16, 2013, pp. 47-49.

31 See Yu Hui, Joint Development of Mineral Resources—An Asian Solution, *Asian Yearbook of International Law*, Vol. 2, 1994, p. 104; Yu Hui, International Law Issues on the Joint Development of Marine Mineral Resources, *Chinese Yearbook of International Law*, 1994, p. 60.

32 Yang Zewei, On the Developing Trends of Joint Maritime Development, *Oriental Law*, 2014, Issue 3, p. 79.

33 See S. P. Jagota, Maritime Boundary and Joint Development Zones: Emerging Trends, Nonliving Resources, 1993, p. 131.

operation management. The joint development management models for offshore oil and gas resources can be categorized into three types: the agency model, the supranational management model, and the joint operation model. The agency model is one in which one state party manages development activities and affairs within the joint development zone on behalf of both parties, with the other party sharing in the proceeds; the supranational management model is one in which the states, through an agreement, transfer their jurisdiction over the joint development zone to an established joint management authority, which is given full responsibility for all relevant management; and the joint operation model is one where each state retains its right to grant licenses or concessions for resource exploration and development, and the concessionaires of each state are responsible for exploration and development of resources within their respective licensed areas and cooperate through a joint operating agreement.[34] Under the different management models for the joint development of offshore oil and gas resources, the choice of applicable law also varies. One approach is for the parties to the agreement to apply the laws of one of the countries, as in the model for the joint development between Malaysia and Vietnam. A second approach is to establish a new, special legal regime and management authority to govern the joint development zone, such as the cooperative model in the case of joint development between Malaysia and Thailand.[35] A

34 See Deng Niya, *A Study on the Legal Issues of Management Models for Join t Maritime Development*, Wuhan University Press, 2019.

35 For a comparison of the Malaysia-Vietnam and Malaysia-Thailand cooperative

third is a hybrid approach, which includes the model used in the Japan-South Korea joint development case, where the joint development zone is divided into several sub-blocks, with the laws of different countries applying to different blocks. It also includes the model of applying the laws of different countries according to the subject matter, such as criminal jurisdiction, civil jurisdiction, customs, immigration and quarantine, and taxation.[36] A number of younger domestic scholars, such as Deng Niya[37], He Hairong[38], and Dong Shijie[39], have in their respective publications, discussed in considerable depth and from various perspectives the issues of law application under these different management models.

Notably, Professor Yang Zewei has explored in considerable detail the issue of law application for the joint development of offshore oil and gas resources. He argues that scenarios involving the application of law relate

---

models, see Yang Zewei (ed.), *A Study on the Theory and Practice of International Law on Joint Maritime Development*, Wuhan University Press, 2018, pp. 350-368; He Hairong, *A Study on the Legal Issues of Joint Maritime Development in the Gulf of Thailand*, Wuhan University Press, 2020.

36 See Yang Zewei (ed.), *Research on International Law Issues of Joint Maritime Development*, Social Sciences Academic Press (China), 2016, pp. 42-52; see David M. Ong, Implications of Recent Southeast Asian State Practice for the International Law on Offshore Joint Development, in Beckman etc. ed., *Beyond Territorial Disputes in the South China Sea: Legal Framework for the Joint Development of Hydrocarbon Resources*, Edward Elgar Publishing Limited 2013, pp. 191-204.

37 See Deng Niya, *A Study on the Legal Issues of Management Models for Joint Maritime Development*, Wuhan University Press, 2019.

38 See He Hairong, *A Study on the Legal Issues of Joint Maritime Development in the Gulf of Thailand*, Wuhan University Press, 2020.

39 See Dong Shijie, The Application of Law in Joint Maritime Development Zones, *Wuhan University International Law Review*, Vol. 17, 2015, pp. 69-87; Dong Shijie, *A Study on the Legal Issues of Existing Petroleum Contracts in Disputed Maritime Areas*, Wuhan University Press, 2019.

primarily to two contexts: the joint development of oil and gas resources in disputed maritime areas and the joint development of transboundary offshore oil and gas resources. Drawing on a comprehensive review of international practice since 1958, he identifies three main types of legal application: separate, joint, and hybrid. The laws applicable to joint development of offshore oil and gas resources consist chiefly of international law, international petroleum development contracts, special laws, and domestic law. In the future, China should select a choice-of-law model for the joint development of offshore gas resources that is favorable to protecting its national interests.[40] His perspectives have offered significant inspiration for the writing of this book.

In sum, a significant body of valuable research on the joint development of offshore oil and gas resources and its law application already exists in both Chinese and international academia. These works provide a solid foundation for the research and further exploration conducted in this book, and the perspectives offered in some of these studies have served as a major source of inspiration. Needless to say, however, there is still potential for the existing body of research on this topic to be further expanded and deepened.

First, the depth of existing research could be further explored. For example, while domestic scholars have produced a relatively large number

40 See Yang Zewei, On the Issue of Applicable Law in Joint Maritime Develop ment Zones, *Journal of Guangxi University (Philosophy and Social Sciences)*, 201 5, Issue 4, pp. 71-78.

of articles from the perspective of international law or international relations on maritime delimitation and joint development in the East and South China Seas, there are comparatively few books and articles that provide an in-depth analysis of the issue of law application for the joint development of offshore oil and gas resources. In terms of articles, Jia Yu, in "Issues and Prospects of Joint Development in the East China Sea between China and Japan," analyzes the history and current realities of joint development in the East China Sea, pointing out that joint development is a provisional arrangement pending delimitation and that political will is the key factor in achieving joint development. He also offered an outlook on the prospects for joint development between China and Japan in the East China Sea.[41] The most notable feature of Zhou Zhonghai's article, "On the Legal Issues of Joint Development in the South China Sea," is its proposal of the "issue of a Nansha joint development zone and the choice of schemes."[42] In his article "The Predicament and Path Forward for the 'Shelving Disputes and Pursuing Joint Development' Principle," Yang Zewei provides a relatively systematic analysis of the predicament facing this principle. He points out that the difficulty in implementing it in practice between China and its neighboring countries is mainly due to a lack of political will, the absence of a pressing practical need, disputes over island sovereignty, the ambiguity of the disputed

41 See Jia Yu, Issues and Prospects of Joint Development in the East China Sea between China and Japan, *Forum of World Economics & Politics*, 2007, Issue 4, pp. 49-54.

42 See Zhou Zhonghai, On the Legal Issues of Joint Development in the South China Sea, *Xiamen University Law Review*, 2003, Issue 5, pp. 190-209.

maritime zones, and interference from external powers. He also proposes that in resolving territorial and maritime disputes with its neighbors in the future, the Chinese government must, on the one hand, continue to advocate for the "Shelving Disputes and Pursuing Joint Development" principle and strive for breakthroughs in its implementation, while on the other hand, also be prepared to utilize other peaceful means of resolving international disputes.[43]

In terms of monographs, the most representative work is Cai Penghong's *Management Models for Joint Development in Disputed Maritime Areas: A Comparative Study*, which at the time was the only monograph in China on joint maritime development. It takes the management models of joint development as its subject of study, discussing various aspects such as fundamental issues, applicable law, and fiscal and tax systems, and provides a detailed analysis of eleven cases of joint development. However, its greatest shortcoming is that it does not offer a forward-looking study of China's own practice of joint maritime development.[44] Another work, Xiao Jianguo's *Joint Development of Petroleum on International Maritime Boundaries*, primarily discusses the origin, development, and characteristics of joint development from the perspective of international law, and particularly the law of the sea. It analyzes the legal basis for joint development, examines

---

43 See Yang Zewei, The Predicament and Path Forward for the "Shelving Disputes and Pursuing Joint Development" Principle, *Journal of Jiangsu University*, 2011, Issue 3, pp. 70-75.
44 See Cai Penghong, *Management Models for Joint Development in Disputed Maritime Areas: A Comparative Study*, Shanghai Academy of Social Sciences Press, 1998.

existing cases and related agreements from around the world, describes the history of China's offshore oil exploration and development, and offers an outlook on China's implementation of joint development in disputed maritime areas. [45] Yu Mincai's *Legal Issues in Marine Petroleum Exploration and Development* systematically explores five main legal issues related to marine petroleum exploration and development: its legal basis, legal approaches, the joint development regime, legal coordination between offshore petroleum activities and fishing and navigation, and the environmental protection regime for offshore petroleum activities. However, its research on the joint development regime is not sufficiently in-depth.[46] Furthermore, there are specialized works on topics such as international petroleum contracts and international oil and gas cooperation.[47] These works are limited to the study of international petroleum contract models or focus solely on the theory and practice of international oil and gas cooperation. They are of some reference value for related legal issues in the joint development of offshore oil and gas resources, such as the choice of contract models and project management.

Second, the systematicity of the research could be further strengthened.

---

45 See Xiao Jianguo, *Joint Development of Petroleum on International Maritime Boundaries*, China Ocean Press, 2006.

46 See Yu Mincai, *Legal Issues in Marine Petroleum Exploration and Developme nt*, China Renmin University Press, 2001.

47 See Wang Nianping, *A Comparative Study of International Petroleum Contract Models*, Law Press China, 2009; He Sha et al., *Legal Foundations of Internatio nal Petroleum Cooperation*, Petroleum Industry Press, 2008; Ge Aiji et al., *Theor y and Practice of International Oil and Gas Cooperation*, Petroleum Industry Pre ss, 2004.

For example, research in international academia on the joint development of offshore oil and gas resources and its law application has always gone hand-in-hand with practice, producing some landmark works with significant international influence. On the whole, however, this research has been rather fragmented. From an academic standpoint, the concept of joint development had its genesis in the 1930s with onshore petroleum extraction activities. At the time, onshore oil extraction in the American West gave rise to certain judicial practices and sparked corresponding research. By the late 1950s and early 1960s, cases of joint development of both offshore and onshore petroleum resources had emerged in the Persian Gulf in the Middle East and on the European continent. It was against the backdrop of this international practice that William T. Onorato, an American petroleum law expert and senior consultant to the World Bank, pioneered a relatively comprehensive theoretical exploration of joint development. In 1968, he officially published the first article on the subject: Apportionment of an International Common Petroleum Deposit.[48] In the 1970s and 1980s, as the practice of joint maritime development grew more frequent, the international community convened two international workshops in 1980 and 1983 respectively, on the development of hydrocarbons in the South China Sea, which brought together a number of academic papers from the fields of law, diplomacy, and geology. Subsequently, the British Institute of International and Comparative

48 See William T. Onorato, Apportionment of an International Common Petroleum Deposit, *International and Comparative Law Quarterly*, Vol. 17, 1968, pp. 85-102.

Law organized a group of academics, petroleum experts, and lawyers to specifically study the issue of joint maritime development, and they completed the drafting of a model agreement for joint development. In 1990, the group's research findings were compiled and published in two volumes as *Joint Development of Offshore Oil and Gas*.[49] This work marked the pinnacle of research on joint maritime development and to this day remains the most in-depth, comprehensive, and authoritative publication on the subject. Since the turn of the 21st century, research on joint maritime development by scholars abroad has not advanced significantly, consisting mainly of fragmented studies.

In view of this, there are still many worthwhile areas to be explored further concerning the issue of law application for the joint development of offshore oil and gas resources. This is particularly true for the new management models for oil and gas exploration and development adopted after the signing of a joint development agreement—models that are distinct from a single country's domestic framework. (Even in the agency model, where the law of one country is applied, the legal basis ultimately differs from that of a management system under purely domestic jurisdiction, especially in areas such as taxation and revenue sharing.) These new models have, to varying degrees, had an impact on the pre-existing domestic laws of the

49 See Hazel Fox etc. ed., *Joint Development of Offshore Oil and Gas: A Model Agreement for States for Joint Development with Explanatory Commentary*, British Institute of International and Comparative Law 1989; Hazel Fox ed., *Joint Development of Offshore Oil and Gas*, Vol. II, British Institute of International and Comparative Law 1990.

relevant countries, raising questions as to how those countries should handle conflicts between their respective domestic laws and the joint development agreements and management systems. In short, the original intention and ultimate goal of this book is to do its utmost to remedy the shortcomings and fill the gaps in the research by both Chinese and international academia on the issue of law application for the joint development of offshore oil and gas resources.

IV. Research Approach and Methodology

(I) Research Approach

Building upon an examination of the historical evolution of the joint development of offshore oil and gas resources, this book explores various scenarios for the application of law in this field. It primarily addresses the application of law to the joint development of offshore oil and gas resources in disputed maritime areas and to that of transboundary offshore oil and gas resources. The book then provides a detailed analysis of international practices in the joint development of offshore oil and gas since 1958, categorizing the main approaches to legal application into three models: separate, joint, and hybrid. It also identifies the principal legal sources applicable to joint development, namely international law, special law, domestic law, and international petroleum development contracts. Finally, after a thorough discussion of the joint development practices between China and its neighboring countries, the book proposes a legal application model for China's future joint development of offshore oil and gas resources that will best serve its national interests.

(II) Research Methodology

This book will employ the following research methods:

1. Case Study Method. To date, there have been nearly 30 international

cases concerning the joint development of offshore oil and gas resources.[50] This book will therefore adopt the case study method. Through an analysis of typical international cases—such as the 1974 Japan-South Korea Joint Development Case, the 1976 United Kingdom-Norway Joint Development Case, the 1979 Malaysia-Thailand Joint Development Case, the 1992 Malaysia-Vietnam Joint Development Case, the 2001 Nigeria-São Tomé and Príncipe Joint Development Case, and the 2002 Australia-East Timor Joint Development Case—it seeks to identify the commonalities, patterns, and characteristics of legal application in the joint development of offshore oil and gas resources. On this basis, the book will propose a legal application model for China to adopt in its future joint maritime development practices with its neighboring countries.

2. Interdisciplinary Research Method. The joint development of offshore oil and gas resources is not only a political proposition but also a legally recognized concept. It is closely intertwined with fields such as international politics, the national economy, and cultural traditions, while also involving numerous areas of law, including public international law, the law of the sea, private international law, labor law, contract law, and petroleum law. Therefore, only through a comprehensive and integrated analysis from political, economic, and legal perspectives can the issue of joint

50 See Yang Zewei (ed.), *A Study on the Theory and Practice of International L aw on Joint Maritime Development*, Wuhan University Press, 2018, p. 2.

maritime development be thoroughly and profoundly examined.

3. Historical Analysis Method. The joint development of offshore oil and gas resources is a product of a specific historical period. This book will conduct a longitudinal analysis of international practices in the joint development of offshore oil and gas resources since the end of the Second World War. It will also analyze the historical processes of maritime delimitation and joint development among neighboring maritime states, striving to predict the development trends of joint offshore oil and gas development between China and its neighbors, and to propose principles and measures for future joint development of offshore oil and gas resources between China and its neighboring countries.

4. Empirical and Comparative Method. Currently, international practice includes cases of the joint development of offshore oil and gas resources in maritime areas with overlapping claims prior to delimitation, as well as cases concerning the joint development of transboundary petroleum resources after delimitation. These precedents contain a wealth of general principles and specific methods applicable to the joint development of offshore oil and gas resources. At the same time, China's maritime neighbors, guided by their own political, economic, security, and strategic considerations, hold various positions, views, and claims regarding maritime disputes and joint development. This book will conduct a comparative analysis of these matters to identify the principles and rules that should govern the application of law

to the joint development of offshore oil and gas resources between China and its neighboring countries.

Chapter 1: The Starting Point for the Application of Law to the Joint Development of Offshore Oil and Gas Resources—The Ownership of Oil and Gas Resources

Some scholars have pointed out that all disputes arising in the course of oil and gas development, in the final analysis, stem from the issue of ownership①. Due to the fluid nature of oil and gas resources, in the early days of the modern petroleum industry, little was known about the size of reserves, the extent of reservoirs, or the migration patterns of these resources deep underground. Consequently, disputes over the ultimate ownership of these subterranean resources have run through the entire process of the formation and development of the legal rules governing the petroleum industry. The history of the industry's development has thus also been a transition from disorderly competition to orderly cooperation, and from a "beggar-thy-neighbor" approach to one of being a "good partner."

The joint development of offshore oil and gas resources has been widely discussed in academia, with the oil and gas cooperation agreement between Saudi Arabia and Bahrain generally considered its inception.② Most of the relevant academic research, however, is conducted from the perspective of international law by scholars who are often unfamiliar with the development and practices of the petroleum industry. Consequently, their studies have tended to overlook the early history of oil and gas resource development and

① See Ralph B. Shank, "Present Status of the Law of Capture", Proceedings of the Annual Institute on Oil and Gas Law and Taxation as It Affects the Oil and Gas Industry, 1955, p. 271.
② See Yang Zewei (ed.), *Research on International Law Issues of Joint Maritim e Development*, Social Sciences Academic Press (China), 2016, p. 2; Yu Hui, Int ernational Law Issues on the Joint Development of Marine Mineral Resources, *C hinese Yearbook of International Law (1994)*, Law Press China, 1995, p. 48.

the evolution of its governing legal rules. In fact, whether it is the Bahrain-Saudi Arabia agreement or issues that have drawn the attention of the International Court of Justice—such as cross-border cooperation in oil and gas development and the joint development of disputed areas—these may be novelties in the field of international law. For the petroleum industry, however, such forms of cooperative development have long been commonplace. The basic legal framework for cooperation in the joint development of offshore oil and gas resources, as discussed in academia today, is basically derived from the long-standing legal practices of the petroleum industry. It simply represents an evolution from domestic to international law and from onshore to offshore contexts. While this process has, of course, seen new developments and the introduction of new provisions to address different circumstances, the fundamental legal principles and framework for cooperation have not changed significantly. Therefore, as a starting point for studying the application of law to the joint development of offshore oil and gas resources, it is essential to examine the evolution of oil and gas resource ownership from the domain of private law to that of public law.

Section One: Ownership of Oil and Gas Resources in Private Law

I. Characteristics of Oil and Gas Resources

When discussing the development and utilization of oil and gas resources, it is essential to first have a basic understanding of their physical forms and how oil and gas fields are created.

Petroleum and natural gas are defined as combustible minerals, primarily composed of hydrocarbons, which are generated and stored in liquid and gaseous states within subterranean rock formations.[③] Oil and gas extracted from the ground in their unprocessed state are generally referred to as crude oil and, more broadly, as hydrocarbons. For convenience, this book will refer to them collectively as "oil and gas resources."

Today, when discussing oil and gas fields buried deep underground, industry professionals generally point out that there are different theories concerning the generation of oil and gas resources. These are primarily divided into two main schools of thought: the organic generation theory and the inorganic generation theory. Within the organic theory, there are further debates on topics such as marine origin of petroleum, terrestrial origin of petroleum, early-stage generation, and late-stage generation. In general terms,

---

③ See China Petroleum and Petrochemical Engineering Institute (ed.), *A Primer on Contemporary Technology in the Petroleum and Petrochemical Industries: Expl oration* (Second Edition), China Petrochemical Press, 2005, p. 1.

however, the process can be broadly summarized as follows: over billions of years of Earth's evolution, tectonic activity led to the formation of sedimentary basins. Within these basins, the continuous accumulation of organic matter underwent complex physical and chemical changes. Through a profound transformation over vast geological timescales, this matter was ultimately converted into the oil and gas resources buried deep underground. The formation of an underground oil and gas field requires four essential elements: source, reservoir, cap, and trap—that is, source rock, reservoir rock, cap rock, and a geological trap. Oil and gas resources are generated in the source rock and then, driven by changes such as formation pressure, migrate to a reservoir rock capable of storing them. Above the reservoir rock lies the cap rock, a layer of dense, impermeable rock that prevents the oil and gas from escaping after entering the reservoir. The trap is the geological structure that confines the migrating oil and gas within a specific area. As oil and gas resources continuously migrate through the reservoir rock, they accumulate and are preserved within this trap, ultimately forming an oil and gas field. The exploration for oil and gas resources is the search for geological traps that may hold them, leading to the discovery of exploitable fields through drilling. Development, on the other hand, is the process of extracting these discovered resources from underground in an economic and efficient manner. In the terminology of the petroleum industry, this is known as the process of resource recovery. An underground oil and gas reservoir is not, as is commonly imagined, a subterranean lake of crude oil, a flowing river, or a vast, empty natural gas tank from which, once a well is drilled, the resources can be easily pumped out like water or air. The nature of these resources can be aptly understood from the literal meaning of the Chinese word for petroleum, shíyóu (石油), which translates to "oil from stone" (or gas from stone). Let us imagine a sponge saturated with water: the oil and gas are the water, and the "sponge" saturated with these resources is the hard rock of the geological strata. Oil and gas are stored within the pores and fractures of various sizes that exist inside this rock. Some of these pores are large enough to be seen with the naked eye, while others require a magnifying glass or microscope. The larger the pores, the more oil and gas they can store. The better the connectivity between the pores—and thus the higher the permeability—the more easily the oil and gas can flow through the rock. Furthermore, the mobility of the oil and gas is also affected by their viscosity, which varies depending on their quality.④

In summary, oil and gas resources are not completely immobile mineral resources like coal or iron ore; rather, they possess a certain mobility. This mobility, however, differs from the complete fluidity of water or air, as it is constrained by geological conditions and is therefore not absolute. Evidently, oil and gas resources are mineral resources characterized by a certain degree of mobility. The foregoing represents our current understanding of these

---

④ See China Petroleum and Petrochemical Engineering Institute (ed.), *A Primer on Contemporary Technology in the Petroleum and Petrochemical Industries: Exploration* (Second Edition), China Petrochemical Press, 2005, pp. 1-34.

resources. However, this understanding—of the principles of hydrocarbon accumulation and of how to develop oil and gas fields economically and effectively—was not achieved overnight; it has developed and evolved continuously through practice. And the evolution of this understanding has, in turn, had a very important and profound impact on the laws applied to oil and gas development.

II. Origins of the Rule of Capture

In the early days of oil and gas development, as the genesis of these resources was not understood, people closely associated petroleum with water. This was because petroleum existed in a fluid state, similar to water. Consequently, when addressing ownership disputes involving subterranean oil and gas resources, it became inevitable to draw an analogy with water resources.[5]

The Rule of Capture is a concept in common law, originally associated with water, particularly groundwater resources. After more than 2,000 years of practice and development, this rule has become an important concept in property law[6] and a core principle for determining the ownership of oil and gas resources and for their exploration and development. As one scholar has noted, "The rule of capture appears at the very beginning of the chain of

⑤ See Terence Daintith, *Finders Keepers? How the Law of Capture Shaped the World Oil Industry*, RFF Press, 2010, p. 41.
⑥ See Dylan O. Drummond, Lynn Ray Sherman & Edmond R. McCarthy, The Rule of Capture in Texas-Still So Misunderstood after All These Years, *Texas Tech Law Review*, Vol. 37, No. 1, 2004, p. 15.

events that has brought us to where we are today, and it has given rise, directly or indirectly, to the characteristic patterns of behavior of oil companies large and small, which in turn have shaped the corrective responses made by government. Like it or not, the rule of capture stands at the starting point of the path of development that the oil industry has in fact taken."[7]

The Rule of Capture is referred to in English by several terms, such as law of capture, rule of capture, and principle of capture; in Chinese, its translations include 捕获规则 (bǔhuò guīzé) and 捕获原则 (bǔhuò yuánzé). The *Comprehensive English-Chinese Dictionary of Petroleum* published in China, omits "law of capture" and "principle of capture," and lists only "rule of capture", translating it as the "principle of possession."[8] This is an interpretative translation that focuses on the term's meaning. I believe, however, that the word "possession" is insufficient to convey the term's origin or historical evolution. Because mobile oil and gas resources were originally analogized to wild animals, the word "capture" more aptly reflects this provenance. Furthermore, "capture" logically implies gaining control and ownership of something previously unowned—or, more precisely, the very act of gaining that control and ownership.[9] Therefore, the full

---

⑦ Aileen McHarg et al. (eds.), *Property and Law in Energy and Natural Resources*, trans. by Hu Desheng, Wei Tiejun, et al. Peking University Press, 2014, p. 195.

⑧ See Editorial Committee of the Comprehensive English-Chinese Dictionary of Petroleum (ed.), *Comprehensive English-Chinese Dictionary of Petroleum*, Petroleum Industry Press, 2001, p. 1231.

⑨ See Dylan O. Drummond, Lynn Ray Sherman & Edmond R. McCarthy, The Rule of Capture in Texas-Still So Misunderstood after All These Years, *Texas Tech Law Review*, Vol. 37, No. 1, 2004, p. 54.

meaning of "capture" is to pursue, obtain, and possess. "Possession" alone is insufficient to encompass the rich legal connotations of the term.

(I) Roman Law

In Roman law, there was no definition of ownership, only the so-called "complete power over a thing" (plena in re potestas). Later commentators defined it from various perspectives, such as "ownership is the right of an owner to dispose of their property," or "ownership is the capacity of an owner to do with an object whatever they wish, subject only to the limits of their own power and the law."[10] An examination of the Roman law interpretation of ownership over things that had never been owned (res quae nullius in bonis sunt)—which fall under the category of unowned things (res sine domino or res nullius)—reveals two main perspectives. One view held that a wild animal, once wounded, belonged to the hunter during the pursuit, reverting to its unowned state or belonging to the next taker if the chase was abandoned. The other held that the hunter became its owner only upon actual capture. Regardless of the perspective, the most fundamental and crucial issue here lies in establishing the basic legal meaning of the ownership of ownerless things: an unowned thing belongs, in principle, to the first occupant.[11]

In the *Theodosian Code*, for the first time, the concept of water rights

⑩ See Zhou Nan, *An Introduction to Roman Law* (Volume 1), The Commercial Press, 2019, pp. 341-342.
11 See Zhou Nan, *An Introduction to Roman Law* (Volume 1), The Commercial Press, 2019, for relevant discussion on pp. 335-337, 456-457, 467-468, and 480.

was linked to that of ownership. This indicates that the Romans had consciously come to regard the right to acquire water resources as a form of ownership, not merely a right of acquisition or use.[12] Marcus Claudius Marcellus held that "no action can be taken against a person who, by digging on their own land, alters a neighbor's water supply." This principle was cited in the English court case of Acton v. Blundell and is regarded as the earliest and most direct origin of the modern Rule of Capture.[13] Justinian's *Digesta* also cites the words of Ulpian: "a landowner who fails to take measures to protect himself against a foreseeable injury has only himself to blame." This principle also represents an important concept of self-help in the development of the Rule of Capture.[14]

(II) English Law

The 1843 English case of Acton v. Blundell (hereinafter the Acton case) was the first court ruling concerning the Rule of Capture in its modern sense. In the Acton case, the plaintiff, Acton, operated a cotton mill on his property, using groundwater from the land to power its machinery. The defendant, a neighboring landowner named Blundell, commenced coal mining operations

---

12 See Dylan O. Drummond, Lynn Ray Sherman & Edmond R. McCarthy, The Rule of Capture in Texas-Still So Misunderstood after All These Years, *Texas Tec h Law Review*, Vol. 37, No. 1, 2004, pp. 15-20.
13 See Dylan O. Drummond, Lynn Ray Sherman & Edmond R. McCarthy, The Rule of Capture in Texas-Still So Misunderstood after All These Years, *Texas Tec h Law Review*, Vol. 37, No. 1, 2004, pp. 22-23.
14 See Dylan O. Drummond, Lynn Ray Sherman & Edmond R. McCarthy, The Rule of Capture in Texas-Still So Misunderstood after All These Years, *Texas Tec h Law Review*, Vol. 37, No. 1, 2004, pp. 23-24.

on his own property. As the mine was dug deeper, it drained the groundwater that supplied the cotton mill. Consequently, Acton sued Blundell, demanding that he stop mining. The plaintiff's counsel argued that as long as the water was located beneath the plaintiff's land, it belonged to the plaintiff under the principle of "Cujas est solum, ejus est usque ad coelum et ad infernos" (Whoever owns the soil, owns up to the sky and down to the depths). However, the precedents cited by the plaintiff's counsel all pertained to surface water cases. The court ultimately ruled that the law applicable to the ownership of groundwater is different from that for surface water and rivers. The legal principle for groundwater ownership, it held, was that a landowner possesses ownership of the land and everything beneath it, and may dispose of the things within their own land as they see fit. If the exercise of this right caused the interception or even depletion of a neighbor's groundwater supply, the resulting inconvenience constituted "damage for which there is no legal remedy", against which the court could take no action. The judgment in the Acton case established two important principles: first, that groundwater resources differ in nature from surface water resources and thus fall within the domain regulated by property rights; and second, that ownership of the surface land simultaneously confers ownership of all subterranean resources beneath it.[15] The importance of this judgment lies in the fact that it created the legal foundation for the application of the modern Rule of Capture and

15 See Dylan O. Drummond, Lynn Ray Sherman & Edmond R. McCarthy, The Rule of Capture in Texas-Still So Misunderstood after All These Years, *Texas Tec h Law Review*, Vol. 37, No. 1, 2004, pp. 35-39.

defined the various rights protected by that rule.[16]

(III) The Application of the Rule of Capture in Modern American Oil and Gas Law

It is widely held that the modern commercial oil industry originated in the United States in 1859.[17] America's early practices had a pivotal influence on the development of the oil and gas industry's practices and legal application. Non-biological resources that exist underground in solid form, such as metals and coal, are immobile and generally remain fixed where they are discovered. Oil and natural gas, however, as liquid or gaseous resources, possess a degree of mobility. Because adjacent surface tracts of land may overlie a common subterranean reservoir, when one landowner drills a well and extracts oil and gas on their own property, the resources originally under other tracts may migrate due to the resulting change in pressure. This can cause detriment to the owners of the surrounding surface land. Therefore, the question of ownership of oil and gas resources became a central concern. How to determine this ownership was a critical issue that the law of the time was compelled to address.

In the 1867 case of Dark v. Johnston, the court held that "petroleum is a

16 See Dylan O. Drummond, Lynn Ray Sherman & Edmond R. McCarthy, The Rule of Capture in Texas-Still So Misunderstood after All These Years, *Texas Tec h Law Review*, Vol. 37, No. 1, 2004, p. 37.

17 See Daniel Yergin, *The Prize: The Epic Quest for Oil, Money & Power*, Free Press, 2008, pp. 19-30.

liquid, and like water, is not the subject of ownership unless actually possessed."[18] The fundamental distinction between the ownership of oil and gas resources and that of land, personal property, intellectual property, and other items is that ownership of oil and gas is derived from ownership of the product flow from a specific reservoir (i.e., the oil and gas resources within that reservoir) and from ownership of the reservoir itself.[19]

The 1889 case of Westmoreland and Cambria Natural Gas Co. v. De Witt (hereinafter the Westmoreland case) was the earliest precedent in American history on the ownership of oil and gas resources and proved to be widely influential.[20] In its ruling on the case, the Supreme Court of Pennsylvania responded to the argument that "since natural gas is a mineral, ownership of the land implies ownership of the gas so long as it remains underground." The relevant passage reads as follows:

"Natural gas is indeed a mineral, but one with peculiar attributes. Water is also a mineral. Water and oil, and especially natural gas, should perhaps be classified as minerals ferae nature. Unlike other minerals, they are more like animals in their ability and tendency to escape without the owner's volition.

---

18 See Bruce M. Kramer and Owen L. Anderson, The Rule of Capture-An Oil a nd Gas Perspective, *Environmental Law*, Vol. 35, 2005, p. 904.

19 See Dean Lueck, The Rule of First Possession and the Design of the Law, *J ournal of Law and Economics*, Vol. 38, 1995, p. 393, as cited in Aileen McHarg et al. (eds.), *Property and Law in Energy and Natural Resources*, trans. by Hu Desheng, Wei Tiejun, et al. Peking University Press, 2014, p. 196.

20 See Bruce M. Kramer and Owen L. Anderson, The Rule of Capture-An Oil a nd Gas Perspective, *Environmental Law*, Vol. 35, 2005, p. 906; Terence Daintith, *Finders Keepers? How the Law of Capture Shaped the World Oil Industry*, RFF Press, 2010, p. 21.

So long as they are upon or within a tract of land, they belong to that land, and thus to its owner, and are under that owner's control; but when they go to other land, or fall under another's control, the title of the former owner is lost. Therefore, possession of a tract of land does not mean possession of the gas (within that land). If a neighboring or even a distant landowner drills a well on his own land, guides your gas (originally in your land) into his wellbore, and brings it under his control, then that gas is no longer yours, but his. Whoever controls the captured gas is its legal owner."[21]

In the above case, the judge analogized oil and gas resources to wild animals, which harkens back to a fundamental legal principle developed in Roman law: the ownership of an unowned object belongs to the first taker. This, precisely, is the original legal meaning of the rule of capture.[22] From then on, the rule of capture was recognized by American courts and became the legislative foundation for subsequent oil and gas development. To this day, it remains the principle of property rights upon which American oil and gas law and regulatory agencies are based.[23]

In 1893, the application of the pure rule of capture was taken to its extreme in the case of Hague v. Wheeler. In that case, the owners of three

---

21 See Bruce M. Kramer and Owen L. Anderson, The Rule of Capture-An Oil a nd Gas Perspective, *Environmental Law*, Vol. 35, 2005, p. 906.

22 See Terence Daintith, *Finders Keepers? How the Law of Capture Shaped the World Oil Industry*, RFF Press, 2010, pp. 32-36.

23 See Aileen McHarg et al. (eds.), *Property and Law in Energy and Natural R esources*, trans. by Hu Desheng, Wei Tiejun, et al. Peking University Press, 2014, p. 192.

adjacent land tracts discovered natural gas from a common underground reservoir, and each drilled wells to produce it. However, only two of them found buyers for their gas; the third did not. Subsequently, the third owner, instead of shutting in the well and halting production, proceeded to burn the gas it extracted. The first two owners sued the third on the grounds that its practice of burning the gas was damaging the profits they were entitled to enjoy. The judgment held that once oil and gas are captured, they belong completely and exclusively to the captor, and the resulting ownership right to their use or disposal is unrestricted by law, even if the captor's method of disposal is wasteful. "The act of burning the natural gas may be immoral, but the moral responsibility for it is not one that can be resolved through civil litigation."[24]

In 1895, when hearing Brown v. Spilman, the U.S. Supreme Court cited the Westmoreland decision, acknowledged the rule of capture as the appropriate doctrine for governing oil and gas ownership, and described that ownership as follows: "Oil and gas are minerals with special properties. So long as they are on or in a tract of land, or under the control of the landowner, they constitute a part of that land and belong to the landowner; but when they escape and go into other land, or come under another's control, the title of the original owner is lost. If a neighboring landowner drills a well on his own

---

24 See Bruce M. Kramer and Owen L. Anderson, The Rule of Capture-An Oil a nd Gas Perspective, *Environmental Law*, Vol. 35, 2005, pp. 908-909.

land and induces the oil and gas into the well he has drilled, they become his property, even if the oil and gas reservoir extends beneath his neighbor's land."[25]

The judgment in the 1897 case of Kelley v. Ohio Oil Co. held that each person has the right to use their own property in their own way, as long as it does not affect the legal rights of others. Therefore, the right to drill for and produce oil and gas on one's own land is absolute and not subject to the supervision of any court or other adjacent landowners. Once oil and gas enter a wellbore, ownership belongs to the owner of that well, regardless of where the resources originally came from. This judgment also held that for a landowner, if their underground resources are being depleted by drilling operations on adjacent land, and if they can neither prohibit this invasive drilling nor be compensated for the loss, their best method of protecting their property line is to drill an offset well (offset drilling) on their own land. That is to say, for neighboring landowners sharing the same oil and gas reservoir, the only solution to secure their own interests is that if the other party drills a well, they must drill a well along the property line on their own side to offset the potential loss.[26]

---

25 See Bruce M. Kramer and Owen L. Anderson, The Rule of Capture-An Oil and Gas Perspective, *Environmental Law*, Vol. 35, 2005, p. 907.

26 See Terence Daintith, *Finders Keepers? How the Law of Capture Shaped the World Oil Industry*, RFF Press, 2010, pp. 28-29; Bruce M. Kramer and Owen L. Anderson, The Rule of Capture-An Oil and Gas Perspective, *Environmental Law*, Vol. 35, 2005, pp. 909-910; Lewis M. Andrews, The Correlative Rights Doctrine in the Law of Oil and Gas, *Southern California Law Review*, Vol. 13, No. 2, 1940, p. 187.

In 1935, Robert Hardwicke, a renowned lawyer in the American oil and gas industry, defined the rule of capture as follows: "The owner of a tract of land has title to the oil and gas resources obtained by drilling on his land, even if there is evidence that a portion of the resources has migrated from adjacent lands." [27] The *Comprehensive English-Chinese Dictionary of Petroleum* offers this explanation for the "principle of possession": "The owner of land or minerals may only drill on his own land and is entitled to the oil and gas produced, but cannot exclude a portion that has migrated from neighboring areas. This principle often encourages the mineral owner to drill and obtain oil and gas from his land as quickly and economically as possible."[28]

In the United States, two different rules of oil and gas ownership, based on different legal rationales, have developed and been adopted by various states and the federal government. One is the ownership-in-place doctrine. Under this doctrine, when oil and gas resources are located beneath a tract of land, they constitute a part of that land, are therefore classified as real property, and can be authorized to be severed and extracted from the surface. Once such authorization is granted, they may be regarded as a corporeal interest in real property. Under the ownership-in-place doctrine, once oil and

27 See Robert E. Hardwicke, The Rule of Capture and Its Implications as Applie d to Oil and Gas, *Texas Law Review*, Vol. 13, 1935, pp. 391, 393; as cited in B ruce M. Kramer and Owen L. Anderson, The Rule of Capture-An Oil and Gas P erspective, *Environmental Law*, Vol. 35, 2005, p. 900.
28 See Editorial Committee of the Comprehensive English-Chinese Dictionary of Petroleum (ed.), *Comprehensive English-Chinese Dictionary of Petroleum*, Petroleu m Industry Press, 2001, p. 1231.

gas resources escape[29] from under a landowner's property, that landowner's title to those resources is lost. This rule is adopted in states such as Texas, Arkansas, Kansas, Michigan, Mississippi, Montana, Ohio, Pennsylvania, Tennessee, and Virginia.[30] The other is the nonownership theory[31], also known as the exclusive right doctrine[32]. According to this doctrine, oil and gas resources, due to their fugacious nature, are considered to have characteristics more akin to common property. When they are produced and controlled, the possessor acquires absolute ownership. This means that the owner of a tract of land, even if that land contains oil and gas, does not have ownership of the resources in place; they can only acquire ownership of those resources by producing them and bringing them under their control. The landowner does, however, have the exclusive right to drill on their property and to take title to any substance produced on their land. This rule is adopted in states such as California, Illinois, Indiana, Kentucky, Louisiana, New York, and Oklahoma, as well as by the U.S. Supreme Court.[33] In effect, however, both the ownership-in-place doctrine and the nonownership theory (or exclusive right doctrine) recognize the rule of capture.[34] For the former, this

29 Here, escape refers to the migration of resources from beneath one tract of la nd to another, not to their extraction from the ground to the surface.
30 See Lewis M. Andrews, The Correlative Rights Doctrine in the Law of Oil a nd Gas, *Southern California Law Review*, Vol. 13, No. 2, 1940, pp. 188-190.
31 See George W. Hardy II, The Doctrine of Correlative Rights: Origins and Mo dern Applications, Annual Institute on Mineral Law, Vol. 35, 1992, p. 170.
32 See Lewis M. Andrews, The Correlative Rights Doctrine in the Law of Oil a nd Gas, *Southern California Law Review*, Vol. 13, No. 2, 1940, p. 190.
33 See Lewis M. Andrews, The Correlative Rights Doctrine in the Law of Oil a nd Gas, *Southern California Law Review*, Vol. 13, No. 2, 1940, pp. 190-192.
34 See Lewis M. Andrews, The Correlative Rights Doctrine in the Law of Oil a nd Gas, *Southern California Law Review*, Vol. 13, No. 2, 1940, p. 192; George

means that if underground oil and gas resources escape, the landowner loses ownership of them; if the resources migrate to another's land, they can be "captured" by the other landowner and become that person's property. For the latter, this means that although a landowner does not own the oil and gas in place, once they produce and bring those resources under their control—that is, "capture" them—they gain ownership, even if there is evidence that the resources migrated from adjacent land.

The application of the rule of capture was not unique to the United States. In the development of France's mineral water industry, disputes over the ownership of water sources had long been a subject of controversy. According to the *French Civil Code* and relevant parliamentary debates, a landowner has the right to do as they wish on their own land, and the rule of capture is a natural expression of the right to dispose of one's property at will.[35] In the late 19th and early 20th centuries, the rule of capture was also widely practiced in the oil and gas industries of America's early competitors—such as Romania, Russia, and the province of Galicia in what was then the Austro-Hungarian Empire (now western Ukraine)—despite their differing systems of land tenure, rules governing mineral ownership, and legal provisions for oil and gas development. In Russia, for example, although subsurface oil and gas resources were owned by the state, its 1904

W. Hardy II, The Doctrine of Correlative Rights: Origins and Modern Application s, Annual Institute on Mineral Law, Vol. 35, 1992, p. 171.
35 See Terence Daintith, *Finders Keepers? How the Law of Capture Shaped the World Oil Industry*, RFF Press, 2010, pp. 87-121.

Mining Law provided that "the system of oil and gas development shall be determined by the developer." This, in effect, legally granted the right of disposal over captured oil and gas to the developers, which led to a situation where derricks proliferated as producers scrambled to develop the resources.[36]

Driven by the benefits of oil and gas development and the "finders keepers" incentive that the rule of capture offered to developers, the American oil and gas industry experienced a period of wild growth. It achieved tremendous expansion and maintained the highest global production levels for a considerable time.[37]

III. Adjacency Rights and Unitization

(I) Problems Arising from the Application of the Rule of Capture and Challenges Thereto

In 1968, Garrett Hardin published a landmark article pointing out that a tragic feature of any common resource is that each party is driven to appropriate as much of it as possible, without regard for its depletion or overexploitation. He termed this practice the "Tragedy of the Commons."[38] In the case of petroleum, a common underground reservoir may be overlain

36 See Terence Daintith, *Finders Keepers? How the Law of Capture Shaped the World Oil Industry*, RFF Press, 2010, pp. 139-167.
37 See Daniel Yergin, *The Prize: The Epic Quest for Oil, Money & Power*, Free Press, 2008, pp. 29-95.
38 Garrett Hardin, The Tragedy of the Commons, *Science*, Vol. 162, 1968. pp. 1 243-1248.

by lands belonging to different surface owners, and the actions of one neighboring party clearly and inevitably affect the others. The "Tragedy of the Commons" means that the owner of each well has an incentive to pump as much oil as possible, as quickly as possible, to make it their own before it can be extracted by other wells. One can imagine the scenario: your neighbor drills a well, so you immediately drill another on your side of the property line adjacent to it, and this process continues with wells lined up against each other, perpetuating a vicious cycle. Journalists at the time reported that under the rule of capture, oil derricks stood in such dense formations as had rarely been seen in the world; a person could supposedly walk from one town to another dozens of miles away by stepping from the base of one derrick to the next, without ever touching the ground.[39]

The result, to be sure, was a rapid rise in oil and gas production and the swift prosperity of the industry. But this disorderly and competitive style of development led to two consequences: one, rapid resource depletion, and two, increasingly high extraction costs and significant resource waste. As early as 1884, a report to the U.S. Congress had already mentioned the danger that over-drilling could lead to resource depletion.[40] Oil and gas development, particularly in its early days, could only utilize underground pressure to push oil and gas up the wellbore to the surface. If wells were properly spaced, high

39 See Terence Daintith, *Finders Keepers? How the Law of Capture Shaped the World Oil Industry*, RFF Press, 2010, p. 63.
40 See Terence Daintith, *Finders Keepers? How the Law of Capture Shaped the World Oil Industry*, RFF Press, 2010, p. 82.

levels of underground pressure could be maintained for a longer period, thereby allowing for the recovery of more oil and gas from the reservoir. Drilling too many wells, however, caused the underground pressure to drop too far and too fast, soon making it difficult for the oil and gas to be forced to the surface. This caused an oilfield's production to decline rapidly until it ceased altogether—a phenomenon known as field depletion. Depleted wells had to be abandoned, and new well locations had to be found. For the developers, the abandonment of recoverable but unproduced underground resources was one form of waste, while the search for more new well locations, the construction of more derricks, and the drilling of more wells meant a further waste of capital investment. In 1914, while the total value of U.S. oil and gas production was just $214 million, losses due to over-drilling amounted to a staggering $50 million, nearly a quarter of the total production value. In 1931, statistics from Oklahoma City showed that the city alone had drilled 765 excess wells; if these wells were to produce at full capacity, their output would have been 20 times the market demand. In a single oilfield, over-drilling caused $70 million in waste. At the time, it was estimated that as many as 4,000 to 5,000 unnecessary wells were being drilled in the United States each year. With 88% of the world's total wells, the U.S. produced only 14% of the world's crude oil, resulting in $80 million to $100 million in waste and demonstrating extremely low economic efficiency. The second consequence was the severe environmental impact. Overproduction exceeded total demand, which not only caused frequent collapses in crude oil prices but also meant that vast quantities of produced oil had to be stored on the surface. Given the relatively primitive storage conditions of the time, this led not only to frequent fires—causing economic losses and air pollution—but also to leaks from improper storage, which further polluted the environment. In 1917 alone, the crude oil lost to these conditions amounted to 20% to 25% of the total U.S. production.[41] These circumstances sparked challenges to the rule of capture. The earliest and most famous opponent of the rule was Henry Doherty. He argued that the rule of capture would lead to over-drilling and the destruction of underground pressure, and, in a letter to the sitting U.S. President, he became the first to advocate for the enactment of compulsory unitization statutes.[42]

(II) The Emergence and Development of Correlative Rights

In Roman law, although ownership was considered the most complete and typical real right, possessing characteristics such as absoluteness and exclusivity, it was also held that the absoluteness of ownership does not mean an owner can exercise their rights without any limitation. Ownership is, first and foremost, subject to the limitations of correlative relations. For example, if a person, by artificial means, altered the natural flow of water in a way that caused damage to another's property, the injured party could sue for compensation. If the construction or demolition of a building was believed

41 See Terence Daintith, *Finders Keepers? How the Law of Capture Shaped the World Oil Industry*, RFF Press, 2010, pp. 8-9.
42 See Bruce M. Kramer and Owen L. Anderson, The Rule of Capture-An Oil and Gas Perspective, *Environmental Law*, Vol. 35, 2005, p. 901.

by a neighbor to be harmful to their interests, they could temporarily halt the work until the rights of both parties were clarified.[43] It is generally held that the rule of correlative rights originates in the common law system. For surface landowners who share a common resource, one party has the right to be free from injury or even the destruction of that resource by another.[44] In the context of water rights, for example, it is held that for underground lakes or artesian systems, the relevant landowners all enjoy a reciprocal right to the reasonable use of these groundwater resources. This right is only a usufructuary right, meaning that if one landowner damages the common resource, their right to use it may be restricted or even prohibited.[45]

As early as the 1862 case of Bassett v. Salisbury Manufacturing Co., the court recognized that the absolute ownership established by the rule of capture could lead to endless strife over the acquisition of groundwater resources. The judgment in that case held that a suitable universal principle should be "the rule of reasonable use," which means exercising one's rights with reason. Because every landowner possesses equal rights, the rights one landowner can enjoy depend on the actions of the surrounding landowners. If neighboring landowners do not restrain themselves, the rights of all will

---

43 See Zhou Nan, *An Introduction to Roman Law* (Volume 1), The Commercial Press, 2019, pp. 343-344.
44 See George W. Hardy II, the Doctrine of Correlative Rights: Origins and Mo dern Applications, Annual Institute on Mineral Law, Vol. 35, 1992, p. 172.
45 See Lewis M. Andrews, The Correlative Rights Doctrine in the Law of Oil a nd Gas, *Southern California Law Review*, Vol. 13, No. 2, 1940, pp. 192-193.

lose their original value. In this sense, these rights are correlative.[46]

In the early 20th century, the problems of waste and pollution caused by the rule of capture had become a matter of great concern to government officials and discerning figures in the oil and gas industry. Consequently, legislation to prevent waste and protect correlative rights began to be developed. The most renowned case establishing correlative rights is the 1900 case of Ohio Oil Co. v. Indiana.

To conserve natural gas resources and meet public demand for lighting and heating, the state of Indiana enacted a statute prohibiting the wanton waste of natural gas produced from underground reservoirs. The Ohio Oil Co.'s business was focused on producing oil, and natural gas held no commercial value for it. However, because oil and gas resources are often found together underground, the company, in the course of its extraction operations, would recover and process the oil while venting the natural gas directly into the atmosphere—in other words, wasting it. In the company's view, based on the rule of capture, all resources produced from underground—both the oil it recovered and the gas it vented—were its property. However, the company's practice of venting natural gas constituted a wasteful act prohibited by Indiana's new law. But since it lacked the means to recover and utilize the gas, the company could not produce the associated

46 See Terence Daintith, *Finders Keepers? How the Law of Capture Shaped the World Oil Industry*, RFF Press, 2010, pp. 39-40.

oil without venting the gas. From its perspective, this prohibition amounted to a taking of its property and an improper interference with private ownership rights, and it therefore sought to have the statute invalidated.

The Indiana Supreme Court and the Federal Supreme Court ultimately affirmed the statute. The Indiana Supreme Court held that ownership of the natural gas resource is acquired only when one takes actual possession of it. Since the Ohio Oil Co. vented the gas, the company never possessed it, and therefore the state statute did not constitute an unreasonable interference with private property rights. The U.S. Supreme Court, however, took a different interpretive path, reasoning that if surface landowners were deemed to have a legal right to dispose of any resource they brought to the surface at will—even to the point of wasting it—then no single landowner over a common underground resource could truly claim ownership of any part of it. This is because such a right would lack one of the most fundamental elements of ownership: the power to prevent others from taking or destroying one's property. The court held that, since surface landowners all have an equal right to drill on their land and extract their share from the common underground resource, the legislature has the power to enact statutes to protect the common resource and prevent waste. Essentially, the Indiana statute was a law for the protection of private property, designed to prevent one owner of a common resource from acting as he pleased in disregard of the rights of the other owners. The "collectively held rights" recognized in this judgment were subsequently replaced in other rulings by the proper noun "correlative rights."

From then on, in the supervision, legislation, and adjudication of oil and gas extraction, the description of correlative rights was based either on the need to prevent waste for the public interest or on the protection of the co-equal rights of the owners of the common resource.[47]

The 1903 court judgment in Louisville Gas Co. v. Kentucky Heating Co. largely reflects the core tenets of the modern rule of correlative rights. It held that a landowner, in using their own property, must have due regard for the rights of their neighbors and should not be permitted to waste resources maliciously for the purpose of injuring them.[48] In its ruling in Louisiana Gas & Fuel Co. v. White Bros. (1925), the court cited the maxim "sic utere tuo ut alienum non laedas" (use your own property in such a way as not to injure that of another).[49]

In the 1948 case of Elliff v. Texon Drilling Co., the plaintiff argued that the defendant, in conducting development on its own land, had negligently caused a blowout, which reduced the oil and gas the plaintiff could have recovered, and therefore sought compensation. The defendant contended that, although its actions had caused the blowout and depleted the oil and gas resources, under the rule of capture, the plaintiff could not claim ownership of un-captured oil and gas and thus no compensation was owed. Since the

---

47 See Terence Daintith, *Finders Keepers? How the Law of Capture Shaped the World Oil Industry*, RFF Press, 2010, pp. 181-184.
48 See Terence Daintith, *Finders Keepers? How the Law of Capture Shaped the World Oil Industry*, RFF Press, 2010, pp. 191-192.
49 See George W. Hardy II, the Doctrine of Correlative Rights: Origins and Mo dern Applications, Annual Institute on Mineral Law, Vol. 35, 1992, pp. 179-180.

concept of correlative rights grants a reasonable opportunity to produce from a common resource, rather than an equal share of that resource[50], the judgment held that every owner over a common reservoir must be afforded a fair opportunity to produce their just and equitable share. The loss caused by the blowout deprived the plaintiff of this opportunity, and therefore compensation was due. The key insight of the judgment was this: although under the rule of capture, a landowner's actual recovery may be reduced when an adjacent landowner drains away underground oil and gas from a common reservoir, that landowner's opportunity to produce and own the resources is not impaired. In this case, however, the blowout destroyed the plaintiff's well, thereby taking away their opportunity to produce and own the reasonable share of the common reservoir that they were entitled to produce and own.[51]

Consequently, in the statutes of some American states, correlative rights are defined as the landowner's right to a reasonable opportunity to produce and capture their just and equitable share of oil and gas from their land without waste.[52]

With the development of the petroleum industry and a deeper understanding of oil and gas development principles, a comprehensive set of

---

50 See Eugene Kuntz, Correlative Rights in Oil and Gas, *Mississippi Law Journa l*, Vol. 30, No. 1, 1958, p. 7.
51 See George W. Hardy II, the Doctrine of Correlative Rights: Origins and Mo dern Applications, Annual Institute on Mineral Law, Vol. 35, 1992, pp. 177-179.
52 See George W. Hardy II, the Doctrine of Correlative Rights: Origins and Mo dern Applications, Annual Institute on Mineral Law, Vol. 35, 1992, pp. 191-192.

solutions for the economically efficient development of oil and gas fields gradually took shape from a professional perspective. These included developing a field with the minimum number of wells and achieving the maximum recovery rate per well, all predicated on the surface area covering the entire field belonging to a single landowner. In the United States at that time, however, most land was privately owned, and oil and gas developers had to contend with a patchwork of different landowners. Only if all landowners treated themselves as a single entity, planning and developing rationally and steadily, could they maximize and equitably share the benefits. Therefore, the content of correlative rights expanded beyond the right to a reasonable opportunity to produce one's fair share of the resource. It evolved to include the right and responsibility of all adjacent parties to implement unitization of the entire common underground resource. According to the scholar Eugene Kuntz, the term "correlative rights" is used to describe the reciprocal rights and duties of the owners in a common source of supply[53]. Correlative rights refers to the duties that exist among all adjacent landowners in the development of a common underground oil and gas reservoir. Correlative rights mainly include four aspects: (1) not to waste substances produced from the common resource; (2) not to damage the common resource; (3) not to maliciously cause the depletion of the common resource; and (4) to have an equal opportunity to produce from the common

53 See George W. Hardy II, the Doctrine of Correlative Rights: Origins and Modern Applications, Annual Institute on Mineral Law, Vol. 35, 1992, pp. 173-174.

resource.[54]

(III) The Development of Unitization

Unitization may be achieved through voluntary agreements. A common practice is to include an authorization clause for pooling in lease agreements for oil and gas development. Such a clause, granted by the lessors (i.e., the various surface landowners participating in the pooling), authorizes the lessee (i.e., the oil and gas developer) to develop resources from a common underground reservoir as a single unit through rational well placement for the purpose of reasonable and centralized development. This is permitted even if this method might affect the legal rights of an individual lessor (specifically, the right to freely develop oil and gas resources on their own land)[55]. However, when dealing with self-interested individuals, this voluntary approach to cooperation is not always successfully realized. In some U.S. states, the government has developed the authority not only to regulate oil and gas production to prevent waste but also to adjust and protect the correlative rights of owners of a common reservoir.[56] For instance, the Louisiana Conservation Act requires the government to appoint a Commissioner of Conservation. The Commissioner's duties include

54 See Eugene Kuntz, Correlative Rights in Oil and Gas, *Mississippi Law Journa l*, Vol. 30, No. 1, 1958, pp. 1-8.
55 See George W. Hardy II, the Doctrine of Correlative Rights: Origins and Mo dern Applications, Annual Institute on Mineral Law, Vol. 35, 1992, p. 184.
56 See Ralph B. Shank, "Present Status of the Law of Capture", Proceedings of the Annual Institute on Oil and Gas Law and Taxation as It Affects the Oil and Gas Industry, 6, 1955, p. 278.

preventing the avoidable depletion of oil and gas resources caused by competitive drilling, ensuring that wells in a unitized field are rationally spaced, and guaranteeing that the production share of each tract participating in the unitization does not exceed its "just and equitable share."[57] Among the 19 oil and gas producing states in the U.S., all recognize correlative rights to varying degrees through legislation: 5 states explicitly define correlative rights in their statutes, 13 states provide for their protection, 7 states equate waste with a violation of these rights, 3 states expressly designate an administrative agency for their protection, and 7 states even provide a clear definition of a "just and equitable" share.[58] For the lessee (i.e., the oil and gas developer), acquiring the exclusive right to develop oil and gas resources comes with the concurrent duty to manage and protect the correlative rights of all lessors participating in the unitization[59].

Of course, whether voluntary or compulsory, the purpose of unitization is to avoid the misallocation of economic resources and eliminate waste.[60] Under a unitization system, the various surface landowners over a single reservoir cooperate to develop the underground reservoir as a whole. Typically, one company serves as the operator responsible for production and

57 See George W. Hardy II, the Doctrine of Correlative Rights: Origins and Modern Applications, Annual Institute on Mineral Law, Vol. 35, 1992, pp. 186-196.
58 See R. O. Kellam, A Century of Correlative Rights, *Baylor Law Review*, Vol. 12, No. 1, 1960, P. 35.
59 See George W. Hardy II, the Doctrine of Correlative Rights: Origins and Modern Applications, Annual Institute on Mineral Law, Vol. 35, 1992, pp. 184-186.
60 See George W. Hardy II, the Doctrine of Correlative Rights: Origins and Modern Applications, Annual Institute on Mineral Law, Vol. 35, 1992, pp. 184-185.

daily management, while the landowners form an operating committee to supervise the oil and gas operations and the operator's activities. Through unitization, unnecessary competition within the same reservoir is avoided. This is a vast improvement over the disorderly competition, inefficient development, and reduced recovery rates under the rule of capture, which result in resource waste. Therefore, from an industry perspective, it is the best management practice and, if properly implemented, also the best way to protect the correlative rights of all landowners.[61] Consequently, the concept of unitization has not only been recognized in U.S. domestic legislation but has also gradually become a consensus within the oil and gas industry, proven by industry practice to be a more scientific, orderly, economical, and environmentally friendly method for developing oil and gas resources while ensuring maximum benefits.

The application and development of the rule of capture and correlative rights are a product not only of the historical logic of the U.S. oil and gas industry but also of the economic and technical logic inherent in developing common reservoirs. The rule of capture and correlative rights are mutually complementary[62], representing two sides of the same coin in the development of common reservoirs. Together, they form the legal rationale for domestic

---

61 See Jacqueline Lang Weaver, *Unitization of Oil and Gas Fields in Texas: A Study of Legislative, Administrative, and Judicial Policies*, RFF Press, 2011, pp. 21-29; George W. Hardy II, the Doctrine of Correlative Rights: Origins and Modern Applications, Annual Institute on Mineral Law, Vol. 35, 1992, pp. 194-195, 203-204.

62 See Eugene Kuntz, The Law of Capture, *Oklahoma Law Review*, Vol. 10, No. 4, 1957, p. 408.

oil and gas development in the United States and determine the cooperative models used in practice. This legal rationale, in turn, has laid the jurisprudential foundation for the development of transboundary oil and gas resources, thereby providing cooperative models that can be drawn upon.

Section Two: Ownership of Oil and Gas Resources in Public International Law

Permanent sovereignty over natural resources is an important and evolving principle of international law. Oil and gas resources, as a component of natural resources, are of course governed by this principle. As discoveries of oil and gas reservoirs have increasingly shifted from being within single countries to being transboundary, and from onshore to offshore, the associated legal questions have also progressively developed within the realm of public international law. These questions pertain to the ownership of offshore oil and gas resources, their unitization—or joint development of transboundary resources—and even the joint development of resources in areas of disputed sovereignty.

I. The Emergence and Development of the Concept of Permanent Sovereignty over Natural Resources

The principle of state sovereignty is the cornerstone of the prevailing international legal order and its most important basic principle, considered to be "the supreme and externally independent power of a state."[63] State

63 See Zhou Gengsheng, *International Law* (Vol. 1), Wuhan University Press, 2009, p. 150.

sovereignty can be understood in two parts: internal and external. Internally, it signifies the supreme authority of the state, which is thereby clearly distinguished from private rights, particularly rights of ownership.[64] Externally, it means independence, free from the coercion or interference of any other authority. Sovereignty is not an abstract concept; it is vested in a specific, independent state with a fixed territory. A state necessarily exercises sovereignty over the territory it possesses, and the two are inseparable. Although a state may not be the owner of all land under its domestic law, in international relations it possesses the absolute right to control and dispose of its territory. The state holds both dominion over and ownership of its territory.[65]

According to the object theory of state territory, the relationship of a state with its territory is similar to that of an individual with their land and property. When a state exercises sovereignty over its territory and the things (res) upon it, the power it exercises is one of management. Although this power cannot be equated with the concept of ownership, in practice it has the characteristics of property rights.[66] If one analyzes from this perspective the sovereignty that a state possesses over its territory—that is, its various rights, powers, privileges, etc.—the term "territorial sovereignty" may be used to

---

64 See Richard Barnes, *Property Rights and Natural Resources*, Hart Publishing, 2009, p. 221.
65 See Zhou Gengsheng, *International Law* (Vol. 1), Wuhan University Press, 2009, p. 275.
66 See Richard Barnes, *Property Rights and Natural Resources*, Hart Publishing, 2009, pp. 221-224.

describe it.[67] Its principal components include the right to possess, the right to use, the right to manage, the right to the income of a thing, the right to the capital of the thing, the duty to prevent harm, and so on. The right to possess refers to the state's power to exercise exclusive physical control over its territory, and it is the most fundamental component of territorial sovereignty. The right to use is the state's autonomous right to the exclusive use of its territory. The right to manage is the state's right to decide how the territory is to be used and by whom. The right to the income of a thing is the state's right to derive various benefits from its territory; this constitutes the fundamental significance of territorial sovereignty and finds concrete expression in the concept of permanent sovereignty over natural resources. The right to the capital of the thing includes the state's right to freely acquire, use, waste, or even destroy the things upon its territory. Of course, although a state possesses permanent sovereignty over the natural resources within its territory and the right to use, waste, or even exhaust them, this right is, in some respects, subject to limitations. The duty to prevent harm, along with other related rights and responsibilities, constitutes a set of concepts: namely, the state has the power and the duty to take various measures to protect its territory and property from infringement by other states (or persons).[68]

Natural resources is a general term for naturally occurring things of

---

67 See Richard Barnes, *Property Rights and Natural Resources*, Hart Publishing, 2009, pp. 224-225.
68 See Richard Barnes, *Property Rights and Natural Resources*, Hart Publishing, 2009, pp. 228-231.

utility value, such as land, mineral deposits, climate, water, biological, and marine resources.[69] When these natural resources are situated within the territory of a state, they of course fall under the concept of "things upon the territory". When we are concerned with the ownership and usufruct of the natural resources upon a state's territory, the core issue is, as described above, that of territorial sovereignty.

After World War II, the old international order was shattered and a new one was gradually established. The decolonization movement flourished, and former colonial countries gained independence one after another, joining the United Nations as sovereign states. However, in these newly independent states, which had long served as resource suppliers for Western colonial powers, the natural resources that formed the material basis for their own survival and development remained under the control of foreign or multinational corporations. As a result, they were unable to achieve economic independence, and their political independence was thus difficult to sustain. When these newly independent states sought to reclaim control over their natural resources, Western nations would often counter that the resources had been obtained through concession contracts. They argued that based on the fundamental principle of international law that "agreements must be kept", these new states should not put forward any claims superior to the agreements. But the vast majority of newly independent states considered such

69 See Xia Zhengnong (ed.), *Cihai*, Shanghai Lexicographical Publishing House, 2000, p. 2286.

agreements to be inequitable. In order to safeguard their national sovereignty and independence and to ensure the survival and development of their peoples, they drew upon the legal rationale of sovereignty to propose the concept of the permanent sovereignty over natural resources, seeking to alter the prevailing situation. Thereafter, this concept gradually gained universal recognition from the international community, becoming an inalienable component of national sovereignty and one of the principles of international law.[70]

A series of resolutions adopted by the United Nations General Assembly is one of the primary legal sources for the principle of permanent sovereignty over natural resources. For instance, at the 8th session of the UN Commission on Human Rights in 1952, several states raised the issue of permanent sovereignty over natural resources. In December of that year, General Assembly Resolution 626 (VII), "Right to exploit freely natural wealth and resources," stated: "States have the right to freely use and exploit their natural resources." In 1960, General Assembly Resolution 1515 (XV) recommended that "the sovereign right of every State to dispose of its wealth and natural resources should be respected in conformity with the rights and duties of States under international law." In the Declaration on the Granting of Independence to Colonial Countries and Peoples, adopted at the same session, it was "reaffirmed that All peoples may, for their own ends, freely dispose of

70 See Yang Zewei, *Analysis of International Law* (5th ed.), China Renmin Univ ersity Press, 2022, pp. 124-125.

their natural wealth and resources without prejudice to any obligations arising out of international economic co-operation, based upon the principle of mutual benefit, and international law." The 1962 Declaration on Permanent Sovereignty over Natural Resources, adopted by the 17th Session of the UN General Assembly, proclaimed "the right of peoples and nations to permanent sovereignty over their natural wealth and resources," emphasized that a state's permanent sovereignty over its natural resources is a fundamental element of the right of self-determination, and set forth the rights and conditions for nationalization. UN General Assembly Resolution 2692 (XXV) of 1970 and Resolution 3016 (XXVII) of 1972 extended the permanent sovereignty of states over their natural resources from land to the resources of adjacent seas and of the waters superjacent to the continental shelf. In 1974, the Sixth Special Session of the UN General Assembly adopted the Declaration on the Establishment of a New International Economic Order and the Programme of Action, drafted by the Group of 77. The Declaration proclaimed the "full permanent sovereignty of every State over its natural resources and all economic activities. In order to safeguard these resources, every State has the right to take suitable measures to exercise effective control over its resources and their exploitation with means suitable to its own situation, including the right to nationalization or the transfer of ownership to its nationals. This right is an expression of the full permanent sovereignty of the State." The Programme of Action not only affirmed in principle permanent sovereignty over natural resources but also provided for putting an end to "all forms of foreign occupation, racial discrimination, apartheid, colonial, neo-colonial and alien domination and exploitation through the exercise of permanent sovereignty over natural resources."

Furthermore, some international treaties also make explicit provision for permanent sovereignty over natural resources. For example, Article 2 of the 1958 Convention on the Continental Shelf points out that the coastal State has the right to explore and exploit the natural resources of the continental shelf. Article 1, paragraph 2 of the 1966 International Covenant on Economic, Social and Cultural Rights provides that "All peoples may, for their own ends, freely dispose of their natural wealth and resources." The 1982 United Nations Convention on the Law of the Sea, in addition to reaffirming the rights provided for in the Convention on the Continental Shelf, also provides in Article 56 that the coastal State has sovereign rights in the exclusive economic zone for the purpose of exploring and exploiting, conserving and managing the natural resources of the waters superjacent to the seabed and of the seabed and its subsoil, as well as sovereign rights with regard to other activities for the economic exploitation and exploration of the zone. The 1994 Energy Charter Treaty recognizes the sovereign rights of states over energy resources, noting that states continue to hold the right to determine which areas within their territory may be made available for energy development and utilization, and provides that the Treaty shall in no way impair the rules of the contracting parties governing the system of ownership of energy resources.

Some international judicial precedents have also affirmed the principle of permanent sovereignty over natural resources. For instance, in the 1977 arbitration case of Libyan American Oil Company (LIAMCO) v. Government of the Libyan Arab Republic, the sole arbitrator held that the Declaration on Permanent Sovereignty over Natural Resources, although not a source of law, represented the latest prevailing trend regarding permanent sovereignty over natural resources and recommended that the sovereign right of states to freely dispose of their natural wealth and resources should be respected.[71] In the 1982 arbitration case of Kuwait v. American Independent Oil Company (AMINOIL), the arbitration tribunal ruled that the decision by the Kuwaiti government to terminate its concession agreement with the AMINOIL for the exploration and exploitation of oil and natural gas was lawful, as the decision was made for the purpose of fully assuming ownership of its oil resources and placing them under state control.[72]

Thus, the concept that permanent sovereignty over natural resources is an inseparable part of state sovereignty—an inherent, inalienable right of a state—was gradually established and became universally recognized by the

71 See Nico Schrijver, *Sovereignty Over Natural Resources: Balancing Rights an d Duties*, Cambridge University Press, 1997, p. 261; Meng Guobi, A Brief Discu ssion on the Theory and Practice of the Principle of Economic Sovereignty, PhD dissertation, Xiamen University, 2000, p. 32.
72 See Yao Meizhen (ed.), *A Study of International Investment Law Cases*, Wuha n University Press, 1989, pp. 125-144.

international community. Its specific contents mainly include that each state or people has, within its jurisdiction, the right to: freely dispose of its natural resources and wealth; freely explore and develop natural resources; restore effective control over natural resources and receive compensation for damages; utilize natural resources for national and popular development; manage natural resources in accordance with national environmental policy; equitably share in the benefits of transboundary natural resources; regulate foreign investment; and expropriate or nationalize foreign investment, among others.[73] Oil and gas resources, as a part of natural resources, are of course governed by this principle of permanent sovereignty over natural resources.

II. The Issue of Ownership in the Development of Offshore Oil and Gas Resources

The legal regime for the sea is different from that for land, and the application of state sovereignty also varies. With respect to the development of offshore oil and gas resources, the question of ownership (title) is critically important. This is because it determines whether a state has the authority to transfer its title to the resources to a developer for the global market, and under what law it may grant resource concessions to developers.[74] For the oil and gas companies acting as developers, given that offshore exploration

---

73 See Yang Zewei, *Analysis of International Law* (5th ed.), China Renmin Univ ersity Press, 2022, pp. 128-134.
74 See Richard Barnes, *Property Rights and Natural Resources*, Hart Publishing, 2009, p. 252.

and development entails long timeframes, high capital costs, substantial technological investment, and high operational risks, it is very difficult for them to decide to participate in a project in any given sea area in the absence of a clear legal regime that defines ownership of the oil and gas resources. Therefore, clarifying the question of oil and gas resource ownership under the maritime legal regime is fundamental to undertaking offshore oil and gas exploration and development, and it is also, of course, a critical issue that must be resolved for the joint development of these resources.

(I) Ownership of Oil and Gas Resources of the Coastal State in the Territorial Sea

According to Article 2 of the United Nations Convention on the Law of the Sea, the sovereignty of a coastal State extends to the seabed and subsoil of the territorial sea, and the exercise of this sovereignty is subject to the Convention and other rules of international law. Accordingly, the coastal State's ownership of the oil and gas resources within its territorial sea is in no way different from its sovereignty over oil and gas resources on its land territory.

(II) Sovereign Rights of the Coastal State over Oil and Gas Resources in the Exclusive Economic Zone[75]

---

75 The coastal State's ownership of oil and gas resources in the contiguous zone is similar to that in the exclusive economic zone and is therefore not elaborated upon here.

According to Article 56 of the United Nations Convention on the Law of the Sea, the coastal State in the exclusive economic zone has "sovereign rights for the purpose of exploring and exploiting, conserving and managing the natural resources, whether living or non-living, of the seabed and its subsoil, and with regard to other activities for the economic exploitation and exploration of the zone, such as the production of energy from the water, currents and winds," and the rights with respect to the seabed and subsoil shall be exercised in accordance with the provisions concerning the continental shelf. At the same time, when exercising its rights and performing its duties in the exclusive economic zone in accordance with the Convention, the coastal State has an obligation to have due regard to the rights of other States.

(III) Sovereign Rights of the Coastal State over Oil and Gas Resources on the Continental Shelf

According to Article 77 of the United Nations Convention on the Law of the Sea, the coastal State exercises sovereign rights over the continental shelf for the purpose of exploring it and exploiting its natural resources; these rights are exclusive in the sense that if the coastal State does not explore the continental shelf or exploit its natural resources, no one may undertake these activities without the express consent of the coastal State; the sovereign rights of the coastal State over the continental shelf do not depend on occupation, effective or notional, or on any express proclamation. Article 81 provides that the coastal State shall have the exclusive right to authorize and regulate drilling on the continental shelf for all purposes; Article 82 provides for payments and contributions in kind with respect to the exploitation of the non-living resources on the outer continental shelf.

Thus, in the exclusive economic zone and on the continental shelf, the coastal State possesses the exclusive sovereign right to explore and exploit offshore oil and gas resources, as well as the sovereign right to regulate the relevant activities. This sovereign right can be understood as the exclusive right of the coastal State to itself explore and develop (or not to explore and develop) the oil and gas resources located in the relevant maritime areas, to permit (or not to permit) others to explore and develop these resources, and to manage the related exploration and development activities and facilities.

Some scholars argue that under the maritime legal regime, there is no ownership offshore, and therefore a coastal State does not own the natural resources of the sea; it may only, in accordance with Articles 56 and 77 of the United Nations Convention on the Law of the Sea, enjoy sovereign rights to explore and exploit these resources. However, many EU countries, such as Denmark, Norway, Spain, and the Netherlands, claim not only the right to regulate offshore oil and gas resources but also ownership.[76] Similarly, Article 27 of Mexico's Constitution provides that the Nation has direct

76 See William Hughes, *Fundamentals of International Oil and Gas Law*, PennWell Corporation, 2016, p. 231.

ownership of all natural resources of the land, the continental shelf, and islands and their continental shelves, particularly oil and gas and other hydrocarbon resources.[77] The United Kingdom, based on its interpretation of international law, has not claimed ownership of unexploited offshore oil and gas resources.[78] According to the U.S. Outer Continental Shelf Lands Act, the U.S. federal government has control of the seabed and subsoil of the sea beyond three nautical miles from the coast and the related oil and gas resources, but in the Act, the U.S. Congress did not make clear whether the federal government has ownership and jurisdiction.[79]

(IV) Ownership of Transboundary Oil and Gas Resources

Due to the fluid nature of oil and gas, an international practice of unitization has gradually formed for transboundary oil and gas resources where boundaries have been delimited. Agreements for unitization implicitly treat the relevant maritime oil and gas resources as "joint property."[80] As a general rule, the management of oil and gas exploration and development on each side of a delimited boundary is conducted in accordance with the respective national laws of each state, while the allocation of the oil and gas

---

77 See Jorge A. Vargas, Mexico's Legal Regime Over Its Marine Space: A Proposal for the Delimitation of the Continental Shelf in the Deepest Part of the Gulf of Mexico, *University of Miami Inter-American Law Review*, Vol. 26, No. 2, 1995, p. 195.
78 See William Hughes, *Fundamentals of International Oil and Gas Law*, PennWell Corporation, 2016, p. 253.
79 See William Hughes, *Fundamentals of International Oil and Gas Law*, PennWell Corporation, 2016, p. 232, 253.
80 See David M. Ong, Joint Development of Common Offshore Oil and Gas Deposits: "Mere" State Practice or Customary International Law? *American Journal of International Law*, Vol. 93, 1999, p. 778.

resources can be resolved equitably and reasonably on a technical basis. For example, Article 2 of the 1993 Maritime Delimitation Treaty between Jamaica and the Republic of Colombia stipulates that if a reservoir is found to straddle the delimitation line, the oil and gas produced shall be apportioned in proportion to the subsoil reserves found on each side.[81] Article 9 of the 2002 Timor Sea Treaty between the Government of East Timor and the Government of Australia, which governs unitization, provides that for any transboundary oil or gas field, the two states shall agree on a method for the equitable sharing of the benefits of development[82]. The agreement with the most detailed provisions, however, is that for the joint development of the Frigg gas field by the UK and Norway. According to this agreement, the British and Norwegian governments were to agree on the apportionment of the field's production. This apportionment is based on an assessment of the gas reserves and is not a one-time, final decision; it is subject to redetermination through periodic reviews and re-evaluations to ensure that the final share of gas received by each country remains consistent with the proportional distribution of the reserves in place.[83] In other words, the entire gas field is divided in two by the maritime boundary, with each country

---

81 See Yang Zewei (ed.), *International Agreements on the Joint Development of Marine Resources* (Chinese-English Bilingual Version) (Vol. I), Social Sciences Academic Press (China), 2016, p. 325.
82 See Yang Zewei (ed.), *International Agreements on the Joint Development of Marine Resources* (Chinese-English Bilingual Version) (Vol. II), Social Sciences Academic Press (China), 2016, p. 524.
83 See Yang Zewei (ed.), *International Agreements on the Joint Development of Marine Resources* (Chinese-English Bilingual Version) (Vol. I), Social Sciences Academic Press (China), 2016, pp. 118-121, 156-158.

possessing an unequal share of the total reserves. Through unitization, the gas produced is allocated according to the apportionment of the subsoil reserves. However, subsoil reserves are ultimately estimates that cannot be measured with precision, and they may also change due to the progress of development, geological shifts, or new geological insights gained during exploitation. Periodic reviews thus allow for adjustments to the apportionment of the remaining reserves, ensuring that the gas production each country receives remains broadly consistent with the division of the subsoil reserves, thereby achieving an equitable and reasonable outcome.

(V) Ownership of Oil and Gas Resources in Areas of Overlapping Claims

In maritime areas with overlapping claims where boundaries have not been delimited, the disputing parties, pursuant to international law including the United Nations Convention on the Law of the Sea, each assert their sovereign rights over the relevant area and, consequently, their exclusive sovereign rights to explore and exploit the oil and gas resources therein. In reality, however, these mutual disputes often lead to protracted standoffs or even confrontation. Should one party insist on unilateral exploration and development by invoking its sovereign rights, this could provoke maritime conflicts or international litigation. Joint development offers a viable solution, allowing the parties to enjoy the economic benefits from exploiting oil and gas resources before the dispute is settled. Under such a provisional arrangement, the parties to the dispute share the oil and gas resources produced and jointly manage development activities, all without prejudice to their respective legal positions, including their claims to ownership of the resources or, in other words, the exclusive right to their exploration and exploitation.[84] Similar to transboundary unitization agreements, existing joint development agreements also implicitly treat the relevant maritime oil and gas resources as "joint property."[85]

For example, Article 16 of the 1974 Agreement between Japan and the Republic of Korea Concerning Joint Development of the Southern Part of the Continental Shelf Adjacent to the Two Countries[86] provides that natural resources extracted and owned by concessionaires in the joint development zone shall be deemed to be natural resources extracted from the continental shelf over which each party exercises sovereign rights.[87] Article 3 of the 1979 Memorandum of Understanding between Malaysia and the Kingdom of Thailand on the Establishment of the Joint Authority for the Exploitation of the Resources of the Sea-bed in a Defined Area of the Continental Shelf of

84 See William Hughes, *Fundamentals of International Oil and Gas Law*, PennWell Corporation, 2016, pp. 2234-2248.

85 See David M. Ong, Joint Development of Common Offshore Oil and Gas Deposits: "Mere" State Practice or Customary International Law? *American Journal of International Law*, Vol. 93, 1999, p. 778.

86 It must be pointed out that this Japan-ROK agreement on joint development infringed upon China's sovereign rights over its continental shelf in the East China Sea and was met with protests from the Chinese government. Although this book refers to the agreement in several places for the purposes of discussion, this does not imply my endorsement of the said agreement.

87 See Yang Zewei (ed.), *International Agreements on the Joint Development of Marine Resources* (Chinese-English Bilingual Version) (Vol. I), Social Sciences Academic Press (China), 2016, p. 72.

the Two Countries in the Gulf of Thailand stipulates that the two countries shall establish a Joint Authority to explore and exploit the non-living resources of the seabed and subsoil within the overlapping area, and that the Joint Authority shall, on behalf of both countries, hold the rights and responsibilities for all non-living natural resources of the seabed and subsoil in this area.[88] Furthermore, Article 5 of the Malaysia-Thailand Joint Authority Act 440 (1991) clarifies that the Joint Authority is vested with and shall assume the exclusive rights, powers, liberties, and privileges related to the exploration and exploitation of natural resources, particularly petroleum resources, in the joint development area.[89]

III. The Issue of the Rule of Capture in International Law

The applicability of the rule of capture in international law is a matter of considerable scholarly debate.

Some scholars argue that the rule of capture is applicable in international law and, by extension, to the development of offshore oil and gas resources under the continental shelf regime. The underlying reasoning is that once an oil company, as a lessee, obtains a concession from a state, it possesses the

88 See Yang Zewei (ed.), *International Agreements on the Joint Development of Marine Resources* (Chinese-English Bilingual Version) (Vol. I), Social Sciences Academic Press (China), 2016, p. 182.
89 See Yang Zewei (ed.), *International Agreements on the Joint Development of Marine Resources* (Chinese-English Bilingual Version) (Vol. I), Social Sciences Academic Press (China), 2016, pp. 231-232.

right to exploit oil and gas resources on that state's continental shelf. It is therefore entitled to extract as much oil and gas as it can from the subsoil, regardless of whether the resources were originally in place in the reservoir or have migrated across a boundary from the subsoil of a neighboring state. Even if an oil company holding a concession from an adjacent state finds its development interests in the same reservoir harmed by the first company's production, the first company may disregard this. It need only concern itself with its own petroleum development contract with the granting state, a contract which would contain no clause prohibiting it from maximizing the recovery of oil and gas resources.[90]

In summarizing the discussions on the relevant issues at the third meeting of the 1985 East-West Center workshops on Southeast Asian maritime problems, scholar Masahiro Miyoshi stated that the consensus among the vast majority of legal experts in attendance was that the rule of capture is inapplicable in international law.[91] These scholars argue that it is precisely because oil and gas resources are fluid that when a subsoil reservoir crosses national (onshore or offshore) boundaries, unilateral development by one party will cause harm to the interests of others. For a single transboundary deposit, they contend, unitization should be pursued through

90 See Joseph W. Morris, the North Sea Continental shelf: Oil and Gas Legal Pr oblems, *International Lawyer*. Vol. 2, 1967, pp. 203-210.
91 See Masahiro Miyoshi, The Basic Concept of Joint Development of Hydrocar bon Resources on the Continental Shelf: With Special Reference to the Discussio ns at the East-West Centre Workshops on the South-East Asian Seas, *Internationa l Journal of Estuarine and Coastal Law*, Vol. 3, No.1, 1988, pp. 5-7.

cooperation to allow each party to receive an equitable and reasonable share. This is the most fundamental element of the concept of joint development of maritime oil and gas resources.[92] Scholar David Ong, meanwhile, argues that with respect to the development of marine living and non-living resources, while many international agreements require coastal states to cooperate, there is no clear legal obligation as to the form and content of this cooperation, making the provisions more declaratory than mandatory. However, according to his review, there is no explicit provision in international law establishing that the rule of capture prevails over the principle of cooperation.[93]

Scholar Logchem thinks that the logic for applying the rule of capture to international law is based on state sovereignty, which entitles a state to act freely and thus to take any action under the rule of capture to maximize production from the oil and gas fields it possesses. However, it is oil companies—merely private actors—that carry out the development of oil and gas fields, whereas international law directly regulates states, not companies. A coastal state possesses sovereign rights over the continental shelf ab initio and de jure. The exploration and development of marine oil and gas resources on the continental shelf is a manifestation of a coastal state's sovereign rights and can therefore only be undertaken by the state itself or with its

92 See Masahiro Miyoshi, The Basic Concept of Joint Development of Hydrocar bon Resources on the Continental Shelf: With Special Reference to the Discussio ns at the East-West Centre Workshops on the South-East Asian Seas, *Internationa l Journal of Estuarine and Coastal Law*, Vol. 3, No.1, 1988, p. 6.

93 See David M. Ong, Joint Development of Common Offshore Oil and Gas De posits: "Mere" State Practice or Customary International Law? *American Journal of International Law*, Vol. 93, 1999, p. 777.

authorization. Under international law, a coastal state may have an Exclusive Economic Zone, and enjoys exclusive sovereign rights therein, including for the exploitation of living and non-living resources. With regard to oil and gas resources located in areas of overlapping claims, each coastal state, in accordance with international law, lawfully possesses sovereignty and jurisdiction over them. If a state, whether acting by itself or through an oil company, takes unilateral action to explore and develop oil and gas resources in an area of overlapping claims without regard for the rights of other states, it will necessarily infringe upon the sovereign rights of those other states—rights that are of equal strength, substance, and validity. For oil and gas resources that straddle a delimited boundary, unilateral development based on the rule of capture will also necessarily infringe upon the sovereign rights of other states to the resources located on their side. The principle of good neighbourliness, which developed from the maxim "sic utere tuo, ut alienum non laedas" (use your own property in such a way as not to injure that of another) and has been accepted into customary international law, provides that a state has an obligation to ensure that activities within its jurisdiction and control respect areas under the jurisdiction of other states and the environment as a whole. Under this principle, a state should avoid having its oil and gas exploration and development activities on its continental shelf infringe upon the sovereign rights of other coastal states over their own continental shelves.[94] Therefore, the rule of capture is not applicable in

94 See Youri van Logchem, The Status of a Rule of Capture Under International

international law.

Of course, the rule of capture, as a foundational principle for the development of the oil and gas industry, still appears from time to time in rules of international law concerning the exploration and development of offshore oil and gas resources. As noted previously, the United Kingdom, according to its interpretation of international law, does not consider itself to have ownership of unextracted offshore oil and gas resources, a position consistent with the rule of capture's concept of "ownership by capture." For another example, many scholars argue that from a practical perspective, the line between a coastal state's exclusive sovereign rights to explore and exploit oil and gas resources in its Exclusive Economic Zone and on its continental shelf, and its ownership of those resources, is not particularly clear.[95] However, the distinction is clarified if explained through the logic of the rule of capture: for the oil and gas resources in the subsoil of the EEZ and continental shelf, the coastal state possesses the sovereign rights to exploration and development; once they are produced, the coastal state naturally acquires ownership by taking control of them. Because the coastal state's relevant sovereign rights are exclusive, its ownership of the oil and gas resources is therefore also quite clear. And the most conspicuous evidence for the application of the rule of capture in offshore oil and gas

---

Law of the Sea with Regard to Offshore Oil and Gas Resource Related Activiti es, *Michigan State International Law Review*, Vol. 26, No. 2, 2018, pp. 202-219.
95 See William Hughes, *Fundamentals of International Oil and Gas Law*, PennW ell Corporation, 2016, p. 231.

development can even be found in the clauses of many joint development agreements. For example, Article 1 of the Timor Sea Treaty between the Government of East Timor and the Government of Australia specifies that its definition of "petroleum" includes not only petroleum that occurs naturally but also petroleum that has been returned to a natural reservoir.[96] In the 2012 Treaty between the Government of the Republic of Seychelles and the Government of the Republic of Mauritius Concerning the Joint Management of the Continental Shelf in the Mascarene Plateau Region, the definition of petroleum in Article 1 also includes petroleum that is naturally formed and that which is returned into a reservoir.[97] Here, petroleum that is "returned" to a reservoir refers to petroleum that may not have originally belonged to the subsoil reservoir of the joint development area, but which migrated into that reservoir from elsewhere after the petroleum in the joint development area began to be produced. This is, in practice, still an application of the rule of capture.

In summary, for offshore oil and gas resources, whether located in transboundary or disputed maritime areas, international law does not support the application of the rule of capture to their exploration and development. Of course, while joint development is not the only option for dealing with the

96 See Yang Zewei (ed.), *International Agreements on the Joint Development of Marine Resources* (Chinese-English Bilingual Version) (Vol. II), Social Sciences A cademic Press (China), 2016, p. 517.
97 See Yang Zewei (ed.), *International Agreements on the Joint Development of Marine Resources* (Chinese-English Bilingual Version) (Vol. II), Social Sciences A cademic Press (China), 2016, p. 668.

development of offshore oil and gas resources, it can be argued that it has become a realistic and viable choice among coastal states precisely because they recognize the harm brought by the rule of capture and seek to avoid unnecessary waste and competition.[98] Consequently, the unitization of transboundary offshore oil and gas resources, and the joint development of resources in areas of overlapping claims, have naturally become an inevitable choice for those relevant coastal states that are eager to develop the resources and enjoy their benefits, yet must also be mindful of each other's interests.

98 See David M. Ong, Joint Development of Common Offshore Oil and Gas Deposits: "Mere" State Practice or Customary International Law? *American Journal of International Law*, Vol. 93, 1999, p. 778.

Chapter Summary

A clear definition of property rights is of paramount importance in oil and gas development. Due to the fluid nature of oil and gas resources, determining ownership is critical in situations where a single underground reservoir underlies surface lands belonging to different owners. In the early days of the modern oil and gas industry, the United States, where the industry originated, adopted the rule of capture to determine ownership. This rule facilitated the rapid development of the industry, becoming a cornerstone of its legal framework. However, the application of the rule of capture also had significant negative consequences, leading to disorderly competition, waste, and pollution. With the emergence and development of the doctrine of correlative rights, the unitization of a single reservoir by different surface landowners became a practical option in the U.S. oil and gas industry and was eventually enshrined in law.

As modern industry developed, countries placed increasing importance on securing oil and gas resources. As newly independent states emerged from colonialism, they came to value the economic and political benefits of these resources. In their struggle with former colonial powers for ownership and control, the concept of permanent sovereignty over natural resources gained prominence. Ownership of oil and gas resources is, of course, a component of this principle.

Due to the differences between the maritime and terrestrial regimes in international law, the issue of ownership is of great importance for the development of offshore oil and gas resources. Pursuant to the rules of international law, including the United Nations Convention on the Law of the Sea, coastal states enjoy varying degrees of sovereignty and sovereign rights over offshore oil and gas resources located in the territorial sea, contiguous zone, exclusive economic zone, and continental shelf. As for transboundary oil and gas resources and those in areas of overlapping claims, the relevant coastal states enjoy joint ownership.

Although the rule of capture laid the legal foundation for the development of the oil and gas industry, it is not applicable in the rules of international law concerning the exploration and development of offshore oil and gas resources. It is precisely because the shortcomings of the rule of capture are recognized—and particularly under the norms of international law requiring due regard for the interests of other parties and the principle of good neighbourliness—that joint development has become a realistic, viable, and inevitable choice for coastal states when developing oil and gas resources in transboundary areas and areas of overlapping claims.

Chapter 2: The Historical Development of Joint Development of Offshore Oil and Gas Resources and Different Scenarios of Its Legal Application

Section One: The Historical Development of Joint Development of Offshore Oil and Gas Resources

As mentioned above, the joint development of offshore oil and gas resources refers to the process whereby two or more states, on the basis of a joint development agreement, jointly explore and develop oil and gas resources in transboundary or disputed maritime areas.①

In February 1958, Bahrain and Saudi Arabia concluded the Bahrain-Saudi Arabia Boundary Agreement② to implement the joint development of offshore oil and gas resources. Since then, the practice of states jointly developing oil and gas resources in transboundary or disputed maritime areas has become a relatively common phenomenon. To date, there have been more than 30 such instances of state practice.

A review of the 60-plus-year evolution of the joint development of offshore oil and gas resources reveals four distinct stages. First, the emergence stage (1958-1969), which saw a total of six cases of joint development in the Persian Gulf and Western Europe. Second, the development stage (1970-1993), featuring a total of 16 cases that involved

① See Yang Zewei (ed.), *A Study on the Theory and Practice of International L aw on Joint Maritime Development*, Wuhan University Press, 2018, p. 1.
② See Bahrain-Saudi Arabia Boundary Agreement, 22 February 1958, available a t http://www.un.org/Depts/los/LEGISLATIONANDTREATIES/PDFFILES/TREATIES/BHR-SAU1958BA.PDF.

27 countries: 11 in Asia, 5 in Europe, 7 in Africa, 3 in the Americas, and Australia in Oceania. Third, the decline stage (1994-1999), with only one such case: the Joint Declaration on Cooperation over Offshore Activities in the South West Atlantic, signed by the United Kingdom and Argentina in September 1995. Fourth, the stabilization stage (2000-present); since the beginning of the 21st century, joint development activities have gradually increased once more, resulting in 15 instances of state practice.

I. The Emergence Stage of Joint Development (1958-1969)

During this stage, a total of six instances of state practice concerning the joint development of offshore oil and gas resources took place in the Persian Gulf and Western Europe.

(I) Joint Development Cases in the 1950s

In the 1950s, state practice in the international community regarding the joint development of offshore oil and gas resources was still in its infancy. There was only one such case during this period: the 1958 Joint Development of the Persian Gulf Continental Shelf by Bahrain and Saudi Arabia.

On February 22, 1958, Bahrain and Saudi Arabia concluded the Bahrain-Saudi Arabia Boundary Agreement. This was the world's first agreement involving the joint development of offshore oil and gas resources. The agreement provided that, in addition to delimiting the continental shelf boundary between them, the oil resources in a hexagonal area of Fasht bu Saafa, which was under Saudi Arabian jurisdiction, would be developed in a manner determined by Saudi Arabia, while the Government of Bahrain would receive one-half of the net government revenue derived therefrom. The agreement also stressed that this arrangement was without prejudice to Saudi Arabia's sovereign rights and administrative jurisdiction in that area.③

(II) Joint Development Cases in the 1960s

In the 1960s, state practice in the joint development of offshore oil and gas resources gradually grew more frequent. There were a total of five such cases during this period.

1. The 1962 Case of Joint Development of Resources in the Ems Estuary by the Netherlands and the Federal Republic of Germany. On May 14, 1962, the Netherlands and the Federal Republic of Germany signed the Supplementary Agreement to the Treaty Concerning Arrangements for Cooperation in the Ems Estuary (Ems-Dollard Treaty), signed between the Kingdom of the Netherlands and the Federal Republic of Germany.④ Under the agreement, the Netherlands and the Federal Republic of Germany were

③ See "The 1958 Case of Joint Development of the Persian Gulf Continental Sh elf by Bahrain and Saudi Arabia," in Yang Zewei (ed.), *International Agreements on the Joint Development of Marine Resources* (Chinese-English Bilingual Versio n) (Vol. I), Social Sciences Academic Press (China), 2016, pp. 3-9; Guan Peifeng, The Case of the Continental Shelf Delimitation and Resource Sharing between Bahrain and Saudi Arabia, in Yang Zewei (ed.), *Research on International Law I ssues of Joint Maritime Development*, Social Sciences Academic Press (China), 20 16, pp. 123-136.

④ See the United Nations, Treaty Series, Vol. 508, footnote 1, p. 20.

to establish an oil and gas development zone along the boundary line. Each party was to exercise its jurisdiction and carry out exploration and development of oil and gas resources on its side of the boundary, but both parties were entitled to an equal share of the oil and natural gas produced, with costs also to be shared in the same proportion.⑤

2. The 1965 Joint Development Case Between Saudi Arabia and Kuwait. On July 7, 1965, Saudi Arabia and Kuwait signed the Agreement between the Kingdom of Saudi Arabia and the State of Kuwait on the Partition of the Neutral Zone. The agreement partitioned the Neutral Zone, established by the 1922 Convention of Al-Uqair between these two countries, into two equal parts, which were annexed respectively to the two countries "as an integral part of its territory." Each country was to exercise rights of administration, legislation, and defense over its portion, while mutually respecting the other's rights to the natural resources in the corresponding portion. In addition, the agreement provided that, unless the parties agreed otherwise, they would have equal rights to a submarine area adjoining the partitioned zone, to be exercised by way of joint development.⑥

---

⑤ See "The 1962 Case of Joint Development of Resources in the Ems Estuary by the Netherlands and the Federal Republic of Germany," in Yang Zewei (ed.), *International Agreements on the Joint Development of Marine Resources* (Chinese-English Bilingual Version) (Vol. I), Social Sciences Academic Press (China), 2016, pp. 10-27.

⑥ See "The 1965 Joint Development Case Between Saudi Arabia and Kuwait," in Yang Zewei (ed.), *International Agreements on the Joint Development of Marine Resources* (Chinese-English Bilingual Version) (Vol. I), Social Sciences Academic Press (China), 2016, pp. 28-38.

3. The 1969 Joint Development Case Between Qatar and Abu Dhabi. On March 20, 1969, Qatar and Abu Dhabi concluded the Agreement on Settlement of Maritime Boundary Lines and Sovereign Rights over Islands between Qatar and Abu Dhabi.[7] The agreement stipulated that the Al-Bunduq field would be "equally shared" by both parties, and that they should consult regularly on all matters concerning the field in order to exercise all rights on an equal basis. In accordance with the agreement, the field was to be developed by the Abu Dhabi Marine Areas (ADMA) Company under the terms of the concession specified in its regulations, with all costs and revenues shared equally by the two governments.[8]

4. The 1967 Joint Development Case Between Iran and Iraq. In January 1967, Iran and Iraq signed the Agreement on the Joint Development of the Khanaqin-Kana-Naft-i-Shah Oilfield to implement the joint development of offshore oil and gas resources between the two countries.[9]

It is worth noting that some scholars also include the joint development implemented under the Agreement between the Government of the Czechoslovakia Republic and the Austria Federal Government Concerning the Working of Common Deposits of Natural Gas and Petroleum[10], signed on

⑦ See Agreement on Settlement of Maritime Boundary Lines and Sovereign Rights over Islands between Qatar and Abu Dhabi, 30 March 1969, ST/LEG/SER. B /16, p. 403.

⑧ See Yu Hui, International Law Issues on the Joint Development of Marine Mineral Resources, *Chinese Yearbook of International Law*, 1994, p. 52.

⑨ See Xiao Jianguo, *Joint Development of Petroleum on International Maritime Boundaries*, China Ocean Press, 2006, p. 8.

⑩ See Agreement Concerning the Working of Common Deposits of Natural Gas

January 23, 1960, as a case from this period. Although this agreement concerned the development of land-based resources, it set a precedent for resolving issues related to the development of transboundary offshore oil and gas resources.[11]

However, why did six instances of state practice concerning the joint development of offshore oil and gas resources emerge in the Persian Gulf and Western Europe during this stage? In my view, this was primarily for the following reasons.

1. The growing awareness among coastal states of the need to safeguard their maritime rights and interests after the Second World War

On the one hand, after the end of the Second World War, the rapid development of the offshore oil industry prompted coastal states to assert the broadest possible claims or demands over the ocean, particularly offshore areas, in order to expand their opportunities for acquiring resources. On the other hand, the proclamation on the continental shelf issued by U.S. President Truman spurred many other countries to enact their own continental shelf laws. In 1945, President Truman issued Proclamation No. 2667, Policy of the United States With Respect to the Natural Resources of the Subsoil and Sea Bed of the Continental Shelf, which asserted the right of a coastal state to the

---

and Petroleum, 23 January 1960, CZECHOSLOVAKIA-AUSTRIA, U.N.T.S. Vol. 495, pp. 134-140; available at https://treaties.un.org/doc/Publication/UNTS/Volume%20495/volume-495-I-7241-English.pdf.

11 See Yu Hui, International Law Issues on the Joint Development of Marine Mineral Resources, *Chinese Yearbook of International Law*, 1994, p. 51.

natural resources of its continental shelf, leading many other nations to follow suit. By the time the Convention on the Continental Shelf was signed in 1958, some 50 countries worldwide had proclaimed their own continental shelf legislation [12] and had begun to consider their economic interests in developing the ocean and its resources.

2. A deeper global understanding of the importance of offshore oil and gas resources

From the mid-to-late 1950s, petroleum and natural gas became the first and third largest components, respectively, of the global primary energy consumption structure, transforming them into vital strategic materials for national economic development, political stability, and military security. However, after decades of large-scale extraction, some land-based oil and gas reserves were exhausted or nearing depletion, becoming increasingly inadequate to meet human demand. Against this backdrop, the development and utilization of offshore oil and gas resources became an urgent matter directly affecting national survival and development. Consequently, countries around the world gradually turned their attention to the oceans, leading to a surge in the exploration and exploitation of seabed oil and gas resources after the Second World War.

---

12 See [Canada] Barry Buzan, *Seabed Politics*, trans. by Shi Fuxin, SDX Joint Publishing Company, 1981, pp. 17-22; Hua Jingxin, *A Course of the Law of the Sea*, China Ocean University Press, 2009, p. 155.

3. Favorable bilateral relations

Stable and amicable relations between states are a key prerequisite for and guarantee of the joint development of offshore oil and gas resources. The countries involved in the joint development cases of this period generally maintained stable and close relationships. For example, Bahrain was historically a major entrepôt for Saudi Arabia, and the two countries have long maintained close economic and trade ties; similarly, Saudi Arabia and Kuwait have a long history of peaceful coexistence. On September 14, 1960, to coordinate petroleum policies and safeguard their common interests, Saudi Arabia, Kuwait, Iran, and Iraq, together with Venezuela, founded the Organization of Petroleum Exporting Countries (OPEC), [13] further advancing relations among the Persian Gulf states. Moreover, the Netherlands and the Federal Republic of Germany, as fellow members of both NATO and the European Community, maintained close political, military, and economic ties.

4. The urgent need for economic development in Middle Eastern countries

During the emergence stage of the joint development of offshore oil and gas resources, a total of five instances of this practice occurred, four of which

13 At present, OPEC has 13 member countries: Algeria, Angola, Congo, Equatori al Guinea, Gabon (joined in 1975, left in 1995, rejoined in 2016), Iran, Iraq, Ku wait, Libya, Nigeria, Saudi Arabia, the United Arab Emirates, and Venezuela. See the OPEC website http: //www.opec.org.

were joint development cases among Persian Gulf states. The fundamental reason for this is that, after the Second World War, many newly independent nations placed a high priority on economic development. Persian Gulf countries such as Iran, Saudi Arabia, and Kuwait, in particular, leveraged their abundant oil and gas resources to formulate similar economic development strategies aimed at using the growth of oil exports and the petroleum processing industry to drive their entire national economies. Consequently, in order to achieve their economic development goals and maximize their economic interests, these countries found it relatively easy to reach agreements on the joint development of offshore oil and gas resources.

In summary, it was the confluence of several factors—a growing awareness among coastal states of their maritime rights, a deeper understanding of the importance of the ocean and its oil and gas resources, favorable interstate relations, and an urgent need for economic development—that fostered a strong willingness and a full spirit of understanding and cooperation to pursue joint development, thereby laying the foundation for the emergence of this practice.

II. The Development Stage of Joint Development (1970-1993)

In its 1969 judgment on the North Sea Continental Shelf cases, the International Court of Justice (ICJ) formally proposed for the first time the solution of joint development for oil and gas resources in disputed maritime areas. This solidified the legal foundation for the further development of international practice in the joint development of offshore oil and gas resources over the subsequent two decades. In this period, from 1970 to 1993, international practice in this area grew more frequent, with a total of 16 joint development cases emerging. These cases involved 27 countries: 11 in Asia, 5 in Europe, 7 in Africa, 3 in the Americas, and Australia in Oceania.

(I) Joint Development Cases in the 1970s

In the 1970s, there were a total of eight cases of joint development of offshore oil and gas resources.

1. The 1971 Joint Development Case Between Iran and the United Arab Emirates. On November 18, 1971, Iran and the United Arab Emirates signed the Memorandum of Understanding Between Iran and Sharjah. [14] In accordance with the provisions of this memorandum, Iran and the United Arab Emirates agreed that petroleum in the Abu Musa Area would be explored and developed by the Buttes Gas and Oil Company, and that the company would deliver the government petroleum resources it extracted to Iran and Sharjah in equal shares.

2. The 1974 Delimitation and Joint Development Case Between France and Spain. On January 29, 1974, France and Spain concluded the Convention

---

14 See Memorandum of Understanding Between Iran and Sharjah, November 197 1, Middle East Economic Survey, Vol. 15, No. 28, 1972, Supplement.

Between the Government of the French Republic and the Government of the Spanish State on the Delimitation of the Continental Shelves of the Two States in the Bay of Biscay. In accordance with the provisions of the agreement, in addition to delimiting the continental shelf between the two countries in the Bay of Biscay, a rectangular zone was established straddling the boundary line. Each party was to exercise sovereign rights over the mineral resources in the portion of the zone on its side of the boundary.[15] Furthermore, Annex II to the agreement stipulated that the French and Spanish parties agreed to an equal sharing of the resources in the entire zone and guaranteed that their respective companies would participate on an equal basis in the development of the mineral resources in the zone.[16]

3. The 1974 Joint Development Case Between Japan and South Korea. On January 30, 1974, Japan and South Korea signed the Agreement Between Japan and the Republic of Korea Concerning Joint Development of the Southern Part of the Continental Shelf Adjacent to the Two Countries. Under the agreement, the parties established a joint development zone, which was divided into nine subzones. Each subzone was to be explored and developed by the concessionaires of both parties under an operating agreement. The concessionaires were to share equally the natural resources extracted from

15 See "The 1974 Delimitation and Joint Development Case Between France and Spain," in Yang Zewei (ed.), *International Agreements on the Joint Development of Marine Resources* (Chinese-English Bilingual Version) (Vol. I), Social Science s Academic Press (China), 2016, pp. 91-102.

16 See Annex II Provisions Applicable to the Zone Defined in Article 3 of This Convention.

the joint development zone and bear the costs of exploration and development. The Japan-Republic of Korea Joint Commission was also established to consult on matters concerning the agreement's implementation.[17]

4. The 1974 Joint Development Case Between Sudan and Saudi Arabia. On May 16, 1974, Sudan and Saudi Arabia signed the Agreement Between Sudan and Saudi Arabia relating to the Joint Exploitation of the Natural Resources of the Sea-Bed and Sub-soil of the Red Sea in the Common Zone.[18] The agreement provided that the exclusive sovereign rights of each country were recognized over the seabed area adjoining its coast to a depth of 1,000 meters. The seabed area between their respective 1,000-meter isobaths was designated as a common zone, where the two governments would have equal and exclusive sovereign rights to all natural resources. The agreement also established a Joint Commission, composed of an equal number of representatives from both sides, to exercise comprehensive functions, including issuing permits, supervising development, and

---

17 See "The 1974 Joint Development Case Between Japan and South Korea," in Yang Zewei (ed.), *International Agreements on the Joint Development of Marine Resources* (Chinese-English Bilingual Version) (Vol. I), Social Sciences Academic Press (China), 2016, pp. 49-90; Liu Jia, On the Implications of the Japan-South Korea Joint Development Case for Sino-Japanese Joint Development in the East China Sea, Master's thesis, Wuhan University, 2015; Deng Niya, The Case of Ja pan-South Korea Joint Development of the East China Sea Continental Shelf and Its Implications for China, *Journal of Ocean University of China* (Social Science s), No. 2, 2016, pp. 65-73.

18 See Agreement Between Sudan and Saudi Arabia Relating to the Joint Exploit ation of the Natural Resources of the Sea-Bed and Sub-soil of the Red Sea in th e Common Zone, 16 May 1974, ST/LEG/SER. B/18, pp. 452-455.

establishing relevant regulations.

5. The 1975 Joint Development Case Between Rwanda and Zaire. On May 3, 1975, Rwanda and Zaire signed the Agreement between the Republic of Rwanda and the Republic of Zaire Concerning the Exploration, Development, and Commercialization of the Natural Gas of Lake Kivu. The agreement provided that the natural gas resources of Lake Kivu were recognized as the common property of the two countries and that, in principle, a joint venture with capital shared equally by both parties would be established to exercise the exclusive rights for the exploration, development, and commercialization of the resources.[19]

6. The 1976 Case of Joint Development of the Frigg Gas Field by the United Kingdom and Norway. On May 10, 1976, the United Kingdom and Norway signed the Agreement Between the Government of the United Kingdom of Great Britain and Northern Ireland and the Government of the Kingdom of Norway Relating to the Exploitation of the Frigg Field Reservoir and the Transmission of Gas therefrom to the United Kingdom. The agreement provided that, with the approval of both governments, the gas field would be developed as a "single unit" by a "single operator" designated by agreement between the licensees of both countries. The two governments would jointly decide the location of each gas well in relation to the boundary

---

19 See Yu Hui, International Law Issues on the Joint Development of Marine Mi neral Resources, *Chinese Yearbook of International Law*, 1994, p. 53.

line and would consult to determine the total reserves of the Frigg field and their apportionment. At the same time, development by the licensees was without prejudice to the jurisdiction of either state over the continental shelf on its side of the boundary line.[20]

7. The 1979 Joint Development Case Between Thailand and Malaysia in the Gulf of Thailand. On February 21, 1979, Thailand and Malaysia signed the Memorandum of Understanding Between Malaysia and the Kingdom of Thailand on the Establishment of the Joint Authority for the Exploitation of the Resources of the Sea Bed in a Defined Area of the Continental Shelf of the Two Countries in the Gulf of Thailand. In accordance with the provisions of the memorandum, the two parties recognized the existence of an overlapping maritime area in the Gulf of Thailand and considered that it was in their best interests to jointly develop the seabed resources of this area through mutual cooperation. The Malaysia-Thailand Joint Authority was established to assume, on behalf of both parties, full responsibility for the exploration and development of the living resources in the overlapping area.[21]

---

20 See "The 1976 Case of Joint Development of the Frigg Gas Field by the Uni ted Kingdom and Norway," in Yang Zewei (ed.), *International Agreements on the Joint Development of Marine Resources* (Chinese-English Bilingual Version) (Vol. I), Social Sciences Academic Press (China), 2016, pp. 103-136; Wang Xinyu, T he UK-Norway Joint Development Case of the Frigg Gas Field and Its Implicatio ns for China, Master's thesis, Wuhan University, 2015.

21 See "The 1979 Joint Development Case Between Thailand and Malaysia in th e Gulf of Thailand," in Yang Zewei (ed.), *International Agreements on the Joint Development of Marine Resources* (Chinese-English Bilingual Version) (Vol. I), So cial Sciences Academic Press (China), 2016, pp. 177-262; Wang Xiaomei, A Stud y on the Joint Development Case between Thailand and Malaysia, Master's thesis,

Additionally, the 1970s also saw the 1975 Joint Development Case Between Iran and Iraq.[22]

(II) Joint Development Cases in the 1980s

In the 1980s, there were a total of five cases of joint development of offshore oil and gas resources. The two most representative cases are as follows.

1. The 1981 Joint Development Case Between Iceland and Norway concerning Jan Mayen. On October 22, 1981, Iceland and Norway signed the Agreement on the Continental Shelf Between Iceland and Jan Mayen. Under the agreement, the two parties agreed to establish a joint development area, which was divided into a Norwegian part, north of the boundary line, and an Icelandic part, south of the boundary line. Each party was to apply its own legislation and petroleum development policy to the part under its jurisdiction, while development and production in the joint development area were to be conducted on the basis of joint venture contracts.[23]

2. The 1989 Joint Development Case Between Australia and Indonesia.

Wuhan University, 2015.

22 See Treaty Concerning the Frontier and Neighbourly Relations Between Iran and Iraq, 13 June 1975, available at http://www.parstimes.com/history/iran_iraq_1975.html; Agreement Between Iran and Iraq Concerning the Use of Frontier Watercourses, 26 December 1975, available at http://www.ucdp.uu.se/gpdatabase/peace/Iran-Iraq%20 19751226b.pdf.

23 See "The 1981 Joint Development Case Between Iceland and Norway concerning Jan Mayen," in Yang Zewei (ed.), *International Agreements on the Joint Development of Marine Resources* (Chinese-English Bilingual Version) (Vol. I), Social Sciences Academic Press (China), 2016, pp. 263-271; Ma Sheng, A Study on the Joint Development Case between Norway and Iceland, Master's thesis, Wuhan University, 2015.

On December 11, 1989, Australia and Indonesia signed the Treaty Between Australia and the Republic of Indonesia on the Zone of Cooperation in an Area Between the Indonesian Province of East Timor and Northern Australia. The treaty placed the disputed area of the Timor Sea within a Zone of Cooperation, where the two countries would share equally in the proceeds of development. The zone was divided into three areas: Area A was to be administered by a Joint Authority responsible for managing exploration, development, and the equal sharing of revenue. In Area B, Australia was entitled to grant licenses and approve leases, etc., while in Area C, Indonesia possessed similar rights.[24] In addition, the treaty included detailed annexes, such as a Petroleum Mining Code and a Model Production Sharing Contract. Many scholars consider this treaty to be "the most detailed treaty on joint development yet concluded in terms of its textual provisions."[25]

In addition to the international cases of joint development of offshore oil and gas resources mentioned above, this period also saw the 1981 Joint Development Case in the Gulf of Maine between the United States and

24 See "The 1989 Joint Development Case Between Australia and Indonesia," in Yang Zewei (ed.), *International Agreements on the Joint Development of Marine Resources* (Chinese-English Bilingual Version) (Vol. I), Social Sciences Academic Press (China), 2016, pp. 272-312; Li Yawei, A Study on the Timor Sea Joint Development Case, Master's thesis, Wuhan University, 2016.

25 Xiao Jianguo, *Joint Development of Petroleum on International Maritime Boundaries*, China Ocean Press, 2006, p. 10.

Canada[26], the 1988 Joint Development Case Between Libya and Tunisia[27], and the 1988 Joint Development Case Between the Yemen Arab Republic and the People's Democratic Republic of Yemen[28].

(III) Joint Development Cases in the 1990s

During this period in the 1990s, there were a total of three cases of joint development of offshore oil and gas resources.

1. The 1992 Joint Development Case Between Malaysia and Vietnam. On June 5, 1992, Malaysia and Vietnam signed the Memorandum of Understanding Between Malaysia and the Socialist Republic of Vietnam for the Exploration and Exploitation of Petroleum in a Defined Area of the Continental Shelf Involving the Two Countries. Under the memorandum, the Malaysian and Vietnamese parties pledged that for the next 40 years, they would equally bear all costs and share all benefits arising from petroleum exploration and exploitation activities in the disputed area. It was decided that the Malaysian National Oil Company (Petronas) and the Vietnam Oil and Gas Group (PetroVietnam) would act as the agencies for their respective

26 See Treaty to Submit to Binding Dispute Settlement the Delimitation of the Maritime Boundary in the Gulf of Maine Area, 29 March 1979, available at http://www.un.org/Depts/los/LEGISLATIONANDTREATIES/PDFFILES/TREATIES/CAN-USA1979GM.PDF, Delimitation of the Maritime Boundary in the Gulf of Maine Area, Judgment, available at http://www.icj-cij.org/docket/files/67/6369.pdf.

27 In August 1988, Libya and Tunisia signed the Agreement on the Delimitation of the Continental Shelf and Joint Development between Libya and Tunisia.

28 On November 19, 1988, the Yemen Arab Republic and the People's Democratic Republic of Yemen signed the Aden Agreement Between the Yemen Arab Republic and the People's Democratic Republic of Yemen. According to the agreement, the two parties were to jointly invest in the exploration and development of potential shared petroleum resources through a jointly owned company.

countries, concluding an agreement to manage the exploration and exploitation of natural resources within the defined area.[29]

2. The 1993 Joint Development Case Between Guinea-Bissau and Senegal. On October 14, 1993, Guinea-Bissau and Senegal signed the Agreement on Management and Cooperation Between the Republic of Guinea-Bissau and the Republic of Senegal. According to the agreement, the two parties agreed to jointly exploit a designated zone, which did not include their respective territorial seas. The resources of the zone were to be apportioned as follows: for fishery resources, Senegal would receive 50% and Guinea-Bissau 50%; for resources of the continental shelf, Senegal would receive 85% and Guinea-Bissau 15%. The joint development agreement would not prejudice the legal rights of either party previously acquired and confirmed by judicial award, nor their previously established title to areas not included in the designated zone.[30]

3. The 1993 Joint Development Case Between Jamaica and Colombia. On November 12, 1993, Jamaica and Colombia signed the Maritime Delimitation Treaty Between Jamaica and the Republic of Colombia. In accordance with the provisions of the treaty, where the jurisdictional

---

29 See "The 1992 Joint Development Case Between Malaysia and Vietnam," in Yang Zewei (ed.), *International Agreements on the Joint Development of Marine Resources* (Chinese-English Bilingual Version) (Vol. I), Social Sciences Academic Press (China), 2016, pp. 313-319.

30 See "The 1993 Joint Development Case Between Guinea-Bissau and Senegal," in Yang Zewei (ed.), *International Agreements on the Joint Development of Mar ine Resources* (Chinese-English Bilingual Version) (Vol. I), Social Sciences Acade mic Press (China), 2016, pp. 329-366.

boundary in a designated area could not be determined, the two countries agreed to establish a Joint Regime Area for the joint management, control, exploration, and exploitation of the living and non-living resources. The two parties also agreed to establish a Joint Commission to implement the relevant provisions of the treaty and to carry out such other functions as the Contracting Parties might assign to it for the purpose of giving effect to the treaty.[31]

In summary, during its second stage from 1970 to 1993, the joint development of offshore oil and gas resources expanded geographically from the Persian Gulf, Western, and Northern Europe to the Red Sea, the Mediterranean, and East Asia, and subsequently to South and Southeast Asia, Africa, and Latin America, evolving into a global international practice. Why, then, did state practice in this area develop so rapidly during this period? I believe this can be attributed to the following factors.

First, the support of international judicial decisions and the advocacy of authoritative international jurists provided a powerful impetus for this rapid growth.

The International Court of Justice first proposed "joint development of offshore oil and gas resources" as a suitable method for resolving resource

31 See "The 1993 Joint Development Case Between Jamaica and Colombia," in Yang Zewei (ed.), *International Agreements on the Joint Development of Marine Resources* (Chinese-English Bilingual Version) (Vol. I), Social Sciences Academic Press (China), 2016, pp. 320-328; Zong Lüqian, A Study on the Joint Developme nt Case between Colombia and Jamaica, Master's thesis, Wuhan University, 2016.

disputes in its 1969 judgment in the North Sea Continental Shelf Cases (Federal Republic of Germany/Denmark; Federal Republic of Germany/the Netherlands). In that judgment, the Court formally stated that the unity of a mineral deposit is a reasonable factor to be considered in the delimitation of the continental shelf, noting, "With respect to the preservation of the unity of a deposit... the last solution (i.e., joint development) appears to be particularly appropriate."[32] In his separate opinion in the case, Judge Jessup also pointed out that joint development is applicable not only where boundary lines have been delimited but also in disputed maritime areas where both parties have legitimate claims, emphasizing that "the principle of joint development is especially applicable where the principle of unity of deposit is concerned."[33] In the 1982 judgment in the Continental Shelf case (Tunisia/Libyan Arab Jamahiriya), Judge ad hoc Evensen also proposed in his separate opinion that establishing a joint development zone in the disputed area for the exploration and exploitation of oil and gas resources is an equitable alternative for resolving maritime boundary disputes. He also made specific suggestions regarding the methods for defining the joint development zone, the allocation of jurisdiction within it, principles of cooperation, and dispute settlement.[34]

32 See the North Sea Continental Shelf Cases (Federal Republic of Germany/Denmark; Federal Republic of Germany/the Netherlands), Judgment of 20 February 1969, available at https://www.icj-cij.org/en/case/51/judgments.
33 See Separate Opinion of Judge Jessup, in the North Sea Continental Shelf Cases (Federal Republic of Germany/Denmark; Federal Republic of Germany/the Netherlands), available at https://www.icj-cij.org/public/files/case-related/51/051-19690220-JUD-01-03-EN.pdf.
34 See Dissenting Opinion of Judge Evensen, in Continental Shelf, Tunisia/Libyan Arab Jamahiriya, available at https://www.icj-cij.org/public/files/case-related/63/063-19820224-JUD-01-06-EN.pdf.

Undoubtedly, the high regard for joint development of offshore oil and gas resources shown in these judicial precedents and by authoritative international jurists served as a catalyst for the rapid development of the practice.

Second, explicit provisions in international legal instruments, such as international treaties, that require the cooperative development and utilization of shared resources also contributed to the rapid growth of international practice in this area.

For example, Article 3 of the Charter of Economic Rights and Duties of States, adopted by the UN General Assembly in 1974, explicitly provides that in the exploitation of natural resources shared by two or more countries, states must cooperate on the basis of a system of information and prior consultations in order to achieve the optimum utilization of such resources without prejudice to the legitimate interests of other countries. Other resolutions passed by the UN General Assembly have also, from the perspective of environmental protection, established principles of cooperation among states with shared resources regarding resource conservation and unitization. In particular, Articles 74, 83, 123, and 142 of the 1982 United Nations Convention on the Law of the Sea all emphasize the principle of cooperation among states. Against the backdrop of increasingly prominent maritime disputes and contention over seabed resources, the support for cooperative development of shared resources in these important international legal instruments promoted the practice of joint development of offshore oil and gas among the states concerned.

Third, the multiple occurrences of global oil crises further stimulated the demand for offshore oil and gas resources and spurred nations to accelerate their exploration of nearshore oil and gas.

The three globally recognized oil crises to date all occurred during this developmental phase of joint offshore oil and gas development (1970-1993). The severe impact of these crises on the world economy gave a strong impetus to countries worldwide—particularly developed nations heavily dependent on energy imports—to accelerate the exploration and development of offshore oil and gas resources as a key means of safeguarding their energy security. This intense demand for energy, to a certain extent, diminished and even overrode political considerations, compelling the relevant countries to conclude joint development arrangements for offshore oil and gas resources. In 1974 alone, following the first oil crisis, three such joint development cases emerged, with one each in 1979 and 1981, and three more after 1990. This clearly demonstrates that the strong demand for oil and gas and concerns over the security of supply played a major role in advancing the practice of joint development of offshore oil and gas resources. It is noteworthy that cases of joint development of offshore oil and gas resources between developed countries were also largely concentrated in this period, including the practices between France and Spain, Japan and South Korea, the United

Kingdom and Norway, and Iceland and Norway. As M. J. Valencia, an expert at the East-West Center at the University of Hawaii, and Japanese scholar Masahiro Miyoshi have pointed out: "Perhaps the most important reason for a nation to choose joint development is a sense of urgency and obligation to protect its interests in its oil and natural gas reserves."[35]

Fourth, good, stable bilateral relations between states also promoted the development of state practice in the joint development of offshore oil and gas resources during this stage.

For example, relations between France and Spain, the United Kingdom and Norway, and Iceland and Norway were all friendly, while Thailand and Malaysia, as founding members of ASEAN, also maintained stable and close relations. Furthermore, since the late 1980s, the shift in Vietnam's relations with its neighboring countries from confrontation to dialogue also laid the foundation for it to conclude a joint development agreement on offshore oil and gas resources with Malaysia.

III. The Decline Stage of Joint Development (1994-1999)

In this stage, there was only one instance of state practice concerning the joint development of offshore oil and gas resources: the 1995 Joint

35 See M. J. Valencia and M. Miyoshi, Southeast Asian Seas: Joint Development of Hydrocarbons in Overlapping Claim Area? *Ocean Development and Internatio nal Law*, Vol. 16, 1986, p. 223.

Development Case between the United Kingdom and Argentina.

On February 27, 1995, the United Kingdom and Argentina signed the Joint Declaration on Cooperation over Offshore Activities in the Southwest Atlantic.[36] This joint declaration is considered the legal instrument for their cooperation on joint development. According to its provisions, the two countries agreed to cooperate to encourage offshore activities in the Southwest Atlantic. The exploration and exploitation of oil and gas resources were to be carried out on the basis of reasonable commercial principles and good oilfield practice, incorporating the experience gained by their respective governments from development in the Southwest Atlantic and the North Sea. The two governments also agreed to cooperate through the various stages of offshore development activities to be undertaken by commercial operators.[37]

Compared with the preceding stage, state practice in the joint development of offshore oil and gas resources entered a period of decline. This was primarily due to the following reasons:

1. The negative impact of the entry into force of the United Nations Convention on the Law of the Sea

On November 16, 1994, the United Nations Convention on the Law of

36 See T. W. Wälde & Andrew McHardy, Argentina-United Kingdom: Joint Declaration on Cooperation over Offshore Activities in the Southwest Atlantic, *International Legal Materials*, Vol. 35, No. 2, 1996, p. 302.

37 See R. R. Churchill, Falkland Islands - Maritime Jurisdiction and Cooperative Arrangements with Argentina, *International and Comparative Law Quarterly*, Vol. 46, Issue 2, 1997, pp. 468-469; Wang Yang, A Study on the Joint Development Case between the United Kingdom and Argentina, Master's thesis, Wuhan University, 2016.

the Sea (hereinafter referred to as the Convention) formally entered into force, which had a distinctly negative impact on state practice in the joint development of offshore oil and gas resources. On the one hand, the Convention's entry into force raised the hopes of sovereign states that they could resolve maritime delimitation issues by applying the Convention or settle disputes through its compulsory third-party procedures, causing the practice of joint development to be relatively neglected[38]. On the other hand, the Convention's entry into force enabled many states with adjacent or opposite coasts to legitimately extend their sovereignty or sovereign rights. Because their claims were now legally grounded, they were inclined in their policy choices to favor delimitation over the joint development of offshore oil and gas resources. This pursuit by states of definitive maritime delimitation treaties dealt a significant blow to the joint development approach. In short, since the United Nations Convention on the Law of the Sea entered into force in 1994, maritime boundary delimitation activities between states have increased, and a large number of related delimitation agreements have appeared, thereby greatly diminishing the urgency and necessity for the joint development of offshore oil and gas resources.

2. Some highly disputed maritime areas involve multiple sovereign states, which has increased the difficulty of concluding agreements for the joint development of offshore oil and gas resources.

---

38 Xiao Jianguo, *Joint Development of Petroleum on International Maritime Boun daries*, China Ocean Press, 2006, p. 12.

By the 1990s, all existing joint development agreements and instances of state practice had involved only two parties; to date, no multilateral joint development agreements or practices have emerged. Moreover, in the more than 20 existing cases of joint development, the conclusion and actual implementation of many agreements were fraught with difficulties. Given that this was the case for bilateral agreements, the difficulty of concluding and implementing multilateral ones is self-evident. However, some of the disputed maritime areas that are currently highly contentious and urgently in need of joint oil and gas development are precisely those involving multiple countries and parties. Therefore, to achieve joint development in such disputed areas requires the concerned states to expend more time and demonstrate greater courage and wisdom.

3. The more that is known about oil and gas reserves, the more likely it is to have a negative impact on the state practice of joint development.

Just as a deeper understanding of oil and gas resources makes it more difficult to conclude a maritime delimitation agreement, this greater knowledge can also affect the conclusion of a joint development agreement. This is because the more certain the states concerned are that the disputed maritime area holds abundant oil and gas reserves, the more they will be inclined to clarify the ownership of the resources, rather than leaving ownership ambiguous and pursuing joint development. It is precisely these complex factors that have caused the practice of joint development of offshore oil and gas to advance slowly since the mid-1990s.

In summary, the evolution of state practice in the joint development of offshore oil and gas resources, from its emergence and growth to its decline, shows that a nation's pressing need for oil and gas resources to fuel economic development and a strong political will to pursue joint development are the key drivers for the gradual expansion of this practice. Conversely, a fundamental reason hindering the joint development of offshore oil and gas is the inherently sole and exclusive nature of sovereignty and sovereign rights, which states are driven to assert.

IV. The Stabilization Stage of Joint Development (2000-Present)

In this phase, state practice in the joint development of offshore oil and gas resources saw a resurgence, with 15 cases emerging in total.

(I) The 2001 Joint Development Case Between Nigeria and São Tomé and Príncipe

On February 21, 2001, Nigeria and São Tomé and Príncipe signed the Treaty Between The Federal Republic of Nigeria and The Democratic Republic of São Tomé e Príncipe on the Joint Development of Petroleum and other Resources, in Respect of Areas of the Exclusive Economic Zone of the

Two States.[39] According to the treaty, the two states parties shall jointly control the exploration and exploitation of resources within the development zone with the aim of achieving maximum commercial utilization; all proceeds and liabilities arising from development activities within the zone shall be apportioned 60% to Nigeria and 40% to São Tomé and Príncipe; and a Joint Authority shall be established to manage activities related to the exploration and exploitation of resources within the zone.[40]

(II) The 2002 Joint Development Case Between East Timor and Australia

On May 20, 2002, the day East Timor restored its independence, it signed the Timor Sea Treaty Between the Government of East Timor and the Government of Australia.[41] The treaty stipulated the establishment of a Joint Petroleum Development Area, where Australia and East Timor, for the benefit of the peoples of both countries, would jointly control, manage, and facilitate the exploration, development, and exploitation of petroleum resources. Australia and East Timor would hold title to all petroleum

---

39 See Treaty Between The Federal Republic of Nigeria and The Democratic Republic of São Tomé e Príncipe on the Joint Development of Petroleum and other Resources, in Respect of Areas of the Exclusive Economic Zone of the Two States, available at http://www.un.org/Depts/los/LEGISLATIONANDTREATIES/PDFFILES/TREATIES/STP-NGA2001.PDF.

40 See "The 2001 Joint Development Case Between Nigeria and São Tomé and Príncipe," in Yang Zewei (ed.), *International Agreements on the Joint Development of Marine Resources* (Chinese-English Bilingual Version) (Vol. II), Social Sciences Academic Press (China), 2016, pp. 367-426; Zhang Huifen, A Study on the Joint Development Case between Nigeria and São Tomé and Príncipe, Master's thesis, Wuhan University, 2015.

41 See Timor Sea Treaty Between the Government of East Timor and the Government of Australia. Australian Treaty Series 2003 No. 13.

produced in the Joint Petroleum Development Area, with 90% of the output belonging to East Timor and 10% to Australia.[42] The two countries subsequently reached the Agreement Between the Government of Australia and the Government of the Democratic Republic of Timor-Leste Relating to the Unitisation of the Sunrise and Troubadour Fields[43] concerning the development of the Greater Sunrise block. On January 12, 2016, Australia and East Timor also signed the Treaty Between Australia and the Democratic Republic of Timor-Leste on Certain Maritime Arrangements in the Timor Sea.[44]

(III) The 2003 Joint Development Case Between Barbados and Guyana

On December 2, 2003, Barbados and Guyana signed the Exclusive Economic Zone Cooperation Treaty Between the Republic of Guyana and the State of Barbados Concerning the Exercise of Jurisdiction in Their Exclusive Economic Zones in the Area of Bilateral Overlap Within Each of Their Outer Limits and Beyond the Outer Limits of the Exclusive Economic Zones of Outer States. According to the treaty, in the overlapping area within their exclusive economic zones, the two countries shall jointly exercise

42 See "The 2002 Joint Development Case Between East Timor and Australia," i n Yang Zewei (ed.), *International Agreements on the Joint Development of Marin e Resources* (Chinese-English Bilingual Version) (Vol. II), Social Sciences Academ ic Press (China), 2016, pp. 499-535; Li Yawei, A Study on the Timor Sea Joint Development Case, Master's thesis, Wuhan University, 2016.

43 See Agreement Between the Government of Australia and The Government of the Democratic Republic of Timor-Leste Relating to the Unitisation of the Sunri se and Troubadour Fields, Australian Treaty Series 2007, No. 11.

44 See Treaty Between Australia and the Democratic Republic of Timor-Leste on Certain Maritime Arrangements in the Timor Sea, Australian Treaty Series 2007, No. 12.

jurisdiction, control, management, exploration, and exploitation over living and non-living resources, as well as other rights and obligations stipulated by the treaty.[45]

(IV) The 2009 Joint Development Case Between Brunei and Malaysia

On March 16, 2009, Brunei and Malaysia resolved a series of land and maritime boundary disputes through an exchange of letters. The relevant letters and the agreement between the national petroleum companies of Brunei and Malaysia have not been made public. However, based on available information, the arrangements primarily included: the demarcation of the maritime boundary between the two countries; the determination of the method for delimiting the land boundary; the establishment of a Commercial Arrangement Area and related arrangements; and the right of unrestricted passage for Malaysian nationals through maritime areas under Brunei's jurisdiction. Under the arrangements, where Malaysia's offshore Blocks L and M overlapped with Brunei's Blocks J and K, the parties confirmed that Brunei would exercise the sovereign rights conferred by the United Nations Convention on the Law of the Sea, and the blocks in question were renamed Blocks CA1 and CA2. Contracts previously tendered by Malaysia were terminated, and the original contracting parties withdrew. Malaysia's national

45 See "The 2003 Joint Development Case Between Barbados and Guyana," in Yang Zewei (ed.), *International Agreements on the Joint Development of Marine Resources* (Chinese-English Bilingual Version) (Vol. II), Social Sciences Academic Press (China), 2016, pp. 594-606.

petroleum company would participate in the oil and gas development of Blocks CA1 and CA2 in Brunei and share the revenue with its Bruneian counterpart[46].

(V) The 2012 Joint Development Case Between the United States and Mexico

On February 20, 2012, the United States and Mexico signed the Agreement Between the United States of America and the United Mexican States Concerning Transboundary Hydrocarbon Reservoirs in the Gulf of Mexico. The agreement mainly provides for its scope of application, management model, decision-making, and dispute resolution procedures.[47] In addition, this agreement differs from previous joint development agreements for offshore oil and gas resources in that it is only a framework agreement; it neither stipulates a ratio for the allocation of benefits nor contains specific provisions on environmental protection and safety measures.[48]

(VI) The 2012 Joint Development Case Between Seychelles and

---

46 See Robert Beckman, et al ed., Beyond Territorial Disputes in the South China Sea: Legal Frameworks for the Joint Development of Hydrocarbon Resources, pp. 2 04-210.

47 See "The 2012 Joint Development Case Between the United States and Mexic o," in Yang Zewei (ed.), *International Agreements on the Joint Development of Marine Resources* (Chinese-English Bilingual Version) (Vol. II), Social Sciences A cademic Press (China), 2016, pp. 616-649.

48 See Huang Tian, A Study on the Joint Development Agreement between the United States and Mexico, Master's thesis, Wuhan University, 2016, p. 1.

Mauritius

On March 13, 2012, Seychelles and Mauritius signed the Treaty Concerning the Joint Management of the Continental Shelf in the Mascarene Plateau Region. According to the treaty, the two countries established a Joint Management Area where they shall jointly control, manage, and promote the exploration of the continental shelf and the protection, development, and exploitation of its natural resources; the two parties shall share equally in the benefits derived from natural resource activities in the area, with 50% of the revenue going to Mauritius and the other 50% to Seychelles.[49]

Additionally, during this period, there were other cases of joint development of offshore oil and gas resources, although many have yet to make substantial progress. These include the 2000 Joint Development Case Between China and Vietnam in the Beibu Gulf[50], the 2001 Joint Development Case Between Thailand and Cambodia[51], the 2002 Joint Development Case

49 See "The 2012 Joint Development Case Between Seychelles and Mauritius," i n Yang Zewei (ed.), *International Agreements on the Joint Development of Marin e Resources* (Chinese-English Bilingual Version) (Vol. II), Social Sciences Academ ic Press (China), 2016, pp. 650-685; Wang Juping, A Study on the Joint Develop ment of the Mascarene Plateau by Seychelles and Mauritius, Master's thesis, Wuh an University, 2016.

50 On December 25, 2000, China and Vietnam signed the Agreement between th e People's Republic of China and the Socialist Republic of Vietnam on the Deli mitation of the Territorial Seas, Exclusive Economic Zones and Continental Shelv es of the Two Countries in Beibu Gulf and the Agreement between the Governm ent of the People's Republic of China and the Government of the Socialist Repu blic of Vietnam on Fishery Cooperation in Beibu Gulf.

51 On June 18, 2001, Thailand and Cambodia signed the Memorandum of Under standing Between the Royal Thai Government and the Royal Government of Cam bodia Regarding the Area of their Overlapping Maritime Claims to the Continent al Shelf.

Between the Republic of the Congo and Angola [52], the 2005 Joint Development Case Between China and North Korea [53], the 2006 Joint Development Case Between Micronesia and the Marshall Islands[54], the 2006 Joint Development Case Between Micronesia and Palau[55], the 2007 Joint Development Case Between Trinidad and Tobago and the Bolivarian Republic of Venezuela[56], the 2008 Joint Development Case Between China and Japan[57], and the 2010 Joint Development Case Between Norway and Russia[58].

Since the beginning of the 21st century, state practice in the joint development of offshore oil and gas resources has seen a resurgence. This is

52 On November 27, 2002, the Republic of the Congo and Angola signed the A greement on the Development of Oil Fields in the Maritime Border Zone.
53 On December 24, 2005, China and North Korea signed the Agreement betwee n the Governments of China and North Korea on the Joint Offshore Developmen t of Petroleum.
54 On June 6, 2006, Micronesia and the Marshall Islands signed the Treaty betw een the Federated States of Micronesia and the Republic of the Marshall Islands Concerning Maritime Boundaries and Cooperation on Related Matters.
55 See Treaty Between the Federated States of Micronesia and the Republic of P alau Concerning Maritime Boundaries and Cooperation on Related Matters, availa ble at http://www.un.org/Depts/los/LEGISLATIONANDTREATIES/PDFFILES/FSM-PALAU.pdf.
56 See Framework Treaty Relating to the Unitisation of Hydrocarbon Reservoirs That Extend Across the Delimitation Line Between the Republic of Trinidad and Tobago and the Bolivarian Republic of Venezuela, 20 March 2007, Republic of T rinidad and Tobago - The Bolivarian Republic of Venezuela, U. N. T. S. Vol. 28 76, pp. 1-24, Available at: https://treaties.un.org/doc/Publication/UNTS/No%20Volu me/50196/Part/I-50196-08000002802bb3a7.pdf.
57 On June 18, 2008, the governments of China and Japan reached the Principle d Consensus on the East China Sea Issue. According to this consensus, the two sides agreed to conduct joint development during a transitional period pending de limitation, without prejudice to the legal positions of either side.
58 On September 15, 2010, Norway and Russia signed the Treaty between the K ingdom of Norway and the Russian Federation concerning Maritime Delimitation and Cooperation in the Barents Sea and the Arctic Ocean, available at http://ww w.un.org/Depts/los/LEGISLATIONANDTREATIES/PDFFILES/TREATIES/NOR-RUS 2010.pdf.

mainly due to the following reasons:

(1) As a provisional arrangement prior to maritime delimitation, the joint development of offshore oil and gas resources still has its inherent advantages.

Although the entry into force of the United Nations Convention on the Law of the Sea in 1994 powerfully encouraged coastal states to resolve their maritime delimitation disputes and demarcate their maritime boundaries in accordance with the procedures stipulated in the Convention, as this trend gradually faded, the reality that "maritime delimitation is a worldwide challenge" once again confronted coastal states[59]. "How to determine the baselines for the territorial sea became a very complex and sensitive issue."[60] Therefore, under these circumstances, since coastal states cannot resolve their maritime delimitation disputes and demarcate clear maritime boundaries in the short term, the joint development of offshore oil and gas resources becomes a second-best option.

(2) Developing oil and gas resources to promote economic growth has been an important factor.

For example, after gaining independence, East Timor faced severe

59 According to statistics, there are over 400 potential maritime boundaries in the world's oceans, of which only about 160 have been formally settled by delimitation agreements. Many countries, including China, Japan, and the United States, have only completed the delimitation of a few of their maritime boundaries with neighboring states.

60 [Australia] Victor Prescott and Clive Schofield, The Maritime Political Boundaries of the World, trans. by Wu Jilu and Zhang Haiwen, China Ocean Press, 2014, p. 3.

economic difficulties and urgently needed to develop the oil and gas resources in the Timor Sea to grow its national economy. It therefore moved quickly to sign the Timor Sea Treaty Between the Government of East Timor and the Government of Australia to pursue the joint development of offshore oil and gas resources. Similarly, in the 2012 Joint Development Case Between the United States and Mexico, the signing of the joint development agreement was closely linked to the significant gap between oil supply and demand in both countries. The United States is the world's largest oil consumer; according to the 2012 BP Statistical Review of World Energy, US oil consumption in 2011 accounted for 20.5% of the global total, making it the world's top consumer by a wide margin.[61] Likewise, Mexico's reliance on petroleum was just as critical. Mexico is one of the world's largest oil producers, and petroleum is a pillar of its economy, accounting for about one-third of the country's fiscal revenue. The fortunes of the oil industry are, to a significant extent, vital to the nation's economic lifeline, with petroleum revenue constituting 33.7% of its public sector income in 2011.[62]

(3) The improvement in relations between states has laid the foundation of public support for signing agreements on the joint development of offshore oil and gas resources.

---

61 See B. Dudley, BP Statistical Review of World Energy, June 2012, London, 2012, pp. 6-9.

62 See Petroleos Mexicanos, Statistical Yearbook 2013, available at http://www.pemex.com/acerca/informes_publicaciones/Documents/anuario_estadistico_2013/statistical_yearbook_2013_131014.pdf.

For example, regarding the 2000 Joint Development Case Between China and Vietnam in the Beibu Gulf, the two countries were able to reach delimitation and fishery agreements in 2000 because their relations had been normalized since the 1990s and were developing in a positive direction. Similarly, in the case of the 2008 Joint Development Case Between China and Japan, a public opinion trend emerged within China in the early 21st century, advocating a "new thinking on relations with Japan" and seeking to further improve ties. In fact, prior to 2008, Sino-Japanese relations had indeed gone through a process of "ice-melting," "welcoming spring," and "warm spring."

Section Two: Different Scenarios for the Application of Law to the Joint Development of Offshore Oil and Gas Resources

Although the joint development of offshore oil and gas resources is mainly divided into two types—joint development in disputed maritime areas and joint development in transboundary areas—a joint development zone may still be located within a maritime area under a state's exclusive jurisdiction or in an area beyond the limits of national jurisdiction. Therefore, the application of law to the joint development of offshore oil and gas resources primarily involves the following five scenarios.

I. Application of Law to Joint Development in Disputed Maritime Areas

In disputed maritime areas or areas of overlapping claims, although no clear maritime boundary line exists, the application of law to joint development in international practice generally follows two approaches: one is to establish a unified law applicable to the joint maritime development area, and the other is to adopt a system of joint jurisdiction by both countries or jurisdiction by the operator's home state.[63] However, the former is more

63 See Yu Mincai, *Legal Issues in Marine Petroleum Exploration and Developme nt*, China Renmin University Press, 2001, p. 146.

difficult, and an agreement is not easily reached in the short term; for the latter, joint jurisdiction is generally implemented by a joint management body.

For example, in the 1979 Joint Development Case Between Malaysia and Thailand, Article 3, Paragraph 2 of the 1979 Memorandum of Understanding Between Malaysia and the Kingdom of Thailand on the Establishment of the Joint Authority for the Exploitation of the Resources of the Sea Bed in a Defined Area of the Continental Shelf of the Two Countries in the Gulf of Thailand provides: "The Joint Authority shall assume all rights and responsibilities on behalf of both Parties for the exploration and exploitation of the non-living natural resources of the sea-bed and subsoil in the overlapping area (hereinafter referred to as the joint development area) and also for the development, control and administration of the joint development area. The assumption of such rights and responsibilities by the Joint Authority shall in no way affect or curtail the validity of concessions or licenses hitherto issued or agreements or arrangements hitherto made by either Party." It is therefore clear that the Joint Authority exercises, on behalf of both Malaysia and Thailand, the rights of exploration, exploitation, control, and administration over the non-living natural resources of the seabed and its subsoil in the joint development area.[64]

A typical example of jurisdiction by the operator's home state is the

---

64 See Article 3 of the Memorandum of Understanding Between Malaysia and th e Kingdom of Thailand on the Establishment of the Joint Authority for the Expl oitation of the Resources of the Sea Bed in a Defined Area of the Continental S helf of the Two Countries in the Gulf of Thailand of 21 February 1979.

1974 Joint Development Case Between Japan and South Korea. According to Article 19 of the 1974 Agreement Between Japan and the Republic of Korea Concerning Joint Development of the Southern Part of the Continental Shelf Adjacent to the Two Countries, "Except where otherwise provided in this Agreement, the laws and regulations of one Party shall apply with respect to matters relating to exploration or exploitation of natural resources in the subzones with respect to which that Party has authorized concessionaires designated and acting as operators."

II. Application of Law to Joint Development in Transboundary Maritime Areas

In the case of joint development of offshore oil and gas resources in transboundary maritime areas, since a common maritime boundary line exists, countries generally exercise jurisdiction and apply their laws in the area on their side of the boundary line within the joint development zone.

For example, in the 1974 Joint Development Case Between France and Spain, Annex II, titled "Provisions Applicable to the Zone of Joint Exploitation Defined in Article 3 of this Convention", of the 1974 Convention between the Government of the French Republic and the Government of the Spanish State on the Delimitation of the Continental Shelves of the two States in the Bay of Biscay expressly provides: "The Contracting Parties shall encourage the exploitation of the zone in such a way as to ensure an equal distribution of its resources; In accordance with this principle, each Contracting Party undertakes to encourage within the framework of its mining regulations, the conclusion of agreements between companies applying for licences to explore the zone, in order to allow such companies having the nationality of the other Party to participate in such exploration on the basis of equal partnership and proportional financing of operations; To this end, whenever either Party receives a request for a licence to conduct explorations within its sector, it shall so notify the other Party. The Party so notified shall have a six-month time-limit within which to designate a company or companies of its nationality to participate, with the other applicants, in the procedure for the granting of licences." It is therefore clear that, in this case, France and Spain "exercise their sovereign rights separately" in their respective parts of the joint oil and gas development zone as stipulated, with each party applying its own laws to the portion of the waters under its jurisdiction.[65]

Again, in the 1981 Joint Development Case Between Iceland and Norway concerning Jan Mayen, Article 5, Paragraph 3 of the 1981 Agreement on the Continental Shelf Between Iceland and Jan Mayen expressly provides: "Norwegian legislation, Norwegian petroleum policy and Norwegian regulations relating to the control of such activities, safety measures and environmental protection shall apply to the activities in the area

65 See Article 3 of the French-Spanish Convention on the Delimitation of the C ontinental Shelves of the Two States in the Bay of Biscay of 29 January 1974.

referred to in the first paragraph. The Norwegian authorities shall also be responsible for enforcement and administration in the said area."; Article 6, Paragraph 2 stipulates: "Icelandic legislation, Icelandic petroleum policy and Icelandic regulations relating to the control of such activities, safety measures and environmental protection shall apply to the activities in the area referred to in the first paragraph. The Icelandic authorities shall also be responsible for enforcement and administration in the said area." Thus, in this case, both Iceland and Norway apply their legislation, petroleum policies, and regulations concerning the control of petroleum exploration and exploitation activities, safety measures, and environmental protection within their respective zones, and their administrative authorities are responsible for administrative jurisdiction in their respective zones.[66]

III. Application of Law to Joint Development within a State's Exclusive Jurisdiction

According to the relevant provisions of the United Nations Convention on the Law of the Sea, the exclusive economic zone and the continental shelf fall under the exclusive jurisdiction of a coastal state, which has exclusive jurisdiction over them. For example, Article 56 of the Convention provides: "In the exclusive economic zone, the coastal State has sovereign rights for

66 See Article 5 and Article 6 of the Agreement between Iceland and Norway o n the Continental Shelf in the Area between Iceland and Jan Mayen of 22 Octob er 1981.

the purpose of exploring and exploiting, conserving and managing the natural resources, whether living or non-living, of the waters superjacent to the seabed and of the seabed and its subsoil, and with regard to other activities for the economic exploitation and exploration of the zone, such as the production of energy from the water, currents and winds." Article 77 of the Convention also points out that the coastal state exercises sovereign rights over the continental shelf for the purpose of exploring it and exploiting its natural resources, such as the mineral and other non-living resources of the seabed and subsoil.

Therefore, exploration and development activities in the exclusive economic zone or on the continental shelf will naturally give rise to a series of new legal relationships among the contracting parties, such as the contractual relationship between the coastal state government and the contractor; the relationship between the operator and the contractor, and between the contractor and third parties; the relationship between the coastal state and third-party flag states; and the relationship between the petroleum exploration and development contract and general laws and regulations.[67] Because these relationships all arise within a state's exclusive jurisdiction, the laws of the coastal state primarily apply. However, oil and gas development activities within a state's exclusive jurisdiction generally fall

67 See Cai Penghong, *Management Models for Joint Development in Disputed M aritime Areas: A Comparative Study*, Shanghai Academy of Social Sciences Press, 1998, pp. 49-50.

under the category of cooperative development of offshore oil and gas resources, and therefore are not the subject of this book.

IV. Application of Law to Joint Development on the Continental Shelf Beyond 200 Nautical Miles

If a joint development zone for offshore oil and gas resources is located on the continental shelf of a coastal state beyond 200 nautical miles, then the application of law is more complex.

On the one hand, Article 76, paragraphs 4 and 5 of the Convention expressly provide: "(a) For the purposes of this Convention, the coastal State shall establish the outer edge of the continental margin wherever the margin extends beyond 200 nautical miles from the baselines from which the breadth of the territorial sea is measured, by either: (i) a line delineated in accordance with paragraph 7 by reference to the outermost fixed points at each of which the thickness of sedimentary rocks is at least 1 per cent of the shortest distance from such point to the foot of the continental slope; or (ii) a line delineated in accordance with paragraph 7 by reference to fixed points not more than 60 nautical miles from the foot of the continental slope. (b) In the absence of evidence to the contrary, the foot of the continental slope shall be determined as the point of maximum change in the gradient at its base. The fixed points comprising the line of the outer limits of the continental shelf on the seabed, drawn in accordance with paragraph 4 (a)(i) and (ii), either shall not exceed 350 nautical miles from the baselines from which the breadth of the territorial sea is measured or shall not exceed 100 nautical miles from the 2,500 metre isobath, which is a line connecting the depth of 2,500 metres." It is clear, therefore, that the continental shelf beyond 200 nautical miles remains within the jurisdiction of the coastal state, which has jurisdiction over it, and its laws are therefore applicable.

On the other hand, Article 82 of the Convention, "Payments and contributions with respect to the exploitation of the continental shelf beyond 200 nautical miles", expressly provides in paragraph 1: "The coastal State shall make payments or contributions in kind in respect of the exploitation of the non-living resources of the continental shelf beyond 200 nautical miles from the baselines from which the breadth of the territorial sea is measured." It is thus clear that, according to the provisions of Article 82, a coastal state must make payments or contributions in kind for the exploitation of non-living resources on the continental shelf beyond 200 nautical miles.

Therefore, development activities in a joint maritime development zone on the continental shelf beyond 200 nautical miles must also be subject specifically to the provisions of Article 82.

V. Application of Law to Joint Development Beyond National Jurisdiction

If the oil and gas resources of a joint development area extend to the high seas—that is, the seabed and ocean floor and the subsoil thereof beyond the limits of national jurisdiction—then the related development activities for such resources will involve both the allocation of jurisdiction between the coastal State or the joint authority and the International Seabed Authority, as well as the application of the relevant provisions of the Convention.

For example, Article 142 of the Convention provides that, "Activities in the Area, with respect to resource deposits in the Area which lie across limits of national jurisdiction, shall be conducted with due regard to the rights and legitimate interests of any coastal State across whose jurisdiction such deposits lie. Consultations, including a system of prior notification, shall be maintained with the State concerned, with a view to avoiding infringement of such rights and interests. In cases where activities in the Area may result in the exploitation of resources lying within national jurisdiction, the prior consent of the coastal State concerned shall be required."[68] Meanwhile, Article 140 of the Convention stipulates that, "Activities in the Area shall, as specifically provided for in this Part, be carried out for the benefit of mankind as a whole, irrespective of the geographical location of States, whether coastal or land-locked, and taking into particular consideration the interests and needs of developing States and of peoples who have not attained full independence or other self-governing status recognized by the United

68 Some scholars argue that the principles and procedures stipulated in Article 1 42 of the Convention provide the legal basis for joint development of transbound ary resources between coastal States and the International Seabed Authority. See Yu Hui, Joint Development of Mineral Resources—An Asian Solution, *Asian Year book of International Law*, Vol. 2, 1994, p. 101.

Nations in accordance with General Assembly resolution 1541 (XV) and other relevant General Assembly resolutions. The Authority shall provide for the equitable sharing of financial and other economic benefits derived from activities in the Area through any appropriate mechanism, on a non-discriminatory basis, in accordance with article 160, paragraph 2(f)(i)."

Therefore, the application of law to joint development areas for offshore oil and gas resources beyond national jurisdiction is also not a subject to be specifically studied in this book.

Chapter Summary

Joint development of offshore oil and gas resources refers to the joint exploration and exploitation of oil and gas resources in transboundary or disputed maritime areas by two or more States, based on a joint development agreement concluded between them. According to this definition, joint development of offshore oil and gas resources can be categorized into two types: that for transboundary resources and that for resources in disputed maritime areas. The practice of joint development of offshore oil and gas resources dates back more than 60 years, originating with the Bahrain-Saudi Arabia Boundary Agreement of 1958. This agreement initiated the state practice of joint development for offshore oil and gas resources. Since then, the state practice of jointly developing oil and gas resources in transboundary or disputed maritime areas has become an increasingly common phenomenon. To date, there have been more than 30 instances of joint development of offshore oil and gas resources in the international community.

We can divide the more than 60-year development history of joint development of offshore oil and gas resources into the following four stages: The first stage, from 1958 to 1969, was the emergence stage, with a total of 6 joint development cases. The second stage, from 1970 to 1993, was the development stage, which saw the emergence of 16 instances of state practice in joint development. The third stage, from 1994 to 1999, was the decline stage, with only 1 joint development case. The fourth stage, from 2000 to the present, has been the stabilization stage, with 15 joint development cases.

While the joint development of offshore oil and gas resources is primarily divided into joint development in disputed maritime areas and joint development of transboundary resources, joint development areas may still be located within maritime zones under a state's exclusive jurisdiction or beyond the limits of national jurisdiction. Therefore, the application of law to the joint development of offshore oil and gas resources primarily involves the following five scenarios: first, the Application of Law to Joint Development in Disputed Maritime Areas; second, the Application of Law to Joint Development in Transboundary Maritime Areas; third, the Application of Law to Joint Development within a State's Exclusive Jurisdiction; fourth, the Application of Law to Joint Development on the Continental Shelf Beyond 200 Nautical Miles; and fifth, the Application of Law to Joint Development Beyond National Jurisdiction. Of these, "the Application of Law to Joint Development within a State's Exclusive Jurisdiction" and "the Application of Law to Joint Development Beyond National Jurisdiction" fall outside the scope of this book. Furthermore, the issue of "Application of Law to Joint Development on the Continental Shelf Beyond 200 Nautical Miles" is quite complex and is also not a primary focus of this book.

Chapter 3: The Jurisprudential Basis and Main Types of Application of Law to the Joint Development of Offshore Oil and Gas Resources

Section One: The Jurisprudential Basis for the Application of Law to the Joint Development of Offshore Oil and Gas Resources

I. The Meaning of Applying Law to Joint Development

(I) The Meaning of "Application of Law"

The application of law is a multifaceted concept with varying interpretations in legal scholarship. Some scholars hold that the subjects of the application of law include organs of state power, administrative organs, and judicial organs, as well as state-authorized entities, such as universities, colleges, and scientific research institutions empowered to confer academic degrees.① The entry on "application of law" in the *Encyclopedia of China: Law*, however, defines it as the activity by which state organs and their public officials, social organizations, and citizens implement legal norms.② Furthermore, some scholars equate the implementation of law with the application of law.③

However, most scholars hold that the application of law refers to "the

---

① See Sun Guohua (ed.), *Fundamental Theories of Law*, China Renmin Universi ty Press, 1987, p. 393.
② See *Encyclopedia of China: Law*, Encyclopedia of China Publishing House, 1 984, p. 83.
③ See Shen Zongling (ed.), *Jurisprudence*, Higher Education Press, 1994, p. 340.

specialized activity whereby state judicial organs, in accordance with their statutory authority and procedures, apply the law to resolve specific cases."[4] Because this activity involves the exercise of judicial power in the name of the state, it is generally referred to simply as "adjudication"; like administrative law enforcement, it is an important form of implementing the law. Therefore, courts and judges are the subjects, or principal actors, in the application of law.

(II) The Concept of Application of Law to the Joint Development of Offshore Oil and Gas Resources

The application of law to the joint development of offshore oil and gas resources refers to the specialized activity, within the state practice of such development, whereby sovereign states, the management institutions for joint development, and legal persons, based on the relevant provisions of a joint development agreement, apply specific legal provisions to handle matters related to joint development activities, such as taxation, revenue sharing, and civil or criminal cases. Furthermore, when international judicial institutions, arbitral tribunals, or domestic courts—acting in accordance with the agreement of the states concerned—apply laws such as international treaties, international custom, general principles of law, judicial precedents, international petroleum contracts, or domestic law to resolve disputes or conflicts arising from the process of joint development of offshore oil and

---

④ See Jurisprudence Editorial Board, *Jurisprudence*, People's Publishing House a nd Higher Education Press, 2010, p. 326.

gas resources, this also constitutes an application of law in this context.

Evidently, the application of law to the joint development of offshore oil and gas resources is quite different from the application of law in a domestic context. In China, for example, according to its Constitution, the People's Courts are the State's adjudicatory organs and independently exercise the State's judicial power in accordance with the law; the People's Procuratorates are the State's legal supervision organs and independently exercise the State's procuratorial power in accordance with the law. Both the People's Courts and the People's Procuratorates are classified as State judicial organs and are responsible for implementing national law. However, the People's Courts focus on representing the State by applying the law to specific cases through the trial and judgment of civil, criminal, and administrative matters, thereby fulfilling the State's judicial function. The People's Procuratorates, in contrast, focus on performing their legal supervision function—by conducting investigations, reviewing and approving arrests, initiating public prosecutions, and carrying out legal supervision over trial and litigation activities—to ensure the uniformity of the State's legal system and the correct implementation of the law.

II. Subjects of the Application of Law to Joint Development

The American sociological jurist Roscoe Pound once stated: "The life of the law is in its enforcement."⑤ The application of law is thus of profound significance. This is as true for domestic law as it is for the state practice of joint development of offshore oil and gas resources. Indeed, the application of law can be considered a crucial step and a fundamental guarantee for the successful implementation of joint development. However, "the application of law is a special legal activity with creative and organizational content."⑥ Moreover, "one of the most important features of the application of law is that only specialized organs (competent authorities) can apply legal norms."⑦ Therefore, the primary subjects of the application of law to the joint development of offshore oil and gas resources include sovereign states, joint authorities, legal persons, international judicial institutions, arbitral tribunals, and domestic courts.

(I) Sovereign States

Sovereign States are both the initiators of joint development activities for offshore oil and gas resources, and the negotiators and parties to the joint development agreements. Therefore, as the most fundamental and, indeed, the most important subjects of international law⑧, sovereign states are also, of course, the subjects of the application of law to the joint development of

⑤ See Roscoe Pound, *Jurisprudence*, Vol. 1, West Publishing Co., 1959, p. 353.
⑥ See [Soviet Union] S. S. Alekseev, *General Theory of Law*, trans. by Huang Liangping, Ding Wenqi, et al., Law Press China, 1988, p. 336.
⑦ See [Soviet Union] S. S. Alekseev, *General Theory of Law*, trans. by Huang Liangping, Ding Wenqi, et al., Law Press China, 1988, p. 338.
⑧ See [UK] Robert Jennings and Arthur Watts (rev.), *Oppenheim's International Law* (Vol. 1, Book 1), trans. by Wang Tieya et al., Encyclopedia of China Publis hing House, 1995, p. 91.

offshore oil and gas resources.⑨

Some scholars also hold that non-state entities can be parties to joint development agreements. This is because, pursuant to Article 305, paragraph 1 of the Convention, non-state political entities may become parties to the Convention and have competence over the matters governed by it. Accordingly, such political entities should be able to become parties to the provisional arrangements (joint development) under Articles 74 and 83 of the Convention. However, according to Article 305 of the Convention, these political entities are limited to those recognized by the United Nations or self-governing entities supervised and approved in accordance with a UN General Assembly resolution.

The Third Workshop on the Southeast Asian Seas of the East-West Center in 1985 held that, from the perspective of international law, joint development treaties should be limited to intergovernmental agreements and distinguished from agreements between a government and a petroleum company for the establishment of a joint venture, or agreements signed by a consortium of petroleum companies to participate in a country's oil and gas development.⑩ From the joint development agreements collected to date, all

⑨ See Zhang Lina, On the Proper Subjects for the Joint Development of Oil an d Gas Resources in the South China Sea, *Law Science Magazine*, No. 11, 2012, p. 108; He Hairong, Five Elements of Joint Development of Oil and Gas Resour ces in Disputed Maritime Areas and Their Implications for China, *Wuhan Univers ity International Law Review*, No. 2, 2016, p. 324; He Hairong, *A Study on the Legal Issues of Joint Maritime Development in the Gulf of Thailand*, Wuhan Uni versity Press, 2020, p. 62.

⑩ See Masahiro Miyoshi, The Basic Concept of Joint Development of Hydrocar

have been signed by representatives of the relevant governments or their diplomatic departments.[11] Therefore, a joint development agreement for offshore oil and gas resources is, in essence, a bilateral or multilateral international treaty signed between states[12], and only sovereign states, as subjects of international law, possess the capacity to conclude such treaties.[13]

(II) The Joint Authority

Academia generally divides the management models for the joint development of offshore oil and gas resources into the following three types: the joint operation model, the joint authority model, and the agency model.[14]

---

bon Resources on the Continental Shelf: With Special Reference to the Discussio ns at the East-West Centre Workshops on the South-East Asian Seas, *Internationa l Journal of Estuarine and Coastal Law*, Vol. 3, No.1, 1988, p. 5.

11 See Yang Zewei (ed.), *International Agreements on the Joint Development of Marine Resources* (Chinese-English Bilingual Version) (Vols. I & II), Social Scien ces Academic Press (China), 2016; Yang Zewei (ed.), *A Sequel to International A greements on the Joint Development of Marine Resources*, Wuhan University Pres s, 2018.

12 See Hazel Fox et al. eds., Joint Development of Offshore Oil and Gas: A M odel Agreement for States with Explanatory Commentary, London, 1989, p. 34.

13 See He Ende, The Basic Legal System for Joint Maritime Development, in Y ang Zewei (ed.), *Research on International Law Issues of Joint Maritime Develop ment*, Social Sciences Academic Press (China), 2016, p. 12.

14 See Robert Beckman eds., *Beyond Territorial Disputes in the South China Se a: Legal Framework for the Joint Development of Hydrocarbon Resources*, Edwar d Elgar Publishing Limited, 2013, p. 145; Yusuf Mohammad Yusuf, Is Joint Dev elopment A Panacea for Maritime Boundary Disputes and for the Exploitation of Offshore Transboundary Petroleum Deposits?, *International Energy Law Review*, V ol. 4, 2009, pp. 132-133; Ana E. Bastida, Adaeze Ifesi-Okoye, Salim Mahmud, J ames Ross, and Thomas Walde, Cross-border Unitization and Joint Development Agreements: An International Law Perspective, *Houston Journal of International Law*, Vol. 29, No. 2, 2007, pp. 416-418; David M. Ong, Joint Development of C ommon Offshore Oil and Gas Deposits: "Mere" State Practice or Customary Inter national Law?, *The American Journal of International Law*, Vol. 93, No. 4, 1999, pp. 788-792; Xiao Jianguo, *Joint Development of Petroleum on International Ma ritime Boundaries*, China Ocean Press, 2006, pp. 122-127; Cai Penghong, *Manage ment Models for Joint Development in Disputed Maritime Areas: A Comparative Study*, Shanghai Academy of Social Sciences Press, 1998.

Of these, "the joint authority model" refers to establishing an entirely new legal mechanism for petroleum development in the joint development area and setting up a joint institution to represent the States concerned in managing the development of oil and gas resources within that area.[15] This "joint authority model" is also termed the "super-national authority" model,[16] meaning that the governments of the two States engaged in joint development agree to transfer their jurisdiction over the joint development area to a supranational institution for management, which in turn establishes the regulations for the issuance and administration of operating licenses. Under the joint authority model, a joint authority is generally established to represent both States and assume full responsibility for all activities within the joint development area. Because the joint authority is endowed with an independent legal personality and capacity to act, it is, of course, a subject of the application of law to the joint development of offshore oil and gas resources.

For example, in the 1979 Joint Development Case Between Thailand and Malaysia in the Gulf of Thailand, according to the Memorandum of Understanding Between Malaysia and the Kingdom of Thailand on the Establishment of the Joint Authority for the Exploitation of the Resources of

---

15 See He Hairong, *A Study on the Legal Issues of Joint Maritime Development in the Gulf of Thailand*, Wuhan University Press, 2020, p. 84.
16 See Xiao Jianguo, *Joint Development of Petroleum on International Maritime Boundaries*, China Ocean Press, 2006, pp. 122-127; Cai Penghong, *Management Models for Joint Development in Disputed Maritime Areas: A Comparative Study*, Shanghai Academy of Social Sciences Press, 1998, pp. 63-65.

the Sea Bed in a Defined Area of the Continental Shelf of the Two Countries in the Gulf of Thailand, the two countries decided to establish a specialized institution—the Malaysia-Thailand Joint Authority—to represent both parties with full responsibility for the exploration and exploitation of the living resources of the overlapping area.[17] Article 3 of the memorandum explicitly provides: "There shall be established a Joint Authority to be known as Malaysia-Thailand Joint Authority for the purpose of the exploration and exploitation of the non-living natural resources of the sea-bed and subsoil in the overlapping area; the Joint Authority shall assume all rights and responsibilities on behalf of both Parties for the exploration and exploitation of the non-living natural resources of the sea-bed and subsoil in the overlapping area and also for the development, control and administration of the joint development area; the Joint Authority shall exercise on behalf of both Parties all the powers necessary for, incidental to or connected with the discharge of its functions relating to the exploration and exploitation of the non-living natural resources of the sea-bed and subsoil in the joint development area; all costs incurred and benefits derived by the Joint Authority from activities carried out in the joint development area shall be equally borne and shared by both Parties." Evidently, the Malaysia-Thailand

17 See "The 1979 Joint Development Case Between Thailand and Malaysia in th e Gulf of Thailand," in Yang Zewei (ed.), *International Agreements on the Joint Development of Marine Resources* (Chinese-English Bilingual Version) (Vol. I), So cial Sciences Academic Press (China), 2016, pp. 177-262; Wang Xiaomei, A Stud y on the Joint Development Case between Thailand and Malaysia, Master's thesis, Wuhan University, 2015.

Joint Authority is responsible for managing joint development affairs, possessing decision-making power on purely commercial matters and broad authority over the administrative management of joint development affairs; however, on major matters, the approval of both governments is required. That is to say, the two governments retain the ultimate decision-making power on major issues.[18]

(III) Legal Persons

It is generally held that legal persons or enterprises are not subjects of international law. This view is supported by the 1952 judgment of the International Court of Justice in the Anglo-Iranian Oil Co. case (United Kingdom v. Iran).[19] However, legal persons are subjects of the application of law to the joint development of offshore oil and gas resources, and indeed important ones. Petroleum companies are the ultimate implementers of the joint development of offshore oil and gas resources. Whether it is the joint development of transboundary offshore oil and gas resources or that in disputed maritime areas, it must ultimately be carried out by petroleum companies.[20]

In joint development, the participating legal persons or enterprises

18 See He Hairong, *A Study on the Legal Issues of Joint Maritime Development in the Gulf of Thailand*, Wuhan University Press, 2020, p. 86.
19 See Anglo-Iranian Oil Co. (United Kingdom v. Iran), available at https://www.icj-cij.org/public/files/case-related/16/016-19520722-JUD-01-00-EN.pdf.
20 See Yang Zewei, On the Issue of Selecting Blocks for Joint Maritime Develo pment, *Presentday Law Science*, No. 3, 2014, pp. 8-9.

primarily include petroleum companies and service providers. Petroleum companies are generally classified as national, international, and private. A national petroleum company is a state-controlled company that manages and develops the country's oil and gas resources. Major international petroleum companies include firms such as ExxonMobil, Shell, and TotalEnergies. Additionally, many smaller private petroleum companies and various specialized firms and service providers in oilfield services and petroleum engineering are active in the international arena.

In a country's domestic oil and gas development, a national petroleum company exercises strong control over the industry under national law. For instance, Petróleos Mexicanos (PEMEX), Mexico's national petroleum company, originally held exclusive rights within the country to conduct oil and gas exploration, development, production, refining, storage, and sales, pursuant to Article 27 of its Constitution and relevant regulations such as the Federal Ocean Act. It was only to facilitate joint development with the United States in the Gulf of Mexico that Mexico amended the relevant laws, allowing foreign petroleum companies to participate in the development of oil and gas on the Mexican side of the unitization area, thereby ending PEMEX's exclusive role in that context[21]. In China, the China National Offshore Oil Corporation (CNOOC) holds the exclusive right for foreign

21 See Jorge A. Vargas, The 2012 U.S.-Mexico Agreement on Transboundary Hydrocarbon Reservoirs in the Gulf of Mexico: A Blueprint for Progress or a Recipe for Conflict?, *San Diego International Law Journal*, Vol. 14, No. 3, 2012, pp. 62-68.

cooperation in offshore oil and gas pursuant to the Regulations of the People's Republic of China on the Exploitation of Offshore Petroleum Resources in Cooperation with Foreign Enterprises.

In transboundary resource development, a national oil company may also, in accordance with the rules for unitization, act as the national oil company, at least for development on its own side of the boundary. However, its original exclusive monopoly and ownership of the oil and gas resources, held as the national oil company of the resource State, are altered to some extent by its cooperation with other countries. As noted above, the domestic monopoly status of Mexico's national petroleum company changed after it signed a joint development agreement with the United States.

In joint development, even when two national petroleum companies exist—for example, the national petroleum companies of Malaysia and Thailand in their joint development case—relative to the Authority, a supranational entity with legal personality, these two companies can hardly be considered "national petroleum companies" (unless a special Authority Petroleum Company is established). Their legal status is no different from that of an ordinary commercial petroleum company.

A more unique case is that of the joint development between Malaysia and Vietnam. In that case, because Vietnam at the time had no domestic petroleum law and its national oil company was still in its nascent stages, lacking management and operational experience, the two countries ultimately chose to apply Malaysian petroleum law. The national oil company of Malaysia and the national oil company of Vietnam each appointed four members to form a coordination committee responsible for daily management and for resolving disputes amicably and in accordance with good oil industry practice. At the same time, Malaysia's national oil company was designated to be responsible for day-to-day operations, while Vietnam's role was limited to supervision and revenue sharing. Only issues that the coordination committee could not resolve amicably were to be referred to the two governments for resolution [22]. Here, the coordination committee established by the two national oil companies played, to some extent, the role of the two governments (or a similar supranational joint authority).

(IV) International Judicial Institutions

International judicial institutions, primarily the International Court of Justice and the International Tribunal for the Law of the Sea, are subjects of the application of law to the joint development of offshore oil and gas resources. On the one hand, numerous joint development agreements for offshore oil and gas resources generally contain "dispute settlement clauses." In these clauses, it is often stipulated that if a dispute arises between the parties in the course of the joint development of offshore oil and gas resources, it shall be submitted to an international judicial institution for settlement.

22 See Robert Beckman, et al. edited, *Beyond Territorial Disputes in the South China Sea: Legal Framework for the Joint Development of Hydrocarbon Resourc es*, Edward Elgar Publishing Limited, 2013, pp. 197-200.

For example, in the 1965 Joint Development Case Between Saudi Arabia and Kuwait, Article 22 of the Agreement between the Kingdom of Saudi Arabia and the State of Kuwait on the Partition of the Neutral Zone provides: "If any dispute arises in connection with the interpretation or application of this Agreement or the rights and obligations of the two Contracting Parties thereunder, the two Parties shall seek to settle it by friendly means, including recourse to the Arab League. If such means do not lead to a settlement, the dispute shall be referred to the International Court of Justice. The two Contracting Parties shall accept the compulsory jurisdiction of the International Court of Justice in this respect. If one of the two Contracting Parties objects to any measure taken by the other Party, the objecting Party may request the International Court of Justice to indicate provisional measures to suspend the action of the other Party or to allow it to continue until the Court has given its final decision. If either of the two Contracting Parties fails to comply with a judgment rendered against it, the other Contracting Party shall be absolved of its obligations under this Agreement."

Again, in the 1974 Joint Development Case Between Sudan and Saudi Arabia, the Agreement Between Sudan and Saudi Arabia relating to the Joint Exploitation of the Natural Resources of the Sea-Bed and Sub-soil of the Red Sea in the Common Zone also explicitly provides that if the States Parties cannot settle a dispute through negotiation, the dispute shall be referred to the International Court of Justice.[23]

On the other hand, in the course of settling disputes over the joint development of offshore oil and gas resources, international judicial institutions will generally apply the relevant laws in accordance with the agreement of the disputing parties to render a judgment and resolve the dispute. If the parties to the dispute have not made such an agreement, the international judicial institution will, in accordance with the relevant provisions of Article 38 of the Statute of the International Court of Justice, apply sources of international law—such as international treaties, international custom, or general principles of law—to render its judgment.

(V) Arbitral Tribunals

Arbitral tribunals are also subjects of the application of law to the joint development of offshore oil and gas resources. This is because arbitration is a frequently used method for resolving disputes arising from such development[24], especially for those between a joint development institution and a contractor, for which "the most commonly used means of settlement is arbitration or commercial arbitration."[25] In such cases, if the States party to the joint development agreement and the home State of the contractor are all

---

23 See Agreement Between Sudan and Saudi Arabia Relating to the Joint Exploit ation of the Natural Resources of the Sea-bed and Subsoil of the Red Sea in the Common Zone of 16 May 1974, ST/LEG/SER.B/18, pp. 452-455.
24 See Hazel Fox et al. eds., Joint Development of Offshore Oil and Gas: A M odel Agreement for States with Explanatory Commentary, London, 1989, p. 288.
25 See Xiao Jianguo, *Joint Development of Petroleum on International Maritime Boundaries*, China Ocean Press, 2006, p. 153.

parties to the 1965 Washington Convention on the Settlement of Investment Disputes between States and Nationals of Other States, the disputing parties may also choose to have their dispute resolved by the International Centre for Settlement of Investment Disputes (ICSID). In the practice of joint development of offshore oil and gas resources, if arbitration is selected, the joint development agreement will generally provide detailed provisions on matters such as the arbitral procedure and the composition of the arbitral tribunal.

For example, in the 1974 Delimitation and Joint Development Case Between France and Spain, Article 5 of the Convention between the Government of the French Republic and the Government of the Spanish State on the Delimitation of the Continental Shelves of the two States in the Bay of Biscay provides detailed provisions for the arbitral procedure: "The Contracting Parties shall endeavour to settle as soon as possible, through the diplomatic channel, any dispute which may arise concerning the interpretation or application of this Convention. Any dispute not settled within four months from the date on which one of the Contracting Parties gave notice of its intention to initiate the procedure provided for in the preceding paragraph shall, at the request of either Contracting Party, be referred to an arbitral tribunal. In each case, the arbitral tribunal shall be constituted in the following manner: each Party shall nominate one arbitrator, and the two arbitrators shall agree on a third arbitrator who shall not be a national of either of the two Parties; this third arbitrator shall act as president of the arbitral tribunal. If the arbitrators have not been nominated within two months from the date on which one of the Contracting States gave notice of its intention to refer the dispute to the tribunal, or if the arbitrators appointed by the two Parties have not agreed within one month from the date of the most recent nomination on the appointment of the third arbitrator, either Party may request the President of the International Court of Justice to make the necessary appointments. If the President of the Court is a national of one of the Parties or is incapacitated for any reason, the appointments shall be made by the Vice-President. If the Vice-President also is a national of one of the Parties or is incapacitated for any reason, the appointments shall be made by the most senior judge of the Court who is not a national of one of the two Parties. Each Contracting Party shall bear the costs of its arbitrator and one half of all other costs. The arbitral tribunal shall determine its own rules of procedure, if the Parties have not determined them within two months from the date of the most recent appointment."[26]

Similarly, in the 2013 Timor-Leste v. Australia arbitration, the Government of Timor-Leste, pursuant to Annex B(b) to Article 23 of the Timor Sea Treaty[27], appointed Lawrence Collins, a former Justice of the UK

26 Yang Zewei (ed.), *International Agreements on the Joint Development of Marine Resources* (Chinese-English Bilingual Version) (Vol. I), Social Sciences Academic Press (China), 2016, p. 94.

27 Annex B(b) to Article 23 of the Timor Sea Treaty provides: "An arbitral tribunal to which a dispute is submitted pursuant to Article 23(b) shall be composed of three arbitrators constituted as follows: (i) Australia and East Timor shall eac

Supreme Court, as arbitrator; Australia appointed Michael Reisman, an American scholar, as arbitrator; and the president of the arbitral tribunal was Tullio Treves, a former judge of the International Tribunal for the Law of the Sea and a professor at the University of Milan, who was jointly recommended by the two countries.[28]

Furthermore, in the 2012 Joint Development Case Between Seychelles and Mauritius, according to Article 21, paragraph 2 of the Treaty Concerning the Joint Management of the Continental Shelf in the Mascarene Plateau Region, signed by Seychelles and Mauritius, "Any dispute which is not settled in the manner set out in paragraph (a) and any unresolved matter relating to the operation of this Treaty under Article 4(b)(ii) shall, at the request of either of the Contracting Parties, be submitted to an Arbitral Tribunal established in accordance with the procedure set out in Annex B."

---

h appoint one arbitrator; (ii) The two arbitrators appointed by Australia and East Timor shall, within sixty (60) days of the appointment of the second of them, by agreement, select a third arbitrator who shall be a citizen, or permanent resident of a third country which has diplomatic relations with both Australia and East Ti mor; (iii) Within sixty (60) days of the selection of the third arbitrator, Australia and East Timor shall approve the selection of that arbitrator who shall act as Ch airman of the Tribunal. Arbitration proceedings shall be instituted upon notice bei ng given through the diplomatic channel by the country instituting such proceedin gs to the other country. Such notice shall contain a statement setting forth in su mmary form the grounds of the claim, the nature of the relief sought, and the n ame of the arbitrator appointed by the country instituting such proceedings. Withi n sixty (60) days after the giving of such notice the respondent country shall not ify the country instituting proceedings of the name of the arbitrator appointed by the respondent country."

28 See On 23 April 2013, the Republic of Timor-Leste Instituted Arbitral Procee dings Against the Commonwealth of Australia under Paragraph (b) of Annex B t o Article 23 of the Timor Sea Treaty between the Government of East Timor an d the Government of Australia of 20 May 2002, available at: https://pcacases.com /web/view/37.

Evidently, the process by which the above-mentioned international judicial institutions or arbitral tribunals—as subjects of the application of law to the joint development of offshore oil and gas resources—apply the law is very similar to the application of law in a domestic context.

(VI) Domestic Courts

Disputes between contractors in the course of joint development activities for offshore oil and gas resources may also be settled by domestic courts. Because contractors are equal commercial entities, in many cases they will also resort to litigation, submitting their disputes for adjudication to the domestic courts with jurisdiction over the joint development area or to the courts of the home State of any of the contractors.[29]

For example, in the 1974 Joint Development Case Between Japan and South Korea, the Agreement between Japan and the Republic of Korea Concerning Joint Development of the Southern Part of the Continental Shelf adjacent to the Two Countries provides in Article 21, paragraphs 1 and 2: "(1) When damage resulting from exploration or exploitation of natural resources in the Joint Development Zone has been sustained by nationals of either Party or other persons who are resident in the territory of either Party, actions for compensation for such damage may be brought by such nationals or persons in the court of one Party (a) in the territory of which such damage has

29 See Hazel Fox et al. eds., Joint Development of Offshore Oil and Gas: A Model Agreement for States with Explanatory Commentary, London, 1989, p. 289.

occurred, (b) in the territory of which such nationals or persons are resident, or (c) which has authorized the concessionaire designated and acting as the operator in the subzone where the incident causing such damage has occurred. (2) The court of one Party in which actions for compensation for such damage have been brought under paragraph 1 of this article shall apply the laws and regulations of that Party."

Similarly, in the 1989 Joint Development Case Between Australia and Indonesia, the Treaty between Australia and the Republic of Indonesia on the Zone of Cooperation in an Area between the Indonesian Province of East Timor and Northern Australia, in Article 28, also made the following corresponding provisions for the resolution, by way of remedies in domestic courts, of disputes arising from civil torts in the course of joint development: "Claims for damages or restitution of expenses as a result of activities in Area A may be brought in the Contracting State which has or whose nationals or permanent residents have suffered the damage or incurred the expense. The court in which the action is brought shall apply the law and regulations of that State."

Therefore, under these circumstances, domestic courts are, of course, also subjects of the application of law to the joint development of offshore oil and gas resources.

In summary, it is clear that the application of law is a special type of state activity or social management activity. As one scholar has stated: "In terms of its social content, the application of law, like the creation of law, is an activity of management—a special kind of social management. However, the application of law is not management in general, but rather a specialized form of management, the purpose of which is to ensure the full realization of the general rules expressly provided for in legal norms."[30]

III. Objects of the Application of Law to Joint Development

The objects of the application of law to the joint development of offshore oil and gas resources refer to those objects or matters that, in the course of such development, require regulation by different types of legal systems, such as international or domestic law. These include petroleum contract models, revenue sharing, taxation, environmental protection, criminal jurisdiction, civil actions, customs and quarantine, health and safety, and employment and training. As a general rule, the States Parties to a joint development will make explicit provisions for the aforementioned objects in the joint development agreement or in subsequent supplementary agreements concerning the joint development.

(I) Petroleum Contract Model

International petroleum contract models are generally divided into types

30 See [Soviet Union] S. S. Alekseev, *General Theory of Law*, trans. by Huang Liangping, Ding Wenqi, et al., Law Press China, 1988, p. 339.

such as the concession (or license) system and the contract system (e.g., production sharing contracts, service contracts) (see Section Four of Chapter 4 for details). Because different countries may adopt different petroleum contract models, the provisions of their relevant domestic legislation also differ greatly. Adopting a model that is consistent among the States Parties is a relatively simple matter. However, adopting a model that differs from a country's own domestic legislation may require cumbersome changes or adjustments in related areas such as the application of domestic law and state administration and enforcement. For any sovereign State involved, this could be a political disaster. Consequently, in joint development negotiations, especially for States Parties that use different petroleum contract models, the choice of a specific contract model to adopt in the joint development area is one of the key focal points and challenges.

For example, in the Joint Development Case Between Malaysia and Thailand, Malaysia's domestic oil and gas exploration and development employed the production sharing contract model, whereas Thailand's domestic system used the concession model. Because the two parties needed to implement a uniform legal system and a uniform petroleum contract model in the joint development area, the choice of a specific contract model to adopt became one of the focal points of the negotiations. For Thailand, the production sharing contract was a completely unfamiliar model; Malaysia, for its part, was unwilling to abandon its established production sharing model and allow the Authority to become a "state within a state." After eleven years of lengthy negotiations, during which they overcame numerous technical and practical difficulties, the parties ultimately adopted the production sharing contract model in the joint development area, which was formally established in the Authority's relevant charter through the issuance of a Production Sharing Contract.[31]

Of course, another solution is for the States Parties to further subdivide the joint development area into smaller blocks during negotiations, applying their respective legal systems, including their petroleum contract models, within each block. For instance, in the Joint Development Case Between Japan and South Korea, the parties subdivided the joint development area into nine smaller blocks, applying the national law corresponding to the nationality of the operator in each block. It is particularly noteworthy that in the Japan-South Korea case, it was stipulated that operators in the various blocks could only be Japanese or South Korean petroleum companies, meaning that the applicable law could only be Japanese or South Korean law. Although the concession model was chosen for the petroleum contracts in this case, this was merely because the domestic petroleum contract models used by both Japan and South Korea at the time happened to be the concession system.

(II) Revenue Sharing

---

31 See Constantinos Yiallourides, *Maritime Disputes and International Law: Disputed Waters and Seabed Resources in Asia and Europe*, Routledge, 2019, pp. 224-225.

"International practice shows that joint development is based on practical considerations and has distinct functional characteristics." [32] Therefore, a major incentive driving coastal States to undertake the joint development of offshore oil and gas resources is economic consideration. Coastal States hope either to enhance their access to oil and gas resources through joint development, thereby better ensuring their national energy security, or to promote their domestic economic growth through the revenues from resource development. As Professor M. J. Valencia of the East-West Center in Hawaii and the Japanese scholar Masahiro Miyoshi have stated, "Perhaps the most important reason for a nation to choose joint development is a sense of urgency and obligation to protect its interests in its oil and natural gas reserves."[33] In other words, "economic factors, such as a State's urgent need for oil and gas resources, will prompt its government to find ways to benefit from development first, rather than allowing the exploitation of resources to be delayed by delimitation negotiations that can sometimes even affect state relations."[34]

Driven by these economic factors, joint development agreements for offshore oil and gas resources generally contain explicit provisions on the

32 See Xiao Jianguo, *Joint Development of Petroleum on International Maritime Boundaries*, China Ocean Press, 2006, p. 50.

33 See M. J. Valencia and M. Miyoshi, Southeast Asian Seas: Joint Development of Hydrocarbons in Overlapping Claim Area? *Ocean Development and International Law*, Vol. 16, 1986, p. 223.

34 See Yu Hui, International Law Issues on the Joint Development of Marine Mineral Resources, *Chinese Yearbook of International Law*, 1994, China Translation & Publishing Corporation (1996), p. 50.

issue of revenue sharing.

For example, in the 2012 Joint Development Case Between Seychelles and Mauritius, Article 5 of the Treaty between the Government of the Republic of Seychelles and the Government of the Republic of Mauritius Concerning the Joint Management of the Continental Shelf in the Mascarene Plateau Region sets forth the following provision on sharing of revenue: "The Contracting Parties shall share revenue received in respect of natural resource activities carried out in the JMA equally, whereby fifty (50) per cent of revenue received shall be remitted to Mauritius and fifty (50) per cent of revenue received shall be remitted to Seychelles."[35] Again, for example, in the 2001 Joint Development Case Between Nigeria and São Tomé and Príncipe, Article 3, paragraph 1 of the Treaty Between The Federal Republic of Nigeria and The Democratic Republic of São Tomé e Príncipe on the Joint Development of Petroleum and other Resources, in Respect of Areas of the Exclusive Economic Zone of the Two States explicitly provides: "Within the Zone, there shall be joint control by the States Parties of the exploration for and exploitation of resources, aimed at achieving optimum commercial utilization. The States Parties shall share, in the proportions Nigeria 60 per cent, São Tome and Principe 40 per cent, all benefits and obligations arising from development activities carried out in the Zone in accordance with this

---

35 See Yang Zewei (ed.), *International Agreements on the Joint Development of Marine Resources* (Chinese-English Bilingual Version) (Vol. II), Social Sciences A cademic Press (China), 2016, p. 672.

Treaty."[36]

Here, several points merit special attention.

First, this "revenue" refers to the "government take," not the total revenue from oil and gas development, as a portion of the total revenue must be paid to the petroleum company responsible for the development. Using a country's domestic petroleum contracts as a reference: under a concession system, the government take includes royalties and special taxes and fees related to oil and gas operations.[37] Under a production sharing contract, the take includes a range of elements, such as various pre-production fees (application fees, bidding fees, signature bonuses, discovery bonuses, and production bonuses)[38], contributions to training and infrastructure, royalties, the government's share of oil, the allocation of profit oil, and various taxes; in some cases, a special windfall profits tax may also be levied when profits increase significantly due to rising oil prices[39]. The remainder is the petroleum company's share.

Second, a distinction must be made between the allocation of resources and the sharing of revenue (or benefits). This point is often misunderstood.

---

36 See Yang Zewei (ed.), *International Agreements on the Joint Development of Marine Resources* (Chinese-English Bilingual Version) (Vol. II), Social Sciences A cademic Press (China), 2016, p. 396.

37 See Wang Nianping, *A Comparative Study of International Petroleum Contract Models*, Law Press China, 2009, p. 49.

38 See Wang Nianping, *A Comparative Study of International Petroleum Contract Models*, Law Press China, 2009, pp. 38-39.

39 See Hazel Fox et al, *Joint Development of Offshore Oil and Gas: A Model A greement for States for Joint Development with Explanatory Commentary*, British Institute of International and Comparative Law, 1989, pp. 245-248.

For example, in the 1993 Joint Development Case Between Guinea-Bissau and Senegal, Article 2 of the Agreement on Management and Cooperation Between the Republic of Guinea-Bissau and the Republic of Senegal provides: "Resources from the exploitation of the Area shall be shared in the following proportions: Fishery resources: Fifty per cent to Senegal, Fifty per cent to Guinea-Bissau; Resources from the continental shelf: Eighty-five per cent to Senegal, Fifteen per cent to Guinea-Bissau. In the event of new discoveries, these proportions shall be revised, and such revision shall depend on the quantity of resources discovered."[40] In this case, the contracting parties are allocating the exploited resources themselves (i.e., the oil, gas, or fish) based on ownership of those resources, rather than sharing the state revenue. After a contracting party receives its allocated share of the physical resources, it must then, in accordance with its own relevant domestic laws, carry out a further allocation with the operator. The portion retained by the State following this second allocation is what constitutes the actual government take. In the 2002 Joint Development Case Between East Timor and Australia, Article 4 of the Timor Sea Treaty between the Government of East Timor and the Government of Australia provided as follows regarding "Production Sharing Contracts": "East Timor and Australia shall have title to all petroleum produced in the Joint Petroleum Development Area (JPDA). Of the petroleum produced in the JPDA, ninety (90) percent shall belong to East

40 See Yang Zewei (ed.), *International Agreements on the Joint Development of Marine Resources* (Chinese-English Bilingual Version) (Vol. I), Social Sciences Ac ademic Press (China), 2016, p. 331.

Timor and ten (10) percent shall belong to Australia." Article 5, on "Fiscal Arrangements and Taxes," stipulates that the two countries shall reach an agreement on the fiscal regime for petroleum projects in the Joint Development Area; if no agreement can be reached, they shall apply their respective fiscal regimes in accordance with the aforementioned allocation ratio[41]. The correct interpretation of this passage is that, assuming 100 barrels of oil and gas are produced in the Joint Development Area, East Timor owns 90 barrels and Australia owns 10. In the absence of a unified fiscal regime, East Timor, in accordance with its relevant domestic petroleum laws, would allocate the 90 barrels it owns between its government and the participating petroleum company, and would collect various taxes and fees from the company; Australia would allocate the 10 barrels it owns in accordance with its domestic law. Out of this total output of 100 barrels, East Timor's government take would necessarily be less than 90 barrels, and Australia's government take would necessarily be less than 10 barrels. Because the two countries have different domestic laws and levy different taxes and fees on the petroleum company, the final ratio of their government takes would inevitably deviate from 90:10.

Third, the principle for revenue sharing is generally either equal division or proportional allocation, but there are exceptions. As discussed in Section Two of Chapter 1, the principle for allocating transboundary oil and gas

41 See Yang Zewei (ed.), *International Agreements on the Joint Development of Marine Resources* (Chinese-English Bilingual Version) (Vol. II), Social Sciences A cademic Press (China), 2016, pp. 501-502.

resources is that, following the unitization of a single reservoir, the allocation ratio for the oil and gas should roughly correspond to the proportion of reserves on each side of the delimitation line. For the revenue from, or allocation of resources under, joint development, most cases involve equal sharing between the States Parties. As noted above, the case of Senegal and Guinea-Bissau is a special exception, as different allocation ratios were adopted for oil and gas resources and for fishery resources. As for the resource allocation ratio in the Joint Development Case Between Timor-Leste and Australia, it is generally considered by scholars to be highly favorable to Timor-Leste. However, this allocation arrangement must be viewed not only in the context of the joint development agreement itself but also from the broader perspective of the overall development of the Greater Sunrise field in the relevant maritime area. From the perspective of international law, the maritime area that Timor-Leste could have claimed included the entire Greater Sunrise oil and gas field. However, for historical and practical reasons, during its negotiations with Australia, Timor-Leste in effect relinquished its claims to the eastern section of the Timor Gap. This resulted in the finally established joint development area covering only a small portion of the Greater Sunrise field.[42] After Timor-Leste and Australia signed the Timor Sea Treaty, they also signed the Agreement relating to the Unitisation of the Sunrise and Troubadour Fields. Under this agreement, 20.1%

42 See Paul Cleary, *Shakedown: Australia's Grab for Timor Oil*, Allen & Unwin, 2007, pp. 34-109.

of the Greater Sunrise field lies within the Joint Development Area, and consequently, 20.1% of all petroleum production is attributed to the joint development area, with the remaining 79.9% attributed to Australia.[43] Based on the 90:10 allocation ratio for the joint development area between Timor-Leste and Australia, this means that only 18.09% of the total production from the entire Greater Sunrise field actually belonged to Timor-Leste.[44] Had Timor-Leste not relinquished its claim, it seems the production allocation for the entire Greater Sunrise field should by no means have been based on an 18:82 ratio that so heavily favored Australia.

(III) Taxation

"Taxation is one of the manifestations of a State's exercise of its sovereign rights,"[45] and an important aspect of joint development activities for offshore oil and gas resources. Therefore, the parties to a joint development agreement for offshore oil and gas resources both attach great importance to the issue of taxation. After the delineation of a joint development zone, they take care to coordinate their respective tax systems to avoid the overlapping exercise of sovereign rights in matters of taxation

---

43 See Yang Zewei (ed.), *International Agreements on the Joint Development of Marine Resources* (Chinese-English Bilingual Version) (Vol. II), Social Sciences Academic Press (China), 2016, p. 536.
44 See Robert Beckman, et al. edited, *Beyond Territorial Disputes in the South China Sea: Legal Framework for the Joint Development of Hydrocarbon Resources*, Edward Elgar Publishing Limited, 2013, pp. 253-256.
45 See Cai Penghong, *Management Models for Joint Development in Disputed Maritime Areas: A Comparative Study*, Shanghai Academy of Social Sciences Press, 1998, p. 72.

within the zone.[46]

For example, in the 2012 Joint Development Case Between Seychelles and Mauritius, Article 6 of the Treaty between the Government of the Republic of Seychelles and the Government of the Republic of Mauritius Concerning the Joint Management of the Continental Shelf in the Mascarene Plateau Region clearly stipulates the following regarding the "Taxation Code": "The Contracting Parties shall agree upon a Taxation Code applicable to income derived from natural resource activities in the Joint Management Area (JMA). Neither Contracting Party may during the life of a natural resource project vary any of the provisions of the Taxation Code applicable to it except by mutual agreement."

(IV) Environmental Protection

Article 194 of the United Nations Convention on the Law of the Sea stipulates: "States shall take, individually or jointly as appropriate, all measures consistent with this Convention that are necessary to prevent, reduce and control pollution of the marine environment from any source, using for this purpose the best practicable means at their disposal and in accordance with their capabilities, and they shall endeavour to harmonize their policies in this connection." Therefore, in the State practice of joint development of offshore oil and gas resources, the States Parties have an

46 See Xiao Jianguo, *Joint Development of Petroleum on International Maritime Boundaries*, China Ocean Press, 2006, p. 136.

obligation to protect the marine environment.

In fact, numerous joint development agreements for offshore oil and gas resources generally include provisions of principle on marine environmental protection. For example, in the 2012 Joint Development Case between Seychelles and Mauritius, Article 12 of the Treaty between the Government of the Republic of Seychelles and the Government of the Republic of Mauritius Concerning the Joint Management of the Continental Shelf in the Mascarene Plateau Region sets out the following detailed provisions on the "Protection of the Seabed Marine Environment": "(1) The Contracting Parties shall co-operate to protect natural resources in the JMA so as to secure seabed biodiversity and prevent pollution and other risks of harm to the environment arising from, or connected with, natural resource activities in the JMA. (2) The Contracting Parties shall apply the precautionary principle in co-operating to conserve and protect the environment and biodiversity of the seabed in the JMA... (3) The Contracting Parties shall co-operate to protect seabed marine habitats and associated ecological communities of the seabed in the JMA... (4) Where pollution of the marine environment occurring in the JMA spreads beyond the JMA, the Contracting Parties shall co-operate in taking prompt and effective action to prevent, mitigate and eliminate such pollution in accordance with international best practices, standards and procedures."

(V) Criminal Jurisdiction

The issue of Criminal Jurisdiction is a matter with pronounced sovereign overtones in the joint development of offshore oil and gas resources. Therefore, joint development agreements for offshore oil and gas resources typically contain explicit provisions on this matter.

For example, in the 2001 Joint Development Case Between Nigeria and São Tomé and Príncipe, the Treaty Between The Federal Republic of Nigeria and The Democratic Republic of São Tomé e Príncipe on the Joint Development of Petroleum and other Resources, in Respect of Areas of the Exclusive Economic Zone of the Two States made very clear provisions on the issue of Criminal Law and Jurisdiction: "(1) Subject to paragraph 3 of this article, a national or permanent resident of a State Party shall be subject to the criminal law of that State Party in respect of acts or omissions occurring in the Zone provided that a permanent resident of a State Party who is a national of the other State Party shall be subject to the criminal law of the latter State Party. A national of both States Parties shall be subject to the criminal law of both. (2) A national of a third State, not being a permanent resident of either State Party, shall be subject to the criminal law of both States Parties in respect of acts or omissions occurring in the Zone. Such a person shall not be subject to criminal proceedings under the law of one State Party if he or she has already been tried and discharged or acquitted by a competent tribunal or already undergone punishment for the same act or omission under the law of the other State Party... This Article is without prejudice to any other basis for the exercise of the criminal jurisdiction of either of the States Parties."

(VI) Civil Actions

In the State practice of joint development of offshore oil and gas resources, numerous joint development agreements also make comparatively explicit provisions for matters concerning Civil Actions.

For example, in the 2001 Joint Development Case Between Nigeria and São Tomé and Príncipe, Article 42 of the Treaty Between The Federal Republic of Nigeria and The Democratic Republic of São Tomé e Príncipe on the Joint Development of Petroleum and other Resources, in Respect of Areas of the Exclusive Economic Zone of the Two States is the clause on "Civil and Administrative Jurisdiction." The article provides: "Unless otherwise provided in this Treaty, each of the States Parties may exercise civil or administrative jurisdiction in relation to development activities in the Zone, or persons present in the Zone for the purposes of those activities, to the same extent as they may do so in relation to activities and persons in their own exclusive economic zone. In the exercise of jurisdiction under paragraph 1, the States Parties shall give effect to the relevant applicable law. This article is without prejudice to any other basis for the exercise of civil or administrative jurisdiction by either of the States Parties."

(VII) Customs and Quarantine

In the State practice of joint development of offshore oil and gas resources, some joint development agreements also make provisions for the Application of Customs and Quarantine Laws.[47]

For example, in the 1989 Joint Development Case Between Australia and Indonesia, Australia and Indonesia signed the Treaty between Australia and the Republic of Indonesia on the Zone of Cooperation in an Area between the Indonesian Province of East Timor and Northern Australia. Article 23 of this treaty was dedicated specifically to the issue of Customs and Quarantine. It provides: "Each Contracting State may, subject to paragraphs 3 and 5 of this Article, apply customs, migration and quarantine laws to persons, equipment and goods entering its territory from, or leaving its territory for, Area A. The Contracting States may adopt arrangements to facilitate such entry and departure... Nothing in this Article prejudices the right of either Contracting State to apply customs, migration and quarantine controls to persons, equipment and goods entering Area A without the authority of either Contracting State. The Contracting States may adopt arrangements to coordinate the exercise of such rights. Goods and equipment entering Area A for purposes related to petroleum operations shall not be subject to customs duties. Goods and equipment leaving or in transit through a Contracting State for the purpose of entering Area A for purposes related to petroleum

47 There are also many cases of joint development of offshore oil and gas resou rces that have not made provisions for Customs and Quarantine matters, such as the 2012 Joint Development Case Between the United States and Mexico.

operations shall not be subject to customs duties. Goods and equipment leaving Area A for the purpose of being permanently transferred to a part of a Contracting State may be subject to customs duties of that Contracting State."

(VIII) Health and Safety

Some joint development agreements for offshore oil and gas resources include provisions of principle on the health and safety of operators or workers in the joint development zone.

For example, in the 2012 Joint Development Case between Seychelles and Mauritius, Article 15 of the Treaty between the Government of the Republic of Seychelles and the Government of the Republic of Mauritius Concerning the Joint Management of the Continental Shelf in the Mascarene Plateau Region is the clause on Health and Safety for Workers. This article clearly stipulates: "The Authority shall develop, and contractors shall apply where required, occupational health and safety standards and procedures for persons employed on installations and structures in the JMA in accordance with internationally accepted standards and best practices. Similar occupational health, safety standards and procedures shall apply to all workers engaged in natural resource activities in the JMA." Furthermore, in the 1989 Joint Development Case Between Australia and Indonesia, Article 25 of the Treaty between Australia and the Republic of Indonesia on the Zone of Cooperation in an Area between the Indonesian Province of East Timor and Northern Australia contains similar provisions.

(IX) Employment and Training

Since the 21st century, in the State practice of joint development of offshore oil and gas resources, the content of the relevant agreements has become increasingly detailed and comprehensive, even including provisions on matters such as Employment and Training.

For example, in the 2001 Joint Development Case Between Nigeria and São Tomé and Príncipe, Article 36 of the Treaty Between The Federal Republic of Nigeria and The Democratic Republic of São Tomé e Príncipe on the Joint Development of Petroleum and other Resources, in Respect of Areas of the Exclusive Economic Zone of the Two States made the following explicit provisions on the matter of Employment and Training: "(1) The Authority may issue guidelines in respect of the employment and training policies to be followed by contractors in the Zone for the purposes of: (a) Enhancing the employment opportunities of nationals of the States Parties consistent with the safe and efficient conduct of petroleum and other development activities; (b) Assisting to the extent practicable the equitable division of employment and training benefits between the States Parties. (2) The terms of development contracts shall comply with such guidelines. (3) The States Parties shall cooperate in the administration of their immigration and employment laws so as to facilitate the issue of visas and work permits for the purposes of development contracts in relation to the Zone."

As another example, in the 2012 Joint Development Case between Seychelles and Mauritius, Article 14 of the Treaty between the Government of the Republic of Seychelles and the Government of the Republic of Mauritius Concerning the Joint Management of the Continental Shelf in the Mascarene Plateau Region is the clause on Employment. The article provides: "The Contracting Parties shall take appropriate measures to ensure that preference is given in employment in the JMA to nationals of both Contracting Parties and to facilitate, as a matter of priority, training and employment opportunities for those nationals."

Section Two: The Main Types for the Application of Law to the Joint Development of Offshore Oil and Gas Resources

As previously mentioned, since the first case of joint development of offshore oil and gas resources was implemented between Bahrain and Saudi Arabia in 1958, there have been more than 30 such instances of State practice to date. A systematic review and summarization of these 30-plus instances of State practice reveals that there are three main types for the application of law to the joint development of offshore oil and gas resources: separate application, joint application, and comprehensive application.

I. Separate Application of Joint Development Law

The separate application of law for the joint development of offshore oil and gas resources can be divided into the absolute separate application and the relative separate application of joint development law.

(I) Absolute Separate Application of Joint Development Law

The absolute separate application of law for the joint development of offshore oil and gas resources refers to partitioning the joint maritime development zone, with each party's national law being applied separately and exclusively within its designated section. For example, in the 1965 Joint Development Case Between Saudi Arabia and Kuwait, Article 3 of the

Agreement between the Kingdom of Saudi Arabia and the State of Kuwait on the Partition of the Neutral Zone explicitly provides: "Subject to the other provisions of the Agreement, and without prejudice to the rights of both Contracting Parties to the natural resources of the whole Neutral Zone, a Contracting Party shall, in the partitioned zone assigned to it, exercise the same administrative, legislative and defence rights as in its own original territory."[48] It is clear that, in this case, the contracting parties agreed that the law of each party would apply to the area of the Neutral Zone belonging to its territory.

As another example, in the 1981 Joint Development Case Between Iceland and Norway concerning Jan Mayen, the Agreement on the Continental Shelf Between Iceland and Jan Mayen made the following provisions for each party to apply its own laws to its respective area of jurisdiction: "In the part of the area defined in Article 2 north of the delimitation line between the two Parties' economic zones (approximately 32 750 sq. km.)... Norwegian legislation, Norwegian petroleum policy and Norwegian regulations relating to the control of such activities, safety measures and environmental protection shall apply to the activities in the area referred to in the first paragraph. The Norwegian authorities shall also be responsible for enforcement and administration in the said area. In the part of the area defined in Article 2 south of the delimitation line between the two

48 See Article 3 of the Agreement Between the State of Kuwait and the Kingdom of Saudi Arabia Relating to Partition of the Neutral Zone of 7 July 1965.

Parties' economic zones (approximately 12 720 sq. km.)... Icelandic legislation, Icelandic petroleum policy and Icelandic regulations relating to the control of such activities, safety measures and environmental protection shall apply to the activities in the area referred to in the first paragraph. The Icelandic authorities shall also be responsible for enforcement and administration in the said area."[49] Clearly, in this case, Norway and Iceland each applied their own national laws within the maritime areas under their respective jurisdiction and control.

(II) Relative Separate Application of Joint Development Law

The relative separate application of law for the joint development of offshore oil and gas resources refers to the situation where, although the joint maritime development zone is partitioned and, in principle, each party's national law is applied separately, there are modifications or adjustments in practice. For example, in the 1974 Joint Development Case Between Japan and South Korea, although each subzone of the joint development zone is subject to the law of only one country, the applicable law is not fixed but rather depends on the nationality of the operator for that subzone. Article 19 of the Agreement between Japan and the Republic of Korea Concerning Joint Development of the Southern Part of the Continental Shelf adjacent to the Two Countries explicitly provides: "Except where otherwise provided in this

49 See Article 5 and Article 6 of the Agreement between Iceland and Norway o n the Continental Shelf in the Area between Iceland and Jan Mayen of 22 Octob er 1981.

Agreement, the laws and regulations of one Party shall apply with respect to matters relating to exploration or exploitation of natural resources in the subzones with respect to which that Party has authorized concessionaires designated and acting as operators."[50] This is what is known as the "operator formula,"[51] which is a special kind of institutional arrangement. As one scholar has pointed out: "The method of allocating jurisdiction in the Japan-South Korea joint development zone is a variation or modification of the principle of governing one's own designated area with one's own national law."[52]

II. Joint Application of Joint Development Law

The joint application of law for the joint development of offshore oil and gas resources refers to the adoption of a single set of laws, mutually agreed upon by both parties, to be applied to the joint development zone. For example, in the 1979 Joint Development Case Between Malaysia and Thailand, Malaysia and Thailand agreed to establish a Joint Authority responsible for exploration and exploitation activities in the joint maritime development zone. Article 3 of the 1979 Memorandum of Understanding

---

50 See Article 19 of the Agreement Between Japan and the Republic of Korea Concerning Joint Development of the Southern Part of the Continental Shelf Adja cent to the Two Countries of 30 January 1974.
51 See Masahiro Miyoshi, The Joint Development of Offshore Oil and Gas in R elation to Maritime Boundary Delimitation, International Boundaries Research Uni t, Maritime Briefing, Vol. 2, No. 5, 1999, p.12.
52 See Sun Binghui, A Study on the Legal Issues of Joint Development of Mari ne Resources, PhD dissertation, China University of Political Science and Law, 2 000, p. 80.

Between Malaysia and the Kingdom of Thailand on the Establishment of the Joint Authority for the Exploitation of the Resources of the Sea Bed in a Defined Area of the Continental Shelf of the Two Countries in the Gulf of Thailand provides: "The Joint Authority shall assume all rights and responsibilities on behalf of both Parties for the exploration and exploitation of the non-living natural resources of the sea-bed and subsoil in the overlapping area (hereinafter referred to as the joint development area) and also for the development, control and administration of the joint development area. The assumption of such rights and responsibilities by the Joint Authority shall in no way affect or curtail the validity of concessions or licenses hitherto issued or agreements or arrangements hitherto made by either Party. The Joint Authority shall consist of two joint-chairmen, one from each country, and an equal number of members from each country. Subject to the provisions of this Memorandum, the Joint Authority shall exercise on behalf of both Parties all the powers necessary for, incidental to or connected with the discharge of its functions relating to the exploration and exploitation of the non-living natural resources of the sea-bed and subsoil in the joint development area."[53]

In 1990, Malaysia and Thailand signed the 1990 Agreement between the Government of Malaysia and the Government of the Kingdom of Thailand on the Constitution and Other Matters Relating to the Establishment of the

53 See Article 3 of the Memorandum of Understanding Between Malaysia and th e Kingdom of Thailand on the Establishment of a Joint Authority for the Exploit ation of the Resources in the Sea-Bed in a Defined Area of the Continental Shel f of the Two Countries in the Gulf of Thailand of 21 February 1979.

Malaysia-Thailand Joint Authority. The agreement detailed how to establish the Malaysia-Thailand Joint Development Area, the rights within that Area, and how to exercise them.[54] At the same time, the Joint Authority also issued the Malaysia-Thailand Joint Authority Procedures for Drilling Operations (1996), the Malaysia-Thailand Joint Authority Procedures for Production Operations (2003), and the Production Sharing Contract, among others. Furthermore, in 1990 Thailand passed the Thailand-Malaysia Joint Authority Act 1990, and Malaysia passed the Malaysia-Thailand Joint Authority Act 1990 (B.E. 2533). The aforementioned legal documents constitute the legal framework jointly applicable in the Malaysia-Thailand joint maritime development zone.

However, Malaysia and Thailand made a special demarcation of their respective criminal jurisdiction within the joint development zone[55], and specifically declared that: "the provisions concerning the scope of criminal jurisdiction shall neither be deemed to constitute the continental shelf boundary line of the Joint Development Area as determined between the Parties in accordance with paragraph 2, nor shall such provisions prejudice the sovereign rights of either Party in the Joint Development Area."[56]

---

54 See 1990 Agreement between the Government of Malaysia and the Governme nt of the Kingdom of Thailand on the Constitution and Other Matters Relating to the Establishment of the Malaysia-Thailand Joint Authority.

55 See Ana E. Bastida et al., Cross-Border Unitization and Joint Development A greements: An International Law Perspective, *Houston Journal of International La w*, Vol. 29, No. 2, 2007, p. 417.

56 See Article 5 of the Memorandum of Understanding Between Malaysia and th e Kingdom of Thailand on the Establishment of a Joint Authority for the Exploit ation of the Resources in the Sea-Bed in a Defined Area of the Continental Shel

Notably, although the initial agreement pertained only to the scope of criminal jurisdiction, in the course of subsequent enforcement, Malaysia and Thailand agreed to extend this to matters of civil jurisdiction.[57]

III. Comprehensive Application of Joint Development Law

The comprehensive application of laws governing the joint development of offshore oil and gas resources involves both separate and joint application. A case in point is the 1989 Joint Development Case Between Australia and Indonesia. According to the Treaty between Australia and the Republic of Indonesia on the Zone of Cooperation in an Area between the Indonesian Province of East Timor and Northern Australia, the established Zone of Cooperation was divided into three areas: A, B, and C. Of these, Area B, adjacent to Australia, was placed under Australian jurisdiction and subject to its laws; Area C, adjacent to Indonesia, was placed under Indonesian jurisdiction and subject to its laws.[58] Area A, however, was jointly administered by both nations and governed by a comprehensive legal framework mutually agreed upon by the two parties, such as Annex B to the Treaty—the Petroleum Mining Code for Area A of the Zone of Cooperation;

f of the Two Countries in the Gulf of Thailand of 21 February 1979.

57 See Datuk Harun Ariffin, The Malaysian Philosophy of Joint Development, E nergy, Vol. 10, 1985, p. 535.

58 See Lian A. Mito, The Timor Gap Treaty as a Model for Joint Development in the Spratly Islands, *American University International Law Review*, Vol. 13, 19 98, pp. 753-755.

Annex C—the Model Production Sharing Contract between the Joint Authority and Contractors; and Annex D—the Taxation Code for the Avoidance of Double Taxation in Respect of Activities Connected with Area A of the Zone of Cooperation.[59]

Notably, the Treaty between Australia and the Republic of Indonesia on the Zone of Cooperation in an Area between the Indonesian Province of East Timor and Northern Australia also explicitly stipulated how the respective laws of Australia and Indonesia would apply within Area A.

For example, Article 23 of the Treaty between Australia and the Republic of Indonesia on the Zone of Cooperation in an Area between the Indonesian Province of East Timor and Northern Australia makes the following explicit provisions concerning the Application of Customs, Immigration and Quarantine Law: "(1) Each Contracting State may, subject to paragraphs 3 and 5 of this Article, apply customs, migration and quarantine laws to persons, equipment and goods entering its territory from, or leaving its territory for, Area A. The Contracting States may adopt arrangements to facilitate such entry and departure. (2) Contractors shall ensure, unless otherwise authorized by the Contracting States, that persons, equipment and goods do not enter structures in Area A without first entering Australia or the Republic of Indonesia, and that their employees and the employees of their

59 See Anthony Bergin, The Australian-Indonesian Timor Gap Maritime Boundary Agreement, *International Journal of Estuarine and Coastal Law*, Vol. 5, 1990, pp. 388-389.

subcontractors are authorized by the Joint Authority to enter Area A. (3) One Contracting State may request consultations with the other Contracting State in relation to the entry of particular persons, equipment and goods to structures in Area A aimed at controlling the movement of such persons, equipment or goods. (4) Nothing in this Article prejudices the right of either Contracting State to apply customs, migration and quarantine controls to persons, equipment and goods entering Area A without the authority of either Contracting State. The Contracting States may adopt arrangements to coordinate the exercise of such rights. (5) (a) Goods and equipment entering Area A for purposes related to petroleum operations shall not be subject to customs duties. (b) Goods and equipment leaving or in transit through a Contracting State for the purpose of entering Area A for purposes related to petroleum operations shall not be subject to customs duties. (c) Goods and equipment leaving Area A for the purpose of being permanently transferred to a part of a Contracting State may be subject to customs duties of that Contracting State."[60]

As another example, Article 27 of the Treaty between Australia and the Republic of Indonesia on the Zone of Cooperation in an Area between the Indonesian Province of East Timor and Northern Australia also sets out relatively detailed provisions on the issue of Criminal Jurisdiction: "(1)

---

60 Yang Zewei (ed.), *International Agreements on the Joint Development of Mari ne Resources* (Chinese-English Bilingual Version) (Vol. I), Social Sciences Acade mic Press (China), 2016, pp. 283-284.

Subject to paragraph 3 of this Article a national or permanent resident of a Contracting State shall be subject to the criminal law of that State in respect of acts or omissions occurring in Area A connected with or arising out of exploration for and exploitation of petroleum resources, provided that a permanent resident of a Contracting State who is a national of the other Contracting State shall be subject to the criminal law of the latter State. (2) (a) Subject to paragraph 3 of this Article, a national of a third State, not being a permanent resident of either Contracting State, shall be subject to the criminal law of both Contracting States in respect of acts or omissions occurring in Area A connected with or arising out of the exploration for and exploitation of petroleum resources. Such a person shall not be subject to criminal proceedings under the law of one Contracting State if he or she has already been tried and discharged or acquitted by a competent tribunal or already undergone punishment for the same act or omission under the law of the other Contracting State or where the competent authorities of one Contracting State, in accordance with its law, have decided in the public interest to refrain from prosecuting the person for that act or omission. (b) In cases referred to in sub-paragraph (a) of this paragraph, the Contracting States shall, as and when necessary, consult each other to determine which criminal law is to be applied, taking into account the nationality of the victim and the interests of the Contracting State most affected by the alleged offence. (3) The criminal law of the flag State shall apply in relation to acts or omissions on board vessels including seismic or drill vessels in, or aircraft in flight over, Area A. (4) (a) The Contracting States shall provide assistance to and cooperate with each other, including through agreements or arrangements as appropriate, for the purposes of enforcement of criminal law under this Article, including the obtaining of evidence and information. (b) Each Contracting State recognizes the interest of the other Contracting State where a victim of an alleged offence is a national of that other State and shall keep that other State informed to the extent permitted by its law of action being taken with regard to the alleged offence. (5) The Contracting States may make arrangements permitting officials of one Contracting State to assist in the enforcement of the criminal law of the other Contracting State. Where such assistance involves the detention of a person who under paragraph 1 of this Article is subject to the jurisdiction of the other Contracting State that detention may only continue until it is practicable to hand the person over to the relevant officials of that other Contracting State."[61]

As can be seen from the above, in the Joint Development Case Between Australia and Indonesia, Areas B and C were part of the territorial seas and territory of Australia and Indonesia respectively, and were therefore governed by their respective domestic laws. Area A, on the other hand, was the joint offshore development zone for Australia and Indonesia, and was thus subject to a legal framework jointly established and mutually recognized by both nations.

---

61 See Article 27 of the Treaty between Australia and the Republic of Indonesia on the Zone of Cooperation in an Area between the Indonesian Province of East Timor and Northern Australia of 11 December 1989.

Chapter Summary

The application of law refers to the specialized activity whereby a state's judicial bodies, in accordance with their statutory authority and legal procedures, apply law to handle specific cases. In the context of the joint development of offshore oil and gas resources, the application of law refers to the specialized activity, within the practice of states, whereby sovereign nations, administrative bodies for joint development, or legal persons, based on the relevant provisions of a joint development agreement, apply specific legal regulations to handle matters related to joint development activities, such as taxation, revenue sharing, and civil or criminal cases. Furthermore, the application of law to the joint development of offshore oil and gas resources also encompasses instances where international judicial bodies, arbitral tribunals, or domestic courts—acting in accordance with the agreements of the states concerned—resolve disputes or conflicts arising from the joint development process by applying sources of law such as international treaties, international custom, general principles of law, judicial precedents, international petroleum contracts, and the domestic laws of the relevant states.

The application of law is a unique legal activity with creative and organizational dimensions, and it holds great significance. It can be said that the application of law is a critical step and a fundamental guarantee for the successful implementation of the joint development of offshore oil and gas resources. The subjects primarily involved in applying the law to such joint development include sovereign states, joint authorities, legal persons, international judicial bodies, arbitral tribunals, and domestic courts. The objects of this legal application refer to the issues or matters that require regulation by different legal systems, such as international or domestic law, during the process of joint development. These include petroleum contract models, revenue sharing, taxation, environmental protection, criminal jurisdiction, civil actions, customs and quarantine, health and safety, and employment and training. Generally, the state parties to a joint development, as the primary subjects applying the law, will make explicit provisions for these objects in the joint development agreement or in subsequent related supplementary agreements.

Based on an examination of the more than 30 instances of state practice in the joint development of offshore oil and gas resources to date, three primary types of legal application can be identified: separate, joint, and comprehensive application. Among these, the separate application of joint development law can be further divided into absolute and relative forms. Absolute separate application refers to the division of the joint development area, where each zone is separately and exclusively governed by the national law of one state. Relative separate application, by contrast, occurs when the joint development area is divided and, while each zone is in principle governed by its respective national law, modifications or adjustments are made in practice. Joint application of joint development law refers to the application of a single legal framework, mutually agreed upon by the parties, to the entire joint development area. The comprehensive application of joint development law incorporates elements of both separate and joint application. A case in point is the 1989 Joint Development Case Between Australia and Indonesia.

Chapter 4: Principal Laws Applicable to the Joint Development of Offshore Oil and Gas Resources

The laws applicable to the joint development of offshore oil and gas resources mainly include international law, domestic law, special law, and international petroleum development contracts. This chapter will provide a specific analysis of each.

Section One: International Law Applicable to the Joint Development of Offshore Oil and Gas Resources

Joint development is a concept of international law that arises from agreements between states.[①] Therefore, the theoretical foundation for joint development in disputed maritime areas, and the principles it follows, are rooted in international law.[②] As an act of international cooperation between states, the joint development of offshore oil and gas resources is undoubtedly subject to regulation and governance by international law.[③] Article 38(1) of the Statute of the International Court of Justice explicitly states: "The Court, whose function is to decide in accordance with international law such disputes as are submitted to it, shall apply: a. international conventions, whether general or particular, establishing rules expressly recognized by the contesting states; b. international custom, as evidence of a general practice accepted as law; c. the general principles of law recognized by civilized

---

① See Rainer Lagoni, as cited in Hazel Fox et al, *Joint Development of Offshore Oil and Gas: A Model Agreement for States for Joint Development with Explanatory Commentary*, British Institute of International and Comparative Law, 1989, p. 44.

② See Yang Zewei (ed.), *Research on International Law Issues of Joint Maritime Development*, Social Sciences Academic Press (China), 2016, pp. 60-70, 108-109; Robert Beckman, et al. edited, *Beyond Territorial Disputes in the South China Sea: Legal Framework for the Joint Development of Hydrocarbon Resources*, Edward Elgar Publishing Limited, 2013, pp. 300-302.

③ See Robert Beckman, et al. edited, *Beyond Territorial Disputes in the South China Sea: Legal Framework for the Joint Development of Hydrocarbon Resources*, Edward Elgar Publishing Limited, 2013, p. 169.

nations; d. subject to the provisions of Article 59, judicial decisions and the teachings of the most highly qualified publicists of the various nations, as subsidiary means for the determination of rules of law." Although the aforementioned provision does not explicitly state the sources of international law, it is generally considered to be an authoritative statement on the matter.④ Therefore, the international law applicable to the joint development of offshore oil and gas resources should undoubtedly include international treaties, international custom, general principles of law, judicial precedents, and the teachings of the most highly qualified publicists. However, given the special nature of joint development activities for offshore oil and gas resources, the international law applicable to such development primarily includes: the fundamental principles of international law, the United Nations Convention on the Law of the Sea, joint development agreements, international legal regimes related to navigation, fishing activities, and environmental protection, international custom, general principles of law, and international judicial precedents.

I. Basic Principles of International Law

(I) The Joint Development of Offshore Oil and Gas Resources Must First and Foremost Comply With and Apply the Basic Principles of

---

④ See Andrew Clapham, *Brierly's Law of Nations: An Introduction to the Role of International Law in International Relations*, 7th edition, Oxford University Press, 2012, p. 54.

International Law.

It is generally held that the basic principles of international law are those legal principles within the international legal system that are recognized by the international community, possess universal binding force, apply to all areas of international law, and constitute the foundation of international law.⑤ As can be seen from this definition, the basic principles of international law not only have universal binding force but are also applicable to all fields of international law. Engaging in maritime cooperation is also a legal obligation stipulated by global international treaties and guided by numerous international instruments, such as the Charter of the United Nations, the United Nations Convention on the Law of the Sea, the 1970 Declaration on Principles of International Law⑥, and the 1992 Rio Declaration on Environment and Development⑦. The Preamble to the United Nations Convention on the Law of the Sea repeatedly emphasizes the importance of strengthening cooperation among States. The principle of maritime cooperation by coastal States permeates the entire Convention, finding expression in its numerous regimes governing navigation, resource

⑤ See Yang Zewei, *International Law* (4th Edition), Higher Education Press, 202 2, p. 285.
⑥ See UN General Assembly, Declaration of Principles of International Law Con cerning Friendly Relations and Co-operation Among States in Accordance with th e Charter of the United Nations, October 1970, available at www.unhcr.org/refwor ld/docid/3dda1f104.html (accessed 19 November 2019).
⑦ Rio Declaration on Environment and Development, China website: http://www.china.com.cn/environment/txt/2003-04/24/content_5320117.htm; Rio Declaration on Environment and Development, United Nations Conference on Environment and Development, 3-14 June 1992, available at www.unep.org/Documents/Multilingual/Default.asp?documentid=78&articleid=1163 (accessed 22 November 2019).

development and conservation, environmental protection, marine scientific research, and the transfer of technology. For example, Article 74, paragraph 3, and Article 83, paragraph 3, concerning maritime delimitation, provide in identical terms: "Pending agreement as provided for in paragraph 1, the States concerned, in a spirit of understanding and cooperation, shall make every effort to enter into provisional arrangements of a practical nature and, during this transitional period, not to jeopardize or hamper the reaching of the final agreement. Such arrangements shall be without prejudice to the final delimitation." This provision is considered an important international legal basis for the joint development of offshore oil and gas resources. Therefore, the basic principles of international law are undoubtedly applicable to the joint development of offshore oil and gas resources. In other words, when engaging in the joint development of offshore oil and gas resources, coastal States must first and foremost comply with and apply the basic principles of international law. As one scholar has pointed out, the Declaration on Principles of International Law, "as an authoritative interpretation and application of the principles of the UN Charter, can have direct legal effect."[8] Moreover, some basic principles of international law—such as the principle of peaceful settlement of international disputes, the principle of international cooperation, the principle of sovereign equality of States, and the principle prohibiting the threat or use of force—have all developed into rules of jus

---

⑧ See James Crawford, *Brownlie's Principles of Public International Law*, 9th e dition, Oxford University Press, 2019, p. 10.

cogens.

In fact, in the existing practice of the joint development of offshore oil and gas resources, the States concerned generally stipulate in their joint development agreements that they must abide by the basic principles of international law.

For example, in the 1979 Joint Development Case Between Thailand and Malaysia in the Gulf of Thailand, Article 2 of the Memorandum of Understanding Between Malaysia and the Kingdom of Thailand on the Establishment of the Joint Authority for the Exploitation of the Resources of the Sea Bed in a Defined Area of the Continental Shelf of the Two Countries in the Gulf of Thailand explicitly provides: "Both Parties agree to continue to resolve the problem of the delimitation of the boundary of the continental shelf in the Gulf of Thailand between the two countries by negotiations or such other peaceful means as agreed to by both Parties, in accordance with the principles of international law and practice... and in the spirit of friendship and in the interest of mutual security. " Furthermore, the preamble to the MOU also specifically emphasizes being "Convinced that such activities can be carried out jointly through mutual cooperation."[⑨] Clearly, the joint development agreement for offshore oil and gas resources signed by

⑨ See Memorandum of Understanding Between Malaysia and the Kingdom of T hailand on the Establishment of a Joint Authority for the Exploitation of the Res ources in the Sea-Bed in a Defined Area of the Continental Shelf of the Two C ountries in the Gulf of Thailand (21 February 1979), Energy, Vol. 6, 1981, pp. 1 356-1358.

Malaysia and Thailand in this case embodies basic principles of international law, such as the principle of international cooperation and the principle of peaceful settlement of international disputes.

As another example, in the 2012 Joint Development Case between Seychelles and Mauritius, Article 21 of the Treaty Concerning the Joint Management of the Continental Shelf in the Mascarene Plateau Region, signed by the two countries, also explicitly requires: "With the exception of disputes falling within the scope of the Taxation Code referred to in Article 6 of this Treaty and which shall be settled in accordance with that Code as agreed by the Contracting Parties, any dispute concerning the interpretation or application of this Treaty shall, as far as possible, be settled amicably through mutual consultation." It is not difficult to see that, in this joint development case, the agreement signed by Seychelles and Mauritius likewise incorporates basic principles of international law, such as the principle of peaceful settlement of international disputes.

In conclusion, the joint development of offshore oil and gas resources must first and foremost comply with and apply the basic principles of international law.

(II) The Basic Principles of International Law Provide a Solid Legal Foundation for the Joint Development of Offshore Oil and Gas Resources.

It is generally held that the principle of international cooperation is the theoretical basis for the joint development of offshore oil and gas resources.[10] However, other scholars have pointed out that the legal foundation for the joint development of offshore oil and gas resources includes basic principles of international law such as the principle of sovereign equality of States, the principle of international cooperation, and the principle of peaceful settlement of international disputes.[11]

In fact, for the joint development of offshore oil and gas resources, upholding basic principles of international law, such as the principle of sovereign equality of States, is of great importance. For instance, adherence to the principle of sovereign equality facilitates not only the conclusion of a joint development agreement but also its implementation. Because sovereign title to the joint development area has not yet been determined, mutual respect and accommodation between the parties are essential. Therefore, the States concerned, on the basis of the principle of sovereign equality and in a spirit of understanding and cooperation, should respect each other's sovereign status and sovereign rights, focus on the substantive equality of each sovereign State, and negotiate in good faith to conclude an agreement. As the International Court of Justice articulated in its judgment in the North

⑩ See Xiao Jianguo, *Joint Development of Petroleum on International Maritime Boundaries*, China Ocean Press, 2006, pp. 79-102.

11 See Yang Zewei (ed.), *A Study on the Theory and Practice of International L aw on Joint Maritime Development*, Wuhan University Press, 2018, p. 1; Yang Z ewei, On the Legal Basis, Development Trends, and China's Implementation Path for Joint Maritime Development, in *Chinese Yearbook of International Law* (201 5), Law Press China, 2016, p. 111.

Sea Continental Shelf Cases, "negotiations are to be meaningful, which will not be the case when either of them insists upon its own position without contemplating any modification of it."[12]

Cooperation in the development of offshore oil and gas resources must also conform to the principles of the law of treaties. The conclusion of a treaty naturally entails the obligation to comply with it. Treaties must be observed, and a State cannot use its domestic law to alter international law. Article 27 of the Vienna Convention on the Law of Treaties provides: "A party may not invoke the provisions of its internal law as justification for its failure to perform a treaty." Once a cooperation agreement is concluded, the contracting States are obligated to comply with it. The domestic application of a treaty is an important component of a contracting State's performance of its treaty obligations. In principle, the manner in which a treaty is applied domestically is left to the discretion of the contracting State. Modern States generally regulate the domestic application of treaties through their national laws. A contracting State cannot fail to perform a cooperation agreement due to a conflict with its domestic law; rather, it must adopt appropriate measures to apply and perform the agreement. To invoke domestic law, or even constitutional law, as a pretext for resisting the performance of a cooperation agreement is to lack the good faith required for such performance.

---

12 See North Sea Continental Shelf Cases (Federal Republic of Germany/Denmar k; Federal Republic of Germany/Netherlands), Judgments, I.C.J. Reports 1969, ava ilable at http://www.icj-cij.org/docket/files/52/5561.pdf.

Furthermore, the implementation of a joint development agreement for offshore oil and gas resources is likewise dependent on the cooperation and support of each sovereign State and its various domestic agencies. If the relevant joint development agreement completely violates the principle of sovereign equality by making arrangements that are manifestly favorable to one party against the will of the other, then it is impossible for such an agreement to be well implemented, and the joint development in question will be difficult to put into practice.

In conclusion, the principle of sovereign equality of States is the cornerstone, the principle of international cooperation is the core, and the principle of peaceful settlement of international disputes is the essential safeguard for the joint development of offshore oil and gas resources. Like a tripod, these principles together constitute the legal foundation for such development.[13]

II. The United Nations Convention on the Law of the Sea

(I) As the Constitution for the Oceans, the United Nations Convention on the Law of the Sea Provides a Universal Normative and Guiding Framework For International Maritime Cooperation, Including the Joint

13 See Yang Zewei (ed.), *A Study on the Theory and Practice of International Law on Joint Maritime Development*, Wuhan University Press, 2018, p. 5.

Development of Offshore Oil and Gas Resources.

Opened for signature on December 10, 1982, the United Nations Convention on the Law of the Sea (hereinafter the Convention) is the most comprehensive international legal instrument to date. It comprises a preamble, 17 parts, 320 articles, and 9 annexes, covering issues such as marine scientific research, the breadth of the 12-nautical-mile territorial sea, rights of passage through straits, the 200-nautical-mile exclusive economic zone, the limits of the continental shelf, the protection and preservation of the marine environment, and the regime for the exploration and exploitation of the international seabed area. It is the outcome of nine years of arduous negotiations at the Third United Nations Conference on the Law of the Sea, forged through the struggles and compromises among different interest groups, and it largely reflects the consensus the international community was able to reach on maritime issues at that time.[14] Although it is undeniable that many provisions in the Convention are imperfect, or even seriously flawed[15], the Convention stands as the fundamental document governing maritime rights, interests, and order in contemporary international society. It establishes the basic legal framework for the use and management of the oceans by humankind, marking the establishment of a new international

14 See Yang Zewei, *International Law* (4th Edition), Higher Education Press, 2022, pp. 158-159.
15 See Jonathan I. Charney, Central East Asian Maritime Boundaries and the Law of the Sea, *American Journal of International Law*, Vol. 89, No. 4, 1995, p. 744.

maritime order.[16]

Therefore, the Convention exercises a regulatory function over activities related to the joint development of offshore oil and gas resources. In other words, states engaged in the joint development of offshore oil and gas resources must not only comply with the relevant provisions of the Convention, but must also ensure that their national legal jurisdiction within the joint development zone is consistent with the rights that coastal States are permitted to exercise in such maritime areas under the Convention.[17]

(II) Articles 74 and 83 of the Convention Provide the Legal Basis for the Joint Development of Offshore Oil and Gas Resources

Article 74 of the Convention addresses the "Delimitation of the exclusive economic zone between States with opposite or adjacent coasts." It explicitly provides: "The delimitation of the exclusive economic zone between States with opposite or adjacent coasts shall be effected by agreement on the basis of international law, as referred to in Article 38 of the Statute of the International Court of Justice, in order to achieve an equitable solution. If no agreement can be reached within a reasonable period of time, the States concerned shall resort to the procedures provided for in Part XV. Pending agreement as provided for in paragraph 1, the States concerned, in a

16 See T. B. Koh, "A Constitution for the Oceans", in UN, The Law of the Sea — Official Text of the United Nations Convention on the Law of the Sea with Annexes and Index, New York, 1983, p. xxiii.

17 See Xiao Jianguo, *Joint Development of Petroleum on International Maritime Boundaries*, China Ocean Press, 2006, p. 147.

spirit of understanding and cooperation, shall make every effort to enter into provisional arrangements of a practical nature and, during this transitional period, not to jeopardize or hamper the reaching of the final agreement. Such arrangements shall be without prejudice to the final delimitation. Where there is an agreement in force between the States concerned, questions relating to the delimitation of the exclusive economic zone shall be determined in accordance with the provisions of that agreement." Article 83 of the Convention, which concerns the "Delimitation of the continental shelf between States with opposite or adjacent coasts," sets out provisions for the delimitation of the continental shelf using wording similar to that of Article 74.

While Articles 74 and 83 of the Convention may not have been specifically established for provisional arrangements such as joint development pending delimitation, they nevertheless furnish a direct legal basis for States to conclude joint development agreements.[18] Furthermore, in terms of their legal nature, treaties can be classified as law-making treaties and contractual treaties. Law-making treaties are those concluded by a large number of states to establish general rules of international law for their mutual observance. Contractual treaties are those concluded between states to define their mutual rights and obligations with regard to general relations

18 See Yu Hui, Joint Development of Mineral Resources—An Asian Solution, *Asian Yearbook of International Law*, Vol. 2, 1994, p. 102.

or specific matters.[19] The distinction between these two types of treaties is not always clear-cut, and many treaties exhibit a dual character—that is, the same treaty may contain some provisions that are contractual in nature and others that are legislative.[20] This situation is sometimes found in agreements on the joint development of offshore oil and gas resources. Therefore, adopting the view of Ian Brownlie, we regard all treaties, and the Convention in particular, as a legal basis for joint maritime development.[21]

(III) Many Agreements on the Joint Development of Offshore Oil and Gas Resources State That They Were Concluded on the Basis of the Convention.

For example, in the 2012 Joint Development Case Between Seychelles and Mauritius, Article 2, paragraph 1 of the Treaty between the Government of the Republic of Seychelles and the Government of the Republic of Mauritius Concerning the Joint Management of the Continental Shelf in the Mascarene Plateau Region explicitly provides: "This Treaty gives effect to international law as reflected in the Convention which under Article 83 requires States with opposite or adjacent coasts to make every effort to enter into provisional arrangements of a practical nature pending agreement on the final delimitation of the continental shelf between them in a manner

19 See Yang Zewei, *International Law* (4th Edition), Higher Education Press, 2022, p. 285.
20 See Zhou Gengsheng, *International Law* (Vol. 2), Wuhan University Press, 2007, p. 512.
21 See James Crawford, *Brownlie's Principles of Public International Law*, 9th edition, Oxford University Press, 2019, pp. 10-11.

consistent with international law. This Treaty is intended to adhere to such obligation."

As another example, in the 2001 Joint Development Case Between Nigeria and São Tomé and Príncipe, the Treaty Between The Federal Republic of Nigeria and The Democratic Republic of São Tomé e Príncipe on the Joint Development of Petroleum and other Resources, in Respect of Areas of the Exclusive Economic Zone of the Two States explicitly states in its preamble: "The Federal Republic of Nigeria and the Democratic Republic of São Tome and Principe, taking into account the United Nations Convention on the Law of the Sea, done at Montego Bay on 10 December 1982 and, in particular, article 74(3) which requires States with opposite coasts, in a spirit of understanding and cooperation, to make every effort, pending agreement on delimitation, to enter into provisional arrangements of a practical nature which do not jeopardize or hamper the reaching of the final agreement on the delimitation of their exclusive economic zones."

In addition, in the 2002 Joint Development Case Between East Timor and Australia, the preamble to the Timor Sea Treaty between the Government of East Timor and the Government of Australia also declares in very clear terms: "Taking into account the United Nations Convention on the Law of the Sea done at Montego Bay on 10 December 1982, which provides in Article 83 that the delimitation of the continental shelf between States with opposite or adjacent coasts shall be effected by agreement on the basis of international law in order to achieve an equitable solution."

III. Joint Development Agreements

International practice in the joint development of offshore oil and gas resources shows that a fundamental condition for undertaking such activities in disputed or transboundary maritime areas is the conclusion of a joint development agreement. This is a prerequisite for the parties to carry out joint development activities. [22] An agreement for the joint development of offshore oil and gas resources is generally concluded in the form of a treaty and sets out principles or specific provisions for the joint development activities. Such agreements not only provide a direct legal basis for the joint development of offshore oil and gas resources but also serve as a guide for action.

Generally, agreements on the joint development of offshore oil and gas resources fall into three main categories: first, joint development clauses within bilateral maritime delimitation treaties; second, memorandums of understanding on the joint development of offshore oil and gas resources; and third, specific agreements dedicated to the joint development of offshore oil and gas resources.

(I) Joint Development Clauses in Bilateral Maritime Delimitation

22 See William T. Onorato, Potential Joint Development of the Methane Gas Res erves of La Kivu, *International and Comparative Law Quarterly*, Vol. 39, 1990, p. 653.

Treaties

For example, in the 1958 Joint Development of the Persian Gulf Continental Shelf by Bahrain and Saudi Arabia, the Bahrain–Saudi Arabia Boundary Agreement signed by the two countries contained provisions for the joint development of offshore oil and gas resources. Article 2 of the agreement explicitly provides: "This area cited and defined above shall be in the part falling to the Kingdom of Saudi Arabia in accordance with the wish of H.H. the Ruler of Bahrain and the agreement of H.M. the King of Saudi Arabia. The exploitation of the oil resources in this area will be carried out in the way chosen by His Majesty on the condition that he grants to the Government of Bahrain one half of the net revenue accruing to the Government of Saudi Arabia and arising from this exploitation, and on the understanding that this does not infringe the right of sovereignty of the Government of Saudi Arabia nor the right of administration over this above-mentioned area."[23]

As another example, in the 1974 Delimitation and Joint Development Case Between France and Spain, Article 3 of the Convention between the Government of the French Republic and the Government of the Spanish State on the Delimitation of the Continental Shelves of the two States in the Bay of Biscay is also a joint development clause for offshore oil and gas

23 Agreement Concerning the Delimitation of the Continental Shelf in the Persia n Gulf Between the Shaykhdom of Bahrain and the Kingdom of Saudi Arabia of 22 February 1958, Energy, Vol. 6, 1981, p. 1330.

resources.[24] Article 3 of this agreement also explicitly provides: "The Contracting Parties agree to apply the supplementary procedures provided for in annex II for the granting of licences for the exploration and exploitation of the natural resources in the zone."

(II) Memorandums of Understanding on the Joint Development of Offshore Oil and Gas Resources

A memorandum of understanding is often concluded to secure an early harvest, serving as an interim achievement that paves the way for the subsequent signing of more detailed agreements. Its validity depends on the agreement between the states concerned.

In the 1979 Joint Development Case Between Thailand and Malaysia in the Gulf of Thailand, Thailand and Malaysia signed the Memorandum of Understanding Between Malaysia and the Kingdom of Thailand on the Establishment of the Joint Authority for the Exploitation of the Resources of the Sea Bed in a Defined Area of the Continental Shelf of the Two Countries in the Gulf of Thailand on February 21, 1979. This memorandum set out general principles for the joint development of offshore oil and gas resources by the two countries in the Gulf of Thailand. After experiencing fluctuations in their bilateral relations and arduous negotiations, it was not until May 30, 1990, that the two countries, building upon the aforementioned memorandum,

24 To this end, France and Spain also established the Provisions Applicable to th e Zone Defined in Article 3 of this Convention as Annex II to the said delimitat ion agreement.

signed the 1990 Agreement between the Government of Malaysia and the Government of the Kingdom of Thailand on the Constitution and Other Matters Relating to the Establishment of the Malaysia-Thailand Joint Authority. The agreement not only stipulated in considerable detail the legal status, composition, and powers and functions of the Malaysia-Thailand Joint Authority, but also clearly defined its relationship with other institutions, as well as financial and taxation matters concerning the joint development of offshore oil and gas resources.[25] To ensure the smooth implementation of this joint development, the governments of Malaysia and Thailand subsequently promulgated a series of legal instruments, including the Thailand-Malaysia Joint Authority Act 1990 (B.E. 2533), the Malaysia-Thailand Joint Authority Act 440, and the Malaysia-Thailand Joint Authority Standards of Petroleum Operations, thereby further improving the legal system for the joint development of offshore oil and gas resources.[26]

In the 1992 Joint Development Case Between Malaysia and Vietnam, after signing the Memorandum of Understanding Between Malaysia and the Socialist Republic of Vietnam for the Exploration and Exploitation of Petroleum in a Defined Area of the Continental Shelf Involving the Two Countries, they did not proceed with further negotiations. Instead, in

25 See Yang Zewei (ed.), *International Agreements on the Joint Development of Marine Resources* (Chinese-English Bilingual Version) (Vol. I), Social Sciences Ac ademic Press (China), 2016, pp. 186-208.

26 See Yang Zewei (ed.), *International Agreements on the Joint Development of Marine Resources* (Chinese-English Bilingual Version) (Vol. I), Social Sciences Ac ademic Press (China), 2016, pp. 209-262.

accordance with Article 3 of the memorandum and by mutual agreement, they authorized their respective national oil companies, Petronas and PetroVietnam, to represent their interests in conducting petroleum exploration and development activities within the defined area and to conclude a commercial arrangement to that effect.

In the Joint Development Case Between Cambodia and Thailand, the two countries signed a memorandum of understanding, but the relevant negotiations have yet to make progress, and the implementation of the joint development remains a distant prospect. China and the Philippines held negotiations on joint development and in 2018 signed the Memorandum of Understanding on Cooperation in Oil and Gas Development.[27] In June 2022, then-Philippine Secretary of Foreign Affairs Teodoro Locsin Jr. announced the termination of the memorandum and the cessation of negotiations with the Chinese side on joint energy development in the South China Sea[28].

(III) Agreements on the Joint Development of Offshore Oil and Gas Resources

Some agreements on the joint development of offshore oil and gas resources are quite simple, such as the 1958 Bahrain-Saudi Arabia Boundary

27 See website of Ministry of Foreign Affairs of the People's Republic of China, https://www.mfa.gov.cn/web/wjb_673085/zzjg_673183/bjhysws_674671/bhfg_674677/201811/t20181127_7671843.shtml (last visited Feb. 23, 2023).

28 See website of Ministry of Foreign Affairs of the People's Republic of China, https://www.mfa.gov.cn/web/wjdt_674879/fyrbt_674889/202206/t20220624_10709637.shtml (last visited Feb. 23, 2023).

Agreement. It contains a total of six articles: Article 1 provides the coordinates for delimitation; Article 2 determines the scope of the joint development zone, the attribution of sovereignty, and the sharing of revenue, and explicitly states that the sharing of resources does not affect the Saudi government's sovereignty and jurisdiction over the joint development zone. Articles 3 to 6 are technical provisions.[29] For agreements that are simple in content, it is often because more detailed provisions may be difficult to reach at the time and require more prolonged negotiations. The parties involved may intend to first codify the main principles of cooperation in a treaty, while simultaneously providing that specific arrangements will be subject to further negotiation and agreement. For example, the Agreement on Management and Cooperation between the Republic of Guinea-Bissau and the Republic of Senegal is also quite simple, containing only nine articles. Article 4 provides that the parties shall establish an international agency to develop the joint development zone, and that the organization and operation of the agency shall be determined by a specific agreement to be concluded by the parties within 12 months of the signing of the aforementioned agreement[30]. The two countries subsequently signed the Protocol to the Agreement of 14 October 1993, concerning the organization and operation of the Management and

29 See Yang Zewei (ed.), *International Agreements on the Joint Development of Marine Resources* (Chinese-English Bilingual Version) (Vol. I), Social Sciences Ac ademic Press (China), 2016, pp. 3-5.

30 See Yang Zewei (ed.), *International Agreements on the Joint Development of Marine Resources* (Chinese-English Bilingual Version) (Vol. I), Social Sciences Ac ademic Press (China), 2016, p. 330.

Cooperation Agency[31] as a supplement. Together, these two documents constitute a complete joint development agreement.

Some joint development agreements are comprehensive treaties with detailed arrangements reached through negotiation. For example, in the 1974 Joint Development Case Between Japan and South Korea, the Agreement between Japan and the Republic of Korea Concerning Joint Development of the Southern Part of the Continental Shelf Adjacent to the Two Countries made quite detailed provisions on matters concerning the joint development of offshore oil and gas resources between them.[32] As another example, in the 1989 Joint Development Case Between Australia and Indonesia, the Treaty between Australia and the Republic of Indonesia on the Zone of Cooperation in an Area between the Indonesian Province of East Timor and Northern Australia contained particularly detailed provisions on matters related to the joint development of offshore oil and gas resources. The treaty is divided into eight parts, with provisions specifically covering "the Zone of Cooperation, exploration and exploitation in the Zone of Cooperation, the Ministerial Council, the Joint Authority, cooperation on certain matters in relation to

---

31 See Yang Zewei (ed.), *International Agreements on the Joint Development of Marine Resources* (Chinese-English Bilingual Version) (Vol. I), Social Sciences Ac ademic Press (China), 2016, pp. 334-346.

32 See Yang Zewei (ed.), *International Agreements on the Joint Development of Marine Resources* (Chinese-English Bilingual Version) (Vol. I), Social Sciences Ac ademic Press (China), 2016, pp. 49-90; Liu Jia, On the Implications of the Japan -South Korea Joint Development Case for Sino-Japanese Joint Development in the East China Sea, Master's thesis, Wuhan University, 2015; Deng Niya, The Case of Japan-South Korea Joint Development of the East China Sea Continental Shelf and Its Implications for China, *Journal of Ocean University of China* (Social Sc iences), No. 2, 2016, pp. 65-73.

Area A, applicable laws, settlement of disputes, and final clauses."[33] In addition, the treaty had detailed annexes, such as a Petroleum Mining Code, a Taxation Code, and a Model Production Sharing Contract. Therefore, scholars consider this treaty to be "the most detailed treaty on joint development yet concluded in terms of its textual provisions." The Timor Sea Treaty between the Government of East Timor and the Government of Australia, which East Timor signed with Australia after gaining independence, and the subsequent related agreements and annexes, largely inherited the main cooperative framework and model of the aforementioned treaty. Reaching such a complete and detailed treaty is a test not only of the wisdom and endurance of the negotiating parties but, most importantly, of their sincere will to overcome all difficulties and resolve all conflicts in order to secure an agreement.

IV. International Legal Regimes Relating to Navigation, Fishing Activities, and Environmental Protection

(I) The Principle against Unjustifiable Interference

Studies show that there are numerous cases where offshore oil and gas development activities interfere with and affect vessel navigation and fishing

33 The Treaty between Australia and the Republic of Indonesia on the Zone of Cooperation in an Area between the Indonesian Province of East Timor and Nort hern Australia of 11 December 1989.

activities. For example, oil development activities in the California Straits have forced vessels to use shipping lanes on the seaward side of the channel islands, causing an increase in shipping costs of $8 million to $10 million; and from 1980 to 1984, there were 55 collisions between vessels and platforms in the Gulf of Mexico. Furthermore, in the case of four oil production platforms on the Norwegian continental shelf, the safety zone around each platform covers 97 square kilometers, and the distance between them is 6 nautical miles. The total effective area in which they obstruct fishing amounts to 494 square kilometers, which is 100 times the area permitted by law. The establishment of facilities and safety zones in previously unobstructed fish migration routes or fishing grounds creates obstacles for fishing operations, thereby leading to a reduction in fishing income for specific areas and particular fishing vessels.[34]

Evidently, joint development activities for offshore oil and gas resources may interfere with other maritime activities, such as navigation and fishing,[35] and therefore require legal regulation. The generally applicable rule for such regulation is the principle prohibiting "unjustifiable interference."

---

34 See He Sha and Qin Yang (eds.), *Legal Foundations of International Petroleum Cooperation*, Petroleum Industry Press, 2008, pp. 63-64.

35 In the 1974 Joint Development Case Between Japan and South Korea, Japan's consideration of whether oil development activities would affect fishing and freedom of navigation, and of the prevention and control of marine pollution, after the establishment of the joint development zone, was also an important factor influencing the Japanese government's approval of the Agreement between Japan and the Republic of Korea Concerning Joint Development of the Southern Part of the Continental Shelf Adjacent to the Two Countries.

In the 1950s, the United Nations International Law Commission, in drafting the Convention on the Continental Shelf, held in-depth discussions on the principle prohibiting "unjustifiable interference." They took the view that the relative importance of the interests involved should be the decisive factor. The International Law Commission explicitly stated in the relevant draft articles: "This is obviously a matter of balancing the relative importance of the interests involved. In some cases, interference with navigation and fishing, even if serious, may be justified. Conversely, if the interference has no connection with the reasonably foreseeable conditions for the exploration and exploitation of the continental shelf, it would be unjustifiable even if such interference is slight."[36]

The principle of prohibiting "unjustifiable interference" is not only reflected in some agreements on the joint development of offshore oil and gas resources[37], but is also reaffirmed in the Convention.

For example, in the 1974 Joint Development Case Between Japan and South Korea, Article 27 of the Agreement between Japan and the Republic of Korea Concerning Joint Development of the Southern Part of the Continental Shelf Adjacent to the Two Countries, signed by the two countries, explicitly provides: "Exploration and exploitation of natural resources in the Joint

---

36 See He Sha and Qin Yang (eds.), *Legal Foundations of International Petroleu m Cooperation*, Petroleum Industry Press, 2008, p. 65.

37 See Masahiro Miyoshi, The Joint Development of Offshore Oil and Gas in R elation to Maritime Boundary Delimitation, International Boundaries Research Uni t, Maritime Briefing, Vol. 2, No. 5, 1999, p. 45.

Development Zone shall be carried out in such a manner that other legitimate activities in the Joint Development Zone and its superjacent waters such as navigation and fisheries will not be unduly affected."

As another example, Article 78 of the Convention, "Legal status of the superjacent waters and air space and the rights and freedoms of other States," also explicitly provides: "The rights of the coastal State over the continental shelf do not affect the legal status of the superjacent waters or of the air space above those waters. The exercise of the rights of the coastal State over the continental shelf must not infringe or result in any unjustifiable interference with navigation and other rights and freedoms of other States as provided for in this Convention."

Therefore, the principle of prohibiting "unjustifiable interference" is an obligation that coastal States must undertake when carrying out joint development of offshore oil and gas resources[38], and it is also a legal principle that should be applied to such activities.

(II) International Legal Regimes for Marine Environmental Protection

Joint development of offshore oil and gas resources must also comply with international legal regimes for marine environmental protection, such as the 1972 Convention on the Prevention of Marine Pollution by Dumping of

38 See He Sha and Qin Yang (eds.), *Legal Foundations of International Petroleum Cooperation*, Petroleum Industry Press, 2008, p. 64.

Wastes and Other Matter[39] and the Guidelines and Standards for the Removal of Offshore Installations and Structures on the Continental Shelf and in the Exclusive Economic Zone, adopted by the International Maritime Organization in 1989.

For example, Article IV of the Convention on the Prevention of Marine Pollution by Dumping of Wastes and Other Matter provides: "In accordance with the provisions of this Convention, Contracting Parties shall prohibit the dumping of any wastes or other matter in whatever form or condition except as otherwise specified below: (a) the dumping of wastes or other matter listed in Annex I is prohibited; (b) the dumping of wastes or other matter listed in Annex II requires a prior special permit; (c) the dumping of all other wastes or matter requires a prior general permit." On this basis, Article V of the Convention further requires that: "The provisions of Article IV shall not apply when it is necessary to secure the safety of human life or of vessels, aircraft, platforms or other man-made structures at sea in cases of force majeure caused by stress of weather or in any case which constitutes a danger to human life or a real threat to vessels, aircraft, platforms or other man-made structures at sea, if dumping appears to be the only way of averting the threat and if there is every probability that the damage consequent upon such dumping will be less than would otherwise occur. Such dumping shall be so

39 The Convention stipulates that the disposal of (oil and gas development) platf orms, classified as "bulky wastes which are liable to sink to the sea-bed and ma y constitute a serious obstacle to fishing or navigation," requires a prior "special permit."

conducted as to minimize the likelihood of damage to human or marine life and shall be reported forthwith to the Organization. A Contracting Party may issue a special permit as an exception to Article IV(1)(a), in emergencies, posing unacceptable risk relating to human health and admitting no other feasible solution. Before doing so the Party shall consult any other country or countries that are likely to be affected and the Organization which, after consulting other Parties, and international organizations as appropriate, shall, in accordance with Article XIV promptly recommend to the Party the most appropriate procedures to adopt. The Party shall follow these recommendations to the maximum extent feasible consistent with the time within which action must be taken and with the general obligation to avoid damage to the marine environment and shall inform the Organization of the action it takes. The Parties pledge themselves to assist one another in such situations."

In addition, with the support of the United Nations Environment Programme's Regional Seas Programme, countries within certain geographical regions have adopted regional conventions for marine environmental protection, such as the 1972 Convention for the Prevention of Marine Pollution by Dumping from Ships and Aircraft (also known as the Oslo Dumping Convention), the 1976 Convention for the Protection of the Mediterranean Sea Against Pollution and its Protocol for the Prevention of Pollution of the Mediterranean Sea by Dumping from Ships and Aircraft (the Barcelona Convention), the 1978 Kuwait Regional Convention for Cooperation on the Protection of the Marine Environment from Pollution, the 1981 Convention for Co-operation in the Protection and Development of the Marine and Coastal Environment of the West and Central African Region (the Abidjan Convention) and the Convention for the Protection of the Marine Environment and Coastal Area of the South-East Pacific, the 1982 Regional Convention for the Conservation of the Red Sea and Gulf of Aden Environment, the 1983 Convention for the Protection and Development of the Marine Environment of the Wider Caribbean Region, the 1985 Convention for the Protection, Management and Development of the Marine and Coastal Environment of the Eastern African Region, and the 1986 Convention for the Protection of the Natural Resources and Environment of the South Pacific Region and its Protocol for the Prevention of Pollution of the South Pacific Region by Dumping. These conventions are also a codification of customary international law. They not only address, to varying degrees, the disposal of oil platforms from the joint development of oil and gas resources, but also encompass a wide array of content on marine environmental protection, and thus have normative significance for joint development activities.

It is worth noting that some joint development agreements for offshore oil and gas resources also explicitly provide that the parties are to strengthen cooperation to prevent or reduce marine pollution and other environmental damage.

For example, in the 1974 Delimitation and Joint Development Case Between France and Spain, Article 7 of the Convention Between the Government of the French Republic and the Government of the Spanish State on the Delimitation of the Continental Shelves of the Two States in the Bay of Biscay provides: "The Contracting Parties shall endeavour to ensure that the exploration of the continental shelf of the Bay of Biscay and the exploitation of its natural resources do not adversely affect the ecological balance and the legitimate uses of the marine environment, and they shall hold consultations to that end."

As another example, in the 2002 Joint Development Case Between East Timor and Australia, Article 10 of the Timor Sea Treaty Between the Government of East Timor and the Government of Australia provides: "East Timor and Australia shall co-operate to protect the marine environment of the JPDA so as to prevent and minimise pollution and other environmental harm from petroleum activities. Special efforts shall be made to protect marine animals including marine mammals, seabirds, fish and coral. East Timor and Australia shall consult as to the best means to protect the marine environment of the JPDA from the harmful consequences of petroleum activities. Where pollution of the marine environment occurring in the JPDA spreads beyond the JPDA, East Timor and Australia shall co-operate in taking action to prevent, mitigate and eliminate such pollution. The Designated Authority shall issue regulations to protect the marine environment in the JPDA. It shall establish a contingency plan for combating pollution from petroleum activities in the JPDA. Limited liability corporations or limited liability entities shall be liable for damage or expenses incurred as a result of pollution of the marine environment arising out of petroleum activities within the JPDA in accordance with: i. their contract, licence or permit or other form of authority issued pursuant to this Treaty; and ii. the law of the jurisdiction (East Timor or Australia) in which the claim is brought."[40]

V. International Custom

International custom is "a legally binding rule of conduct formed through the practice of states."[41] With regard to the joint development of offshore oil and gas resources, international custom primarily refers to the international commercial practices that have gradually formed through long-term energy activities. Because they have been recognized by the international community, these practices are legally binding and thus have normative significance for joint development activities.

With regard to the joint development of offshore oil and gas resources, such practices derive primarily from the following five sources: practices arising from the trade in oil and natural gas among oil-producing states, oil

---

40 Some scholars consider this article to be of great significance, as it indicates that the contracting parties recognized that while oil and gas development activiti es within the joint development area would not necessarily cause pollution, envir onmental damage could nevertheless occur. See David M. Ong, The New Timor Sea Arrangement 2001: Is Joint Development of Common Offshore Oil and Gas Deposits Mandated Under International Law?, *International Journal of Marine & Coastal Law*, Vol. 17, No. 1, 2002, p. 101.

41 See Liang Xi (ed.), *International Law*, Wuhan University Press, 2000, p. 45.

companies, and oil-consuming states; practices arising from the dealings between states and oil companies; practices formed through joint petroleum development undertaken by oil-producing states in disputed maritime areas; practices that have gradually developed from business operations among oil companies; and practices established by judges, arbitrators, or lawyers in resolving disputes over petroleum activities or in interpreting joint development agreements for offshore oil and gas resources.[42]

VI. General Principles of Law and International Judicial Decisions

(I) General Principles of Law

Article 38 of the Statute of the International Court of Justice provides that the Court, in deciding cases, shall apply "the general principles of law" recognized by civilized nations. As for the meaning of "general principles of law," some scholars believe it has at least the following seven different interpretations: (1) general principles of justice; (2) natural law; (3) principles derived by analogy from private law; (4) general principles of comparative law; (5) general principles of international law (a view held by some Soviet scholars); (6) general theories of law; and (7) general legal concepts.[43] In

42 See Nwosu E. Ikenna, International Petroleum Law: Has It Emerged as a Dist inct Legal Discipline?, *African Journal of International and Comparative Law*, Vo l. 8, No. 2, 1996, p. 432; Yang Zewei, *On Legal Safeguard of China's Energy S ecurity*, China University of Political Science and Law Press, 2009, pp. 231-232.
43 See I. A. Shearer, *Starke's International Law*, Butterworths, 1994, p. 29.

reality, judging from international practice, both the International Court of Justice and international arbitral institutions have rarely applied "general principles of law" on their own to adjudicate the cases concerned.[44]

General principles of law serve as both a legal basis for the joint development of offshore oil and gas resources and as principles governing the application of law to such activities. For example, general principles of law such as "agreements must be kept" (pacta sunt servanda), "estoppel," "prohibition of the abuse of rights" (jus abutendi), "one must not harm others when exercising one's own rights" (qui jure sus utitur, neminin facit injuriam), and "a right does not arise from wrongdoing" (ex injuria jus non oritur) can fill the gaps in the application of treaties or international custom to joint development activities.

In fact, some general principles of law are already clearly reflected in the relevant provisions of the United Nations Convention on the Law of the Sea. For example, Article 56, paragraph 2 of the Convention provides: "In exercising its rights and performing its duties under this Convention in the exclusive economic zone, the coastal State shall have due regard to the rights and duties of other States and shall act in a manner compatible with the provisions of this Convention." Evidently, this provision is consistent with the substance of general principles of law such as "prohibition of the abuse

---

44 See Yang Zewei, *International Law* (4th Edition), Higher Education Press, 2022, p. 35.

of rights" and "one must not harm others when exercising one's own rights."

(II) International Judicial Decisions

According to Article 38 of the Statute of the International Court of Justice, the Court, in deciding cases, may apply "judicial decisions" as a subsidiary means for the determination of rules of law, subject to the provisions of Article 59 that "the decision of the Court has no binding force except between the parties and in respect of that particular case." "Judicial decisions" primarily refer to the rulings of international judicial bodies and arbitral tribunals. The decisions of international judicial bodies have played an important role in authenticating and interpreting the rules of international law, thereby promoting the development of international law.

International judicial decisions related to joint development activities for offshore oil and gas resources mainly include the 1969 North Sea Continental Shelf Cases, the 1982 Tunisia-Libya Continental Shelf case, the 2009 Case Concerning Maritime Delimitation in the Black Sea (Romania v. Ukraine) Judgment, and the 2012 Territorial and Maritime Dispute (Nicaragua v. Colombia).

In the North Sea Continental Shelf Cases, the judgment of the International Court of Justice proposed a solution for the joint development of overlapping areas: "In a sea like the North Sea, with its special configuration, and in view of the particular geographical situation of the coastlines of the coastal States concerned, the method chosen by the parties to delimit their respective boundary lines may lead to overlapping areas of territory in certain regions. The Court considers that this situation must be accepted as a reality and be resolved by agreement or, failing agreement, by an equal division of the overlapping areas, or by an agreement for joint development. The last solution appears particularly appropriate when it comes to maintaining the integrity of the mineral deposit."[45] Judge Jessup, in his separate opinion in the case, further emphasized that the method of joint development is more suitable for continental shelf areas that are disputed but undelimited and have partially overlapping territories.[46] It can be said that the judgment in the North Sea Continental Shelf Cases "provided legal support for the future widespread application of the joint development of offshore oil and gas resources,"[47] and gave a powerful impetus to the growth of this practice worldwide.[48]

In addition, the International Court of Justice also supported the

---

45 The North Sea Continental Shelf Cases (Federal Republic of Germany/Denmark; Federal Republic of Germany/Netherlands), Judgments, I.C.J. Reports 1969, available at http://www.icj-cij.org/docket/files/52/5561.pdf.

46 See Separate Opinion of Judge Jessup, in The North Sea Continental Shelf Cases (Federal Republic of Germany/Denmark; Federal Republic of Germany/Netherlands), Judgments, I.C.J. Reports 1969, available at http://www.icj-cij.org/docket/files/52/5561.pdf.

47 See Xiao Jianguo, *Joint Development of Petroleum on International Maritime Boundaries*, China Ocean Press, 2006, p. 9.

48 On the one hand, in terms of geographical scope, after the 1969 judgment in the North Sea Continental Shelf Cases, the practice of joint development of offshore oil and gas resources expanded from the Persian Gulf and Northwestern Europe to regions such as the Red Sea, the Mediterranean, East Asia, South Asia, Southeast Asia, North Africa, and Latin America. On the other hand, in terms of number, in the 25 years between the 1969 judgment and the entry into force of the United Nations Convention on the Law of the Sea in 1994, a total of 12 offshore joint development agreements emerged, averaging almost one every two years.

principle of joint development of offshore oil and gas resources in the Tunisia-Libya Continental Shelf case. In particular, Judge Evensen noted in his separate opinion: “It would seem advisable that the Parties ... should incorporate provisions on unitization where a petroleum field is situated across the boundary line or the lines of a joint development zone as proposed above.” [49] Domestic judicial precedents are particularly important in common law countries, which operate on the principle of stare decisis.

In summary, judicial decisions have played an important role in authenticating and interpreting the rules on the joint development of offshore oil and gas resources, thereby promoting its development.

In fact, international judicial decisions, as a subsidiary source of international law, not only influence the selection of zones for the joint development of offshore oil and gas resources but are also closely related to the law applicable to these activities. For example, in the 1989 Joint Development Case Between Australia and Indonesia, Indonesia had accepted Australia’s claim based on the principle of natural prolongation of the continental shelf in the 1972 Seabed Agreement it concluded with Australia. However, in the 1989 joint development agreement between the two countries, Indonesia firmly opposed this claim. The reason for Indonesia’s change in position was primarily the influence of two ICJ judgments: the

49 See Dissenting Opinion of Judge Evensen, in The Tunisia and Libya Continen tal Shelf Case, Judgment of 24 February 1982, available at http://www.icj-cij.org/docket/files/63/6281.pdf.

conclusion of the 1972 Seabed Agreement was influenced by the 1969 North Sea Continental Shelf Cases, which had affirmed the principle of natural prolongation. The 1989 joint development agreement, in contrast, was related to the 1985 Libya-Malta Continental Shelf case, in which the ICJ emphasized that for the continental shelf within 200 nautical miles, the structure of the seabed is not a relevant factor.[50]

Furthermore, resolutions of some important intergovernmental organizations also have significant reference and guidance value for the application of law to the joint development of offshore oil and gas resources.[51] For example, since the 1970s, the UN General Assembly has adopted numerous resolutions setting forth general principles for cooperation among states that share natural resources, such as UN General Assembly Resolution 2295 of 1972 on cooperation between States in the field of the environment, and UN General Assembly Resolution 3129 of 1973 on co-operation in the field of the environment concerning natural resources shared by two or more States. Although resolutions of the UN General Assembly are

---

50 See Case Concerning the Continental Shelf (Libyan Arab Jamahiriya/Malta, 3 June 1985), available at http://www.icj-cij.org/docket/files/68/6415.pdf.

51 Some scholars argue that important "resolutions of international organizations" should also be a highly valuable subsidiary means for determining rules of law; and that, given their broad representativeness and their value as expressions of w orld opinion, their status and role in international judicial practice should rank hi gher than those of "judicial decisions" and "the teachings of the most highly qua lified publicists." See [UK] Robert Jennings and Arthur Watts (rev.), *Oppenheim's International Law* (Vol. 1, Book 1), trans. by Wang Tieya et al., Encyclopedia of China Publishing House, 1995, p. 27; Liang Xi (ed.), *International Law*, Wuhan University Press, 2000, p. 49; Wang Tieya (ed.), *International Law*, Law Press C hina, 1995, pp. 18-20.

generally recommendatory in nature and not legally binding, they "reflect the will of governments, are a cumulative and concentrated expression of world opinion, have great political effect ... they represent a universal conviction and can serve as strong evidence of the formation of international custom."[52] In particular, Article 3 of the Charter of Economic Rights and Duties of States, adopted by the General Assembly in 1974, explicitly requires: "In the exploitation of natural resources shared by two or more countries, each State must co-operate on the basis of a system of information and prior consultations in order to achieve optimum use of such resources without causing damage to the legitimate interest of others." Some scholars believe that this provision "constitutes a direct legal basis for the principle of offshore joint development."[53] In addition, international organizations such as the United Nations Environment Programme and the European Union have also successively adopted relevant resolutions advocating for the joint development of transboundary natural resources. Therefore, the resolutions of some important intergovernmental organizations undoubtedly have significant normative importance for the application of law to the joint development of offshore oil and gas resources.

---

52 See Liang Xi, *Liang Xi's Law of International Organizations* (7th ed.), revised by Yang Zewei, Wuhan University Press, 2022, p. 42.

53 Gao Zhiguo, The Legal Concept and Aspects of Joint Development in International Law, Nonliving Resources, 1998, p.117.

Section Two: Domestic Law Applicable to the Joint Development of Offshore Oil and Gas Resources

I. Domestic Law Applicable to Joint Development in Transboundary Maritime Areas

In the international practice of joint development of transboundary offshore oil and gas resources, the maritime boundary between the two coastal states has already been delimited, and the scope of their respective maritime jurisdictions clearly defined, before a joint development agreement is signed. Under these circumstances, the parties' attention tends to focus on how to conduct the joint development of the oil and gas resources and how to allocate the resulting revenues. Therefore, the question of applicable law for the joint development of transboundary offshore oil and gas resources is relatively straightforward: each state party generally applies its own domestic law to the portion of the joint development zone on its side of the boundary line.[54]

For example, in the 1974 Delimitation and Joint Development Case Between France and Spain, Annex II, "Provisions Applicable to the Zone Defined in Article 3 of This Convention," of the Convention between the

54 See Yang Zewei (ed.), *Research on International Law Issues of Joint Maritim e Development*, Social Sciences Academic Press (China), 2016, p. 40.

Government of the French Republic and the Government of the Spanish State on the Delimitation of the Continental Shelves of the Two States in the Bay of Biscay explicitly provides: "In accordance with this principle, each Contracting Party undertakes to encourage within the framework of its mining regulations, the conclusion of agreements between companies applying for licences to explore the zone, in order to allow companies having the nationality of the other Party to participate in such exploration on the basis of equal partnership and proportional financing of operations."[55]

As another example, in the 1976 Case of Joint Development of the Frigg Gas Field by the United Kingdom and Norway, Article 9 of the Agreement between the Government of the United Kingdom of Great Britain and Northern Ireland and the Government of the Kingdom of Norway relating to the Exploitation of the Frigg Field Reservoir and the Transmission of Gas therefrom to the United Kingdom provides: "Each Government may charge tax, in accordance with the tax law of that Government, on the whole of the profits arising by virtue of its own licences from the exploitation of the Frigg Field Reservoir in accordance with the principles set out in the following paragraph, regardless of whether this refers to production carried out on the Continental Shelf of the other State, but shall not charge to tax any such profits arising by virtue of the licences of the other Government."

---

55 See Annex II Provisions Applicable to the Zone Defined in Article 3 of This Convention.

Furthermore, in the 1981 Joint Development Case Between Iceland and Norway concerning Jan Mayen, Articles 5 and 6 of the Agreement on the Continental Shelf between Iceland and Jan Mayen respectively stipulate that Norway and Iceland shall apply their domestic laws in the areas under their respective jurisdictions.[56]

II. Domestic Law Applicable to Joint Development in Disputed Maritime Areas or Areas of Overlapping Claims

With respect to oil and gas exploration and development, based on the principle of permanent sovereignty over natural resources, oil and gas resources belong to the state. For a resource state, it is crucial not only to secure the economic benefits derived from developing these resources but also to manifest national sovereignty through the administration of exploration and development activities. Therefore, the governing law for such fundamental matters as resource ownership, government revenue, taxation, criminal law, and civil law becomes one of the core issues in joint

56 Article 5 of the Agreement on the Continental Shelf between Iceland and Jan Mayen provides: "Norwegian legislation, Norwegian petroleum policy and Norweg ian regulations relating to the control of such activities, safety measures and envi ronmental protection shall apply to the activities in the area referred to in the fir st paragraph. The Norwegian authorities shall also be responsible for enforcement and administration in the said area"; Article 6 provides: "Icelandic legislation, Ice landic petroleum policy and Icelandic regulations relating to the control of such a ctivities, safety measures and environmental protection shall apply to the activities in the area referred to in the first paragraph. The Icelandic authorities shall also be responsible for enforcement and administration in the said area."

development negotiations. In disputed maritime areas or areas of overlapping claims, the application of domestic law to the joint development of offshore oil and gas resources is more complex and primarily falls into the following types.

(I) Application of a Single State's Domestic Law

In the 1969 Joint Development Case Between Qatar and Abu Dhabi, the Agreement on Settlement of Maritime Boundary Lines and Sovereign Rights over Islands between Qatar and Abu Dhabi, signed on March 20, 1969, stipulated that the two parties, Qatar and Abu Dhabi, would "equally share" the al-Bunduq field. The field was to be developed by the Abu Dhabi Marine Areas (ADMA) Company under the concession terms established by its regulations, with all costs and revenues to be shared equally between the two governments.[57] In this case, Qatar and Abu Dhabi were undertaking the joint development of the al-Bunduq field, which straddled their maritime boundary, after their maritime delimitation had already been completed. Both countries held equal ownership rights to the field; they agreed that Abu Dhabi would authorize its national company, the Abu Dhabi Marine Areas Company, to be responsible for the field's exploration and development activities.[58] Because the al-Bunduq field was developed entirely by the national oil company

57 See Article 6 and Article 7 of Agreement on Settlement of Maritime Boundar y Lines and Sovereign Rights over Islands between Qatar and Abu Dhabi, 20 M arch 1969, ST/LEG/SER. B/16, p. 403.
58 See Yu Hui, International Law Issues on the Joint Development of Marine Mi neral Resources, *Chinese Yearbook of International Law*, 1994, p. 52.

authorized by Abu Dhabi, with Qatar only sharing in the revenues, only the domestic law of Abu Dhabi was applied to the joint development zone.

Qatar's consent for the Abu Dhabi Marine Areas Company to manage the development of the al-Bunduq field and to apply only Abu Dhabi's domestic law stemmed from two main reasons: First, Qatar and Abu Dhabi were both British colonies and Arab nations, and they enjoyed good bilateral relations. Second, the Abu Dhabi Marine Areas Company had been established as early as 1962, whereas the Qatar Petroleum Company was only formed in 1974. Thus, at the time the delimitation agreement was signed, Qatar did not yet have a national oil company of its own.[59]

In the 1992 Joint Development Case Between Malaysia and Vietnam, Article 3 of the Memorandum of Understanding Between Malaysia and the Socialist Republic of Vietnam for the Exploration and Exploitation of Petroleum in a Defined Area of the Continental Shelf Involving the Two Countries provides: "For the purpose of this Memorandum of Understanding, Malaysia and the Socialist Republic of Vietnam agree to nominate PETRONAS and PETROVIETNAM, respectively, to undertake, on their respective behalves, the exploration and exploitation of petroleum in the Defined Area; Malaysia and the Socialist Republic of Vietnam shall cause PETRONAS and PETROVIETNAM, respectively, to enter into a

59 See http://www.qapco.com.qa/about-qapco; Dong Shijie, The Application of La w in Joint Maritime Development Zones, *Wuhan University International Law Re view*, Vol. 2, 2015, p. 74.

commercial arrangement as between them for the exploration and exploitation of petroleum in the Defined Area." As Vietnam had not yet established a legal system for offshore oil exploration and development at the time, ultimately, with the approval of both the Vietnamese and Malaysian governments, the PETRONAS was authorized to administer the entire joint development zone for offshore oil and gas resources and to apply Malaysian petroleum law. On August 25, 1993, the PETRONAS and the PETROVIETNAM signed a commercial agreement, deciding to establish the co-ordination commission, composed of eight members, which would be specifically responsible for formulating the implementing regulations for the management of petroleum operations within the joint development zone.[60]

The reasons for Vietnam making such a significant concession[61] on the issue of applicable law are several-fold: First, at the time, the PETROVIETNAM had only recently been established and lacked the capital, technology, and administrative experience for offshore oil and gas development. Furthermore, Vietnam's domestic laws and regulations concerning petroleum exploration and development were still in the drafting stage. Consequently, the Vietnamese side had little foundation for

60 See He Hairong, *A Study on the Legal Issues of Joint Maritime Development in the Gulf of Thailand*, Wuhan University Press, 2020, pp. 138-139; Nguyen Ho ng Thao, Vietnam and Joint Development in the Gulf of Thailand, *Asian Yearboo k of International Law*, Vol. 8, 1999, p. 143.
61 See Yang Zewei (ed.), *Research on International Law Issues of Joint Maritim e Development*, Social Sciences Academic Press (China), 2016, p. 46.

negotiations with the Malaysians. Second, Vietnam hoped to leverage the joint development to acquire technology and administrative experience in offshore oil and gas exploration and development, and to foster its national economic growth through the sharing of revenues. Third, Vietnam aimed, through this cooperative approach, to secure the political support of Malaysia, a founding member of ASEAN, in its bid for early accession to the organization.[62] Vietnam subsequently enacted its first Petroleum Law in 1993 and became a full member of ASEAN in 1995. The boom in Vietnam's offshore oil and gas exploration and development in the early 21st century can arguably be traced back to this initiative. Moreover, given that the Malaysia-Vietnam MOU explicitly stated that the arrangement concerned "joint development in a disputed area" with "equal sharing of revenues" and was "without prejudice to the respective sovereignty over the area concerned," Vietnam's sovereignty claims were not actually harmed. When weighed against the substantial political and economic returns it received, the major political concession made by the Vietnamese side on the question of applicable law was well worth the cost.

(II) Concurrent Application of the Domestic Laws of Both State Parties

As is well known, criminal jurisdiction is a key manifestation of a state's sovereignty. Therefore, in joint development in disputed maritime areas or

62 In 1986, Vietnam initiated its renovation and opening-up process and officially became a member of ASEAN in 1995.

areas of overlapping claims, the state parties generally each assert their own criminal jurisdiction. Accordingly, in some international practices of joint development in disputed maritime areas, the criminal laws of both state parties are applicable within the joint development zone.

For example, in the 2001 Joint Development Case Between Nigeria and São Tomé and Príncipe, Article 40 "Criminal Law and Jurisdiction" of the Treaty Between The Federal Republic of Nigeria and The Democratic Republic of São Tomé e Príncipe on the Joint Development of Petroleum and other Resources, in Respect of Areas of the Exclusive Economic Zone of the Two States explicitly provides: "Subject to paragraph 3 of this article, a national or permanent resident of a State Party shall be subject to the criminal law of that State Party in respect of acts or omissions occurring in the Zone provided that a permanent resident of a State Party who is a national of the other State Party shall be subject to the criminal law of the latter State Party. A national of both States Parties shall be subject to the criminal law of both. A national of a third State, not being a permanent resident of either State Party, shall be subject to the criminal law of both States Parties in respect of acts or omissions occurring in the Zone. Such a person shall not be subject to criminal proceedings under the law of one State Party if he or she has already been tried and discharged or acquitted by a competent tribunal or already undergone punishment for the same act or omission under the law of the other State Party."

(III) Separate Application of the Domestic Laws of Both State Parties

In the area of civil jurisdiction, a more common practice is for the domestic laws of both state parties to be applied separately within the joint development zone.

For example, in the 1993 Joint Development Case Between Jamaica and Colombia, Article 3, paragraph 5 of the Maritime Delimitation Treaty between Jamaica and the Republic of Colombia provides: "The Parties agree that in the Joint Regime Area, each Party has jurisdiction over its nationals and vessels flying its flag or over which it exercises management and control in accordance with international law."[63]

As another example, in the 2001 Joint Development Case Between Nigeria and São Tomé and Príncipe, Article 42 "Civil and Administrative Jurisdiction" of the Treaty Between The Federal Republic of Nigeria and The Democratic Republic of São Tomé e Príncipe on the Joint Development of Petroleum and other Resources, in Respect of Areas of the Exclusive Economic Zone of the Two States provides: "Unless otherwise provided in this Treaty, each of the States Parties may exercise civil or administrative jurisdiction in relation to development activities in the Zone, or persons present in the Zone for the purposes of those activities, to the same extent as they may do so in relation to activities and persons in their own exclusive

---

63 See Article 3(5) of Maritime Delimitation Treaty between Jamaica and the Re public of Colombia, 12 November 1993.

economic zone. In the exercise of jurisdiction under paragraph 1, the States Parties shall give effect to the relevant applicable law. This article is without prejudice to any other basis for the exercise of civil or administrative jurisdiction by either of the States Parties."

It is noteworthy that the application of domestic law to matters such as "Customs, Immigration, Quarantine, and Taxation" differs somewhat. Generally, the common practice is that persons, vessels, and goods moving from the joint oil and gas development zone into the maritime area under the jurisdiction of a contracting state, or from that contracting state's jurisdictional area into the joint development zone, are subject to the customs, immigration, and quarantine laws and tax laws of that particular state. For example, in the 2002 Joint Development Case Between East Timor and Australia, Article 15 "Customs, Quarantine and Migration" of the Timor Sea Treaty between the Government of East Timor and the Government of Australia provides: "East Timor and Australia may, subject to paragraphs (c), (e), (f) and (g), apply customs, migration and quarantine laws to persons, equipment and goods entering its territory from, or leaving its territory for, the JPDA. East Timor and Australia may adopt arrangements to facilitate such entry and departure."[64]

(IV) Unspecified Application of Domestic Law

---

64 See Article 15 of Timor Sea Treaty between the Government of East Timor a nd the Government of Australia. Australian Treaty Series 2003 No. 13.

In the 1974 Joint Development Case Between Sudan and Saudi Arabia, Article 7 of the Agreement Between Sudan and Saudi Arabia relating to the Joint Exploitation of the Natural Resources of the Sea-Bed and Sub-soil of the Red Sea in the Common Zone granted the "joint commission" extensive powers to formulate the rules necessary to perform its functions.[65] However, in fact, this joint development treaty could not cover all matters; for instance, it did not specify which country's domestic law would apply to relevant issues in the spheres of criminal and civil jurisdiction.

The reason why the Sudan-Saudi Arabia Joint Development Case did not explicitly stipulate how domestic law should be applied was primarily that Sudan and Saudi Arabia enjoyed good relations, coupled with the fact that there were no relevant precedents in previous joint development agreements to draw upon. Consequently, it was anticipated that the joint commission would have to actively "create law" in its future practice to fill the relevant legal gaps.[66]

Additionally, in the 2003 Joint Development Case Between Barbados and Guyana, Article 3 "Exercise of Civil and Administrative Jurisdiction in the Co-operation Zone" of the Exclusive Economic Zone Cooperation Treaty

---

65 See Article 7(g) of the Agreement between Sudan and Saudi Arabia Relating to the Joint Exploitation of the Natural Resources of the Sea-Bed and Sub-soil of the Red Sea in the Common Zone, 16 May 1974, Sudan-Saudi Arabia, UNTS, Vol. 952, p. 193, available at https://treaties.un.org/doc/Publication/UNTS/Volume%20952/volume-952-I-13605-English.pdf.

66 See Dong Shijie, The Application of Law in Joint Maritime Development Zon es, *Wuhan University International Law Review*, Vol. 2, 2015, p. 77.

Between the Republic of Guyana and the State of Barbados Concerning the Exercise of Jurisdiction in Their Exclusive Economic Zones in the Area of Bilateral Overlap Within Each of Their Outer Limits and Beyond the Outer Limits of the Exclusive Economic Zones of Outer States also explicitly provides: "The Parties shall exercise joint civil and administrative jurisdiction within and in relation to the Co-operation Zone. In exercising their jurisdiction the Parties shall act at all times in accordance with generally accepted principles of international law and the Convention. The exercise of joint jurisdiction by the Parties in any particular instance shall be evidenced by their agreement in writing, including by way of an exchange of diplomatic notes. For further clarity, the failure of the Parties to reach agreement in writing in relation to the exercise of their joint jurisdiction in the Co-operation Zone in any particular instance means that neither Party can exercise its jurisdiction in that instance."[67]

Evidently, in the Barbados-Guyana Joint Development Case, where jurisdiction is to be exercised jointly, the applicable domestic law can only be the intersection of the corresponding branches of law of both Barbados and Guyana. Furthermore, it is not difficult to see from this case that its provisions concerning the joint exercise of civil and administrative jurisdiction are unlikely to serve as a model. This is because Barbados and

67 See Article 3 of Exclusive Economic Zone Cooperation Treaty Between the Republic of Guyana and the State of Barbados Concerning the Exercise of Jurisdiction in Their Exclusive Economic Zones in the Area of Bilateral Overlap Within Each of Their Outer Limits and Beyond the Outer Limits of the Exclusive Economic Zones of Outer States, 2 December, 2003.

Guyana are both members of the Commonwealth of Nations, enjoy close relations, have similar legal systems, and the joint oil and gas development zone they delimited is relatively small, with few matters requiring jurisdiction.[68]

68 See Yang Zewei (ed.), *Research on International Law Issues of Joint Maritim e Development*, Social Sciences Academic Press (China), 2016, p. 45.

Section Three: Special Law Applicable to the Joint Development of Offshore Oil and Gas Resources

The parties to the joint development of offshore oil and gas resources are generally unwilling to apply the domestic law of another party as the governing law for the joint development zone, as doing so could be construed as an acceptance of that party's judicial jurisdiction over the disputed maritime area. At the same time, while the law of a third country could theoretically become the applicable law for a joint development zone, the parties involved also tend to reject this option in order to safeguard their respective national interests.

Therefore, creating a new and unique set of laws specifically for the development activities in the joint development zone has become an acceptable compromise for the parties involved.

The most typical examples of this are the Joint Development Between Australia and Indonesia and the Joint Development Between Thailand and Malaysia in the Gulf of Thailand. An analysis of these two classic cases reveals that the special law applicable to the joint development of offshore oil and gas resources is primarily concerned with matters such as fiscal and tax systems and the management of oil and gas exploration.

I. Fiscal and Tax System

(I) Joint Development Case Between Australia and Indonesia

In the Joint Development Case Between Australia and Indonesia, Annex D to the Treaty is the Taxation Code for the Avoidance of Double Taxation in respect of Activities Connected with Area A of the Zone of Cooperation. This Tax Code stipulates in detail the terms of taxation in Area A and the avoidance of double taxation. It applies to the legal persons and residents of the two Contracting States, as well as to legal persons and residents of non-Contracting States with a direct or indirect connection to the exploration for and exploitation of petroleum in Area A.

(II) Joint Development Case between Thailand and Malaysia in the Gulf of Thailand

In the Joint Development Case between Thailand and Malaysia in the Gulf of Thailand, Chapter VI of the 1990 Agreement between the Government of Malaysia and the Government of the Kingdom of Thailand on the Constitution and Other Matters relating to the Establishment of the Malaysia-Thailand Joint Authority (hereinafter referred to as the 1990 Agreement) is titled "Customs and Excise, and Taxation." For example, regarding "Customs Matters," Article 16 of the 1990 Agreement stipulates: "The rate of export duty payable by the contractor in respect of the contractor's share of profit oil sold outside Malaysia and the Kingdom of

Thailand shall be ten per centum; the Customs and Excise Authorities shall continue to exercise all powers in relation to all matters relating to the regulation of the movement of goods imported into or exported from the Joint Development Area in accordance with the existing legislation of Malaysia or the Kingdom of Thailand, as the case may be, subject to the following: (i) customs approved goods, equipment and materials for use in the Joint Development area shall be accorded duty exemption if they are imported by the Joint Authority or any person authorized by it: Provided that where one of the Governments proposes to impose any duties or taxes on any such customs approved goods, equipment and materials, it may impose such duties or taxes after consultation with the other Government; Malaysia and the Kingdom of Thailand shall collect their respective duties and taxes collectible under their respective legislation but shall reduce the applicable rates by fifty per centum."

Regarding "Taxation," Article 17 of the 1990 Agreement also clearly stipulates: "For the purpose of Part X of the Acts, the Revenue Authorities of the Governments shall, subject to the following, continue to impose and collect taxes in respect of income from the Joint Development Area in accordance with the existing tax legislation of Malaysia and the Kingdom of Thailand, as the case may be: the taxation of such income of any person who holds the right to explore and exploit any petroleum in the Joint Development Area under a contract awarded by the Joint Authority shall be in accordance with the following rates: 0% of taxable income for the first 8 years of

exploration and development in Area A, as well as on other general matters related to such operations.

(II) Joint Development Case between Thailand and Malaysia in the Gulf of Thailand

In the Joint Development Case between Thailand and Malaysia in the Gulf of Thailand, Malaysia and Thailand signed the Memorandum of Understanding Between Malaysia and the Kingdom of Thailand on the Establishment of the Joint Authority for the Exploitation of the Resources of the Sea Bed in a Defined Area of the Continental Shelf of the Two Countries in the Gulf of Thailand in 1979; in 1990, the two governments signed the 1990 Agreement Between the Government of Malaysia and the Government of the Kingdom of Thailand on the Constitution and Other Matters Relating to the Establishment of the Malaysia-Thailand Joint Authority (hereinafter referred to as the 1990 Agreement).

The 1990 Agreement specifically provides for the "powers and functions of the Joint Authority," which include: "The Joint Authority shall control all exploration and exploitation of the non-living natural resources in the Joint Development Area and shall be responsible for the formulation of policies for the same... Without prejudice to the generality of the foregoing, the powers and functions of the Joint Authority shall include the following: (a) to decide on the plan of operation and the working programme for the administration of the Joint Development Area; (b) to permit operations and to conclude transactions or contracts for or relating to the exploration and exploitation of the non-living natural resources in the Joint Development Area subject to the approval of the Governments; in respect of any contract referred to in subparagraph (b) for the exploration and exploitation of petroleum: (i) to approve and extend the period of exploration and exploitation; (ii) to approve the work programmes and budgets of the contractor; and (iii) to approve the production programmes of the contractor, including the production costs, conditions and schedules of the production... (c) to approve and award tenders and contracts relating to goods and services required in carrying out petroleum operations in the Joint Development Area."[71]

From the above, it is clear that the management of oil and gas exploration is one of the important components of the special law applicable to the joint development of offshore oil and gas resources.

71 See Article 7 of the 1990 Agreement Between the Government of Malaysia and the Government of the Kingdom of Thailand on the Constitution and Other Matters Relating to the Establishment of the Malaysia-Thailand Joint Authority.

Section Four: Petroleum Contracts Applicable to the Joint Development of Offshore Oil and Gas Resources

The primary purpose of the joint development of offshore oil and gas resources is to acquire the oil and gas resources within the offshore joint development zone. To this end, petroleum contracts are necessary to regulate the relationship of rights and obligations between the development institution and the contractors (petroleum companies). Therefore, a petroleum contract is primarily defined as an agreement between the joint development institution (which can be either the government of a state party or a joint authority) and the petroleum companies as contractors, governing activities related to oil and gas exploration, development, and production.

I. Petroleum Contracts

A petroleum contract is a contract used to handle the relationship between the owner of petroleum resources and the user of those resources. An international petroleum contract refers to a type of international cooperation contract concluded in accordance with law between a resource country's government (or its national oil company) and a foreign oil company for the cooperative exploitation of the country's oil and gas resources, and it encompasses exploration, development, production, and sales.[72]

Scholars have classified international petroleum contracts in different ways. For example, Bernard Taverne believes that international petroleum contracts mainly include Production Sharing Contracts, Risk Service Contracts, and Non-Risk Service Contracts.[73] Charles J. Johnson, in turn, classifies international petroleum contracts into Joint Venture Contracts, Production Sharing Contracts, Service Contracts, and composite contracts of the various types mentioned above.[74] Chinese scholar Gao Zhiguo points out that international petroleum contracts primarily comprise the following types: Modern Concession Contracts, Production Sharing Contracts, Service Contracts, Joint Venture Contracts, and composite contracts.[75]

From the perspective of oil and gas resource ownership, I am more inclined to classify international petroleum contracts into two main models: the license system and the contract system. Under the license system, ownership of the oil and gas resources is transferred to the petroleum company in the form of a concession or license from the resource country; whereas under the contract system, the resource country retains ownership of the oil and gas resources.[76] A resource country will typically choose a

72 See Wang Nianping, *A Comparative Study of International Petroleum Contract Models*, Law Press China, 2009, p. 10.
73 See Bernard Taverne, An Introduction to the Regulation of the Petroleum Ind ustry, Graham & Trotman / Martinus Nijhoff Publishers, 1994, p. 20.
74 See Charles J. Johnson, Establishing an Effective Production Sharing Type Re gime for Petroleum, Energy, Vol. 7, No. 2, 1981, pp. 129-141.
75 See Gao Zhiguo, International Petroleum Contracts: Current Trends and New Directions, Graham & Trotman / M. Nijhoff, 1994, p. 20.
76 See Wang Guohua (ed.), *Maritime Regulations and International Petroleum Co*

1. The Product Sharing Contract (or Production Sharing Contract)

The Product Sharing Contract (PSC), which originated in Indonesia in the 1960s[83], is a new model of international petroleum cooperation that emerged in tandem with the development of the concept of permanent sovereignty over natural resources and the pursuit of sovereignty and national self-determination by newly independent nation-states.

A Product Sharing Contract is an exploration and development contract for a petroleum block signed between a foreign oil company and the government or national oil company of a resource country. This model presupposes that the resource country possesses ownership of and exclusive rights to its oil and gas resources. The foreign oil company bears the costs of exploration, development, and production. In return, the resulting production is shared between the parties according to predetermined terms.[84] Under this system, title to the oil and gas resources remains with the resource country. The resource country grants its national oil company exclusive rights and management and supervisory authority over petroleum exploration, development, transportation, and sales. The foreign oil company, as the contractor, signs a petroleum contract with the national oil company to conduct exploration and development activities within the contract area. The

83 In August 1966, IIAPCO (the Independent Indonesian American Petroleum Co mpany) signed the world's first product sharing contract with PERMINA (the Ind onesian state oil company, now known as PERTAMINA).

84 See [US] Daniel Johnston, *International Petroleum Fiscal Systems and Product ion Sharing Contracts*, Seismological Press, 1999, pp. 32-41.

contractor provides all the necessary funding and technology, and assumes the exploration risks as well as the costs of development and production. Once production begins, the total output is first allocated to "cost oil," a pre-determined portion used to reimburse the contractor for its expenditures. The remainder, or "profit oil," is then shared between the resource country's national oil company and the contractor according to a contractually agreed ratio. In addition, the contractor is required to pay various taxes and fees to the resource country as stipulated in the contract. All facilities and assets for petroleum operations constructed within the contract area become the property of the resource country (or its national oil company).[85]

In a Product Sharing Contract, the oil and gas resources are, in essence, owned by the resource country. The contractor is entitled only to a share of the physical product, paid by the resource country as reimbursement for its exploration and development expenditures and as its allotted share of the profit. Title to the contractor's share of oil and gas resources is transferred from the resource country at a contractually specified delivery point.[86] Compared to the concession system, this type of contract upholds the resource country's sovereignty and jurisdiction over its oil and gas resources and the related exploration and development activities, which is why it has been accepted and adopted by many developing countries. This contractual

85 See Wang Guohua (ed.), *Maritime Regulations and International Petroleum Co operation*, Petroleum Industry Press, 2016, pp. 123-124.
86 See Wang Nianping, *A Comparative Study of International Petroleum Contract Models*, Law Press China, 2009, p. 65.

cogens) and the fundamental principles of international law. In addition, Article 10 of the Charter of Economic Rights and Duties of States also clearly stipulates: "All States are juridically equal and, as equal members of the international community, have the right to participate fully and effectively in the international decision-making process in the solution of world economic, financial and monetary problems ... and to share in the benefits resulting therefrom."

In fact, when disputes arise between foreign petroleum companies and host state governments over the interpretation of international petroleum development contracts, international treaties are also commonly used to resolve their disagreements. For example, Article 47 of the *Law on the Use of Subsurface Resources of the Kyrgyz Republic* stipulates that if an international treaty provides otherwise, the provisions of the international treaty shall apply. Similarly, Article 30(8) of the *Petroleum Law of Kazakhstan* also states that the application of Kazakhstan's Petroleum Law and its law on the use of mineral resources must not conflict with the relevant provisions of international treaties to which Kazakhstan is a party.[92]

(2) International Custom

In this context, international custom refers to commercial practices in international oil and gas cooperation. Its application is subject to three

92 See Wang Nianping, *A Comparative Study of International Petroleum Contract Models*, Law Press China, 2009, p. 79.

preconditions: first, the absence of express provisions in international treaties; second, the absence of governing provisions in host state law; and third, the custom must be a universally accepted international practice in international oil and gas cooperation. For example, in Article 13 on Commercial Discovery of the exploration contract between Kazakh Potential Petroleum Company and the government, the provisions regarding the discovery of reserves, submission and approval procedures, and the post-approval development period are all universally accepted customary practices in the petroleum industry.[93]

(III) Domestic Law

As part of the superstructure, law often serves the ruling class. Therefore, in international petroleum development contracts, host states—whether to safeguard national interests or to assert their sovereign rights—generally prefer the application of their own domestic law. For example, the *Petroleum (Production) Regulations 1982* of the United Kingdom stipulate that petroleum development contracts are to be governed by and interpreted in accordance with English law. The *Petroleum Act of the Republic of Nigeria* also provides that disputes arising from its implementation shall be interpreted by the Nigerian judiciary, and that petroleum contracts may contain conciliation and arbitration clauses for the resolution of such disputes.

93 See Wang Nianping, *A Comparative Study of International Petroleum Contract Models*, Law Press China, 2009, p. 80.

contract—the Joint Authority and the Operator; and legal clauses will often cover contract effectiveness and termination, applicable law, force majeure, the language of the contract, the working language, and dispute resolution.

IV. Differences and Similarities between International Petroleum Contracts and Joint Development Agreements

An international petroleum contract is a contract signed between a resource state and a petroleum company. Pursuant to the Vienna Convention on the Law of Treaties, an international petroleum development contract is undoubtedly not an international treaty. The International Court of Justice, in its judgment in the Anglo-Iranian Oil Co. Case, also explicitly stated that the contract signed between the Iranian government and the Anglo-Iranian Oil Co. was merely a concession agreement between a state government and a foreign company, and not a treaty.[98]

Joint development agreements for offshore oil and gas resources, by contrast, are by nature international treaties. They are governed by international law, and their procedures for conclusion, entry into force, observance, application, amendment, interpretation, termination, and invalidity generally comply with the relevant provisions of the Vienna

98 See "The Anglo-Iranian Oil Co. Case," in International Court of Justice: Repo rts of Judgments, Advisory Opinions and Orders, Leyden, 1952, p. 112.

Convention on the Law of Treaties. For example, in the 1974 Joint Development Case Between Japan and South Korea, Article 31 of the Agreement between Japan and the Republic of Korea concerning Joint Development of the Southern Part of the Continental Shelf adjacent to the Two Countries clearly stipulates: "This Agreement shall be ratified. The instruments of ratification shall be exchanged at Tokyo as soon as possible. This Agreement shall enter into force as from the date on which such instruments of ratification are exchanged; This Agreement shall remain in force for a period of fifty years and shall continue in force thereafter until terminated in accordance with paragraph 3 of this article; Either Party may, by giving three years' written notice to the other Party, terminate this Agreement at the end of the initial fifty-year period or at any time thereafter... DONE in duplicate at Seoul in the English language, this thirtieth day of January of the year one thousand nine hundred and seventy-four."

On the other hand, with regard to the content of joint development agreements for offshore oil and gas, considering the main clauses included in the model text designed by the British Association of Comparative Law—such as "joint development zone," "principles of joint development," "without prejudice clause," "the joint commission," "financial terms of development contracts," "customs and duty exemptions," "employment and training of personnel," "health and safety," "protection of the marine environment," "third party rights," "dispute settlement," and "entry into force

only; and cases where the application of domestic law is not expressly provided for.

The primary purpose of the joint development of offshore oil and gas resources is to obtain the oil and gas resources within the joint development zone. To this end, a petroleum contract is required to govern the rights and obligations between the development authority within the joint development zone and the contractors. A petroleum contract primarily refers to an agreement between the development authority (which can be the state parties themselves or a Joint Authority) and an oil company as the contractor, concerning activities such as oil and gas exploration, development, and production. Petroleum contracts generally fall into types such as license systems and contract systems, with the specific choice depending on the discretion of the resource state. A petroleum contract is substantially different from a joint development agreement for offshore oil and gas resources: the former is a transnational economic contract, whereas the latter is a treaty under international law. However, there is also a certain comparability between them, in that a joint development agreement can be viewed as a standard-form petroleum contract negotiated by the state parties for petroleum companies to participate in the development of oil and gas in the relevant area.

management[3] and policy-making authority in purely commercial matters[4], with the application of a special law as the primary approach. The primary reason for this was that Thailand and Malaysia had comparable levels of economic development and were on par in their capacity for marine resource development. Furthermore, both countries had relatively sound legal systems for offshore oil and gas development. Therefore, to reflect their equal status, the two nations were inclined to specially formulate a body of special law applicable to their joint development of offshore oil and gas resources.

It is worth mentioning that, applying the principle that special law prevails over general law, Thailand and Malaysia also granted the special law for joint development precedence in the event of a conflict with their respective domestic laws.[5] For example, Section 3 of Thailand's Thailand-Malaysia Joint Authority Act B.E. 2533 stipulates: "All other laws, by-laws and regulations in so far as they have already been provided in this Act or are contrary to or inconsistent with the provisions of this Act shall be replaced by this Act." Similarly, Section 25 of Malaysia's Malaysia-Thailand Joint Authority Act No. 440 requires: "Where any provision of this Act is in

③ See Article 7(1) and Article 7(2)(c, d, f, i, j, k) of the 1990 Agreement Between the Government of Malaysia and the Government of the Kingdom of Thailand on the Constitution and Other Matters Relating to the Establishment of the Malaysia-Thailand Joint Authority, 30 May 1990.

④ See Article 7(1) and Article 7(2) of the 1990 Agreement Between the Government of Malaysia and the Government of the Kingdom of Thailand on the Constitution and Other Matters Relating to the Establishment of the Malaysia-Thailand Joint Authority, 30 May 1990.

⑤ See He Hairong, *A Study on the Legal Issues of Joint Maritime Development in the Gulf of Thailand*, Wuhan University Press, 2020, p. 90.

conflict or is inconsistent with any provision of any other law, the provision of this Act shall prevail."

(II) Application of a Single State's Law: The Joint Development Case Between Malaysia and Vietnam

In the 1992 Joint Development Case Between Malaysia and Vietnam, in accordance with the provisions of the Memorandum of Understanding Between Malaysia and the Socialist Republic of Vietnam for the Exploration and Exploitation of Petroleum in a Defined Area of the Continental Shelf Involving the Two Countries, the Malaysian National Oil Company (Petronas) and the Vietnamese National Oil and Gas Company (PetroVietnam), as agents for their respective countries, were to sign an agreement to manage exploration and exploitation activities for natural resources within the defined area.⑥ However, at the time, Vietnam had not yet established its own legal system for offshore oil exploitation and was essentially in a state of having no applicable law. Furthermore, the establishment and improvement of such a legal system requires time and cannot be accomplished overnight. Therefore, in this case, the application of law to the joint development—originally envisioned during negotiations as applying the laws of both countries—shifted to the sole application of Malaysia's mature domestic legal system for offshore oil development. For Vietnam, this was a decision

⑥ See Article 3 of Memorandum of Understanding Between Malaysia and the Socialist Republic of Vietnam for the Exploration and Exploitation of Petroleum in a Defined Area of the Continental Shelf Involving the Two Countries, 5 June 1992.

born of necessity.[7]

(III) Application of Different Laws to Different Activities: The Joint Development Case Between Guinea-Bissau and Senegal

In the 1993 Joint Development Case Between Guinea-Bissau and Senegal, in accordance with the Agreement on Management and Cooperation between the Republic of Guinea-Bissau and the Republic of Senegal, the two countries adopted an approach of applying different laws to different activities within the joint development zone. The laws of Senegal apply to the exploration and exploitation of mineral and petroleum resources, as well as to surveys and scientific research in the fields of exploration and petroleum; whereas the laws of Guinea-Bissau apply to the exploitation of fishery resources and to surveys and scientific research in the fisheries sector.[8] This rather unusual method of "applying different laws to different activities" was adopted because the two countries had different degrees of reliance on the fishery and the oil and gas resources within the joint maritime development zone: Guinea-Bissau was more focused on fishery resources, while Senegal placed greater importance on oil and gas resources.

Thus, it is evident that although the nature and purpose of joint

---

⑦ See He Hairong, *A Study on the Legal Issues of Joint Maritime Development in the Gulf of Thailand*, Wuhan University Press, 2020, p. 91.

⑧ See Article 24 of the Protocol to the Agreement Between the Republic of Guinea-Bissau and the Republic of Senegal Concerning the Organization and Operation of the Management and Cooperation Agency Established by the Agreement of 14 October 1993.

development activities for offshore oil and gas resources are fundamentally the same, "most joint development agreements for offshore oil and gas resources adopt different legal frameworks."⑨

II. Law Applied to Joint Development Is Based on International Law

Joint development activities for offshore oil and gas resources are also a form of intergovernmental cooperation and must therefore be governed and regulated by general international law, including the rules of treaty law.

(I) The Selection of Blocks for the Joint Development of Offshore Oil and Gas Resources Must Comply with International Law

Whether for the joint development of offshore oil and gas resources in disputed maritime areas or in transboundary maritime areas, the selection of blocks must comply with international law, including the relevant provisions of the Convention.

Generally speaking, a key prerequisite for selecting "blocks" for the joint development of offshore oil and gas resources is the existence of a maritime area of overlapping claims that is expressly recognized between the states party. However, the legitimacy of such claims asserted by the states

⑨ Robert Beckman et al., eds., *Beyond Territorial Disputes in the South China Sea: Legal Framework for the Joint Development of Hydrocarbon Resources*, Ed ward Elgar Publishing Limited, 2013, p. 237.

party is judged according to the principles and rules of modern international law. In other words, a maritime claim by one state party can be recognized by the other and can form the basis for their negotiations on joint development only if it is founded upon the principles and rules of modern international law.[10] In summary, the legitimacy of the maritime claims of the states party is of critical importance in defining the "blocks" for joint development.[11]

For example, in the 1979 Joint Development Case Between Thailand and Malaysia in the Gulf of Thailand, the preamble to the Memorandum of Understanding Between Malaysia and the Kingdom of Thailand on the Establishment of the Joint Authority for the Exploitation of the Resources of the Sea Bed in a Defined Area of the Continental Shelf of the Two Countries in the Gulf of Thailand explicitly states: "Recognising that as a result of overlapping claims made by the two countries regarding the boundary line of their continental shelves in the Gulf of Thailand, there exists an overlapping area on their adjacent continental shelves;" and designates this overlapping area as the "block" for the joint development of offshore oil and gas resources between the two nations.

As another example, in the 1995 Joint Development Case Between the

⑩ See Yang Zewei, On the Issue of Selecting Blocks for Joint Maritime Develo pment, *Presentday Law Science*, No. 3, 2014, p. 7.
11 See Robert Beckman et al., eds., *Beyond Territorial Disputes in the South Chi na Sea: Legal Framework for the Joint Development of Hydrocarbon Resources*, Edward Elgar Publishing Limited, 2013, p. 141.

United Kingdom and Argentina, the Joint Declaration on Cooperation over Offshore Activities in the South West Atlantic signed by the UK and Argentina provides: "The Government of the United Kingdom of Great Britain and Northern Ireland and the Government of the Argentine Republic agreed that the following formula on sovereignty, based on that contained in the Joint Statement issued at Madrid on 19 October 1989, applies to this Joint Declaration and to its results. Nothing in the content of the present Joint Declaration or of any similar subsequent Joint Statements and meetings shall be interpreted as: (a) a change in the position of the United Kingdom with regard to sovereignty or territorial and maritime jurisdiction over the Falkland Islands, South Georgia and the South Sandwich Islands and the surrounding maritime areas. (b) a change in the position of the Argentine Republic with regard to sovereignty or territorial and maritime jurisdiction over the Falkland Islands, South Georgia and the South Sandwich Islands and the surrounding maritime areas. (c) recognition of or support for the position of the United Kingdom or the Argentine Republic with regard to sovereignty or territorial and maritime jurisdiction over the Falkland Islands, South Georgia and the South Sandwich Islands and the surrounding maritime areas."[12]

---

12 See "Joint Declaration of 27 September 1995 on Cooperation Over Offshore Activities in the South West Atlantic", available at http://www.fiaassociation.com/shopimages/pdfs/7_%201995%20Joint%20Declaration%20on%20Cooperation%20Over%20Offshore%20Activities%20in%20the%20South%20West%20Atlantic.pdf; T.W. Wälde & Andrew McHardy, Argentina-United Kingdom: Joint Declaration on Cooperation over Offshore Activities in the Southwest Atlantic, *International Legal Materials*, Vol. 35, No. 2, 1996, p. 302.

Thus, it is clear that in the Joint Development Case Between the United Kingdom and Argentina, both the UK and Argentina acknowledged the dispute over sovereignty and jurisdiction concerning the Falkland (Malvinas) Islands and their surrounding maritime areas. They agreed, without prejudice to their respective sovereign positions, to designate a portion of the maritime area as a "block" for the joint development of offshore oil and gas resources.[13]

In summary, a prerequisite for the selection of a "block" for the joint development of offshore oil and gas resources in a disputed maritime area is the recognition by the states party that a disputed area or an area of overlapping claims exists[14], and that the claims of both sides are legitimate and based on international law.

(II) The Conclusion, Application, and Modification of Joint Development Agreements Are Also Subject to the Relevant Rules of the Vienna Convention on the Law of Treaties

As a type of treaty, a joint development agreement for offshore oil and gas resources must not, in its conclusion, violate the general provisions of the Vienna Convention on the Law of Treaties, such as the prohibition against

13 See Patrick Armstrong and Viv Forbes, Calming the Ripples: The Cooperative Management of Ocean Resources - The Falkland Islands Example and Some Southeast Asian Comparisons, in Gerald Blake et al., eds., Boundaries and Energy: Problems and Prospects, Kluwer Law International, 1998, p. 350.

14 See Robert Beckman et al., eds., *Beyond Territorial Disputes in the South China Sea: Legal Framework for the Joint Development of Hydrocarbon Resources*, Edward Elgar Publishing Limited, 2013, p. 140.

conflicting with peremptory norms of general international law[15]. Similarly, the application, interpretation, modification, and termination of such agreements must also be governed by the relevant rules of the Vienna Convention on the Law of Treaties.[16]

As is well known, the more common titles for treaties in international law include the following: treaty, convention, agreement, protocol, charter, covenant, statute, exchange of notes, declaration, joint statement, joint communique, memorandum of understanding, act, general act, final act, modus vivendi, and arrangement, as well as minutes of meetings and provisional rules.[17] Although the titles of the foregoing instruments differ, there is no essential difference in their legal nature.

Generally, joint development agreements for offshore oil and gas resources primarily adopt titles such as "treaty," "agreement," "protocol," "memorandum of understanding," "exchange of notes," "declaration," or "joint statement." Fundamentally similar to treaties, a joint development agreement for offshore oil and gas resources is also typically structured in four parts: a preamble, substantive clauses, final clauses, and a concluding section.[18]

---

15 See Article 53 of Vienna Convention on the Law of Treaties.
16 See Vasco Becker-Weinberg, *Joint Development of Hydrocarbon Deposits in th e Law of the Sea*, Springer-Verlag Berlin Heidelberg, 2014, p. 35.
17 See Yang Zewei, *International Law* (4th Edition), Higher Education Press, 202 2, pp. 284-285.
18 See He Hairong, *A Study on the Legal Issues of Joint Maritime Development in the Gulf of Thailand*, Wuhan University Press, 2020, pp. 109-110.

These agreements generally contain provisions on their implementation, interpretation, modification, and termination.

For example, in the 1974 Joint Development Case Between Japan and South Korea, Article 30 of the Agreement between Japan and the Republic of Korea concerning Joint Development of the Southern Part of the Continental Shelf adjacent to the Two Countries provides for the "implementation" of the agreement: "The Parties shall take all necessary internal measures to implement this Agreement." Article 31 provides for the "ratification," "period of validity," "interpretation," and "termination" of the agreement: "This Agreement shall be ratified. The instruments of ratification shall be exchanged at Tokyo as soon as possible. This Agreement shall enter into force as from the date on which such instruments of ratification are exchanged; This Agreement shall remain in force for a period of fifty years and shall continue in force thereafter until terminated in accordance with paragraph 3 of this article; Either Party may, by giving three years' written notice to the other Party, terminate this Agreement at the end of the initial fifty-year period or at any time thereafter. Notwithstanding the provisions of paragraph 2 of this article, when either Party recognizes that natural resources are no longer economically exploitable in the Joint Development Zone, the Parties shall consult with each other whether to revise or terminate this Agreement. If no agreement is reached as to the revision or termination of this Agreement, this Agreement shall remain in force during the period as provided for in paragraph 2 of this article."[19]

As another example, in the 2012 Joint Development Case Between Seychelles and Mauritius, Article 22 of the Treaty between the Government of the Republic of Seychelles and the Government of the Republic of Mauritius concerning the Joint Management of the Continental Shelf in the Mascarene Plateau Region provides for the "amendment" of the treaty: "This Treaty may be amended at any time by written agreement between the Contracting Parties." Article 23 provides for the "duration of the Treaty": "This Treaty shall remain in force until a permanent delimitation of the continental shelf is agreed between the Contracting Parties or for thirty (30) years from the date of its entry into force, whichever is sooner. This Treaty may be renewed by agreement between the Contracting Parties. Natural resource projects commenced under this Treaty shall continue, notwithstanding that this Treaty is no longer in force, under conditions that are consistent with those that are provided for under this Treaty." Article 24 is the clause for the "entry into force": "Each of the Contracting Parties shall notify the other, by means of exchange of diplomatic notes, the completion of the procedures required by its law for the bringing into force of this Treaty. The Treaty shall enter into force on the date of receipt of the later notification. Upon entry into force, the Treaty shall be taken to have effect, and all of its

19 See Article 30 and Article 31 of the Agreement Between Japan and the Repu blic of Korea Concerning Joint Development of the Southern Part of the Contine ntal Shelf Adjacent to the Two Countries, 30 January 1974.

provisions shall be taken to have applied, from the date of signature."[20]

III. States Generally Favor the Application of Their Own Domestic Law in the Practice of Joint Development

As a provisional arrangement, the joint development of offshore oil and gas resources does not affect the conclusion of a final delimitation agreement by the coastal states for the relevant maritime area. This principle is not only affirmed by Articles 74 and 83 of the Convention and supported by judicial practice, such as the judgment of the International Court of Justice in the 1969 North Sea Continental Shelf cases[21], but has also been enshrined in numerous joint development agreements for offshore oil and gas resources.

For example, in the 2003 Joint Development Case Between Barbados and Guyana, the preamble to the Exclusive Economic Zone Cooperation Treaty Between the Republic of Guyana and the State of Barbados Concerning the Exercise of Jurisdiction in Their Exclusive Economic Zones in the Area of Bilateral Overlap Within Each of Their Outer Limits and Beyond the Outer Limits of the Exclusive Economic Zones of Outer States

---

20 See Articles 22, 23, and 24 of the Treaty Concerning the Joint Management of the Continental Shelf in the Mascarene Plateau Region; Yang Zewei (ed.), *International Agreements on the Joint Development of Marine Resources* (Chinese-English Bilingual Version) (Vol. II), Social Sciences Academic Press (China), 2016, pp. 650-691.

21 See "The North Sea Continental Shelf Cases (Federal Republic of Germany/Denmark; Federal Republic of Germany/the Netherlands)," available at https://www.icj-cij.org/public/files/case-related/51/051-19690220-JUD-01-03-EN.pdf.

explicitly states: "Recognising the relevance and applicability of paragraph 3 of Article 74 of the Convention, which establishes that, pending such delimitation, States, in a spirit of understanding and co-operation, shall make every effort to enter into provisional arrangements of a practical nature and, during this transitional period, not to jeopardize or hamper the reaching of the final agreement; Recognizing that such provisional arrangements shall be without prejudice to the final delimitation." The treaty's Article 1, paragraphs 2 and 3, also specially emphasize: "This Treaty and the Co-operation Zone established thereunder are without prejudice to the eventual delimitation of the Parties' respective maritime zones in accordance with generally accepted principles of international law and the Convention. The Parties agree that nothing contained in the Treaty nor any act done by either Party under the provisions of the Treaty will represent a derogation from or diminution or renunciation of the rights of either Party within the Co-operation Zone or throughout the full breadth of their respective exclusive economic zones."[22]

However, the joint development of offshore oil and gas resources is closely related to national sovereignty.[23] Consequently, when it comes to the application of law in joint development, the relevant coastal states are all inclined to extend their own judicial jurisdiction and apply their domestic law.

22 See "The 2003 Joint Development Case Between Barbados and Guyana," in Yang Zewei (ed.), *International Agreements on the Joint Development of Marine Resources* (Chinese-English Bilingual Version) (Vol. II), Social Sciences Academic Press (China), 2016, pp. 594-606.

23 See Yang Zewei, On the Issue of Applicable Law in Joint Maritime Develop ment Zones, *Journal of Guangxi University (Philosophy and Social Sciences)*, 201 5, Issue 4, p. 77.

This is as true for the joint development of transboundary offshore oil and gas resources as it is for joint development in disputed maritime areas.

For example, in the 1981 Joint Development Case Between Iceland and Norway concerning Jan Mayen, Article 5 of the Agreement on the Continental Shelf between Iceland and Jan Mayen signed by Iceland and Norway stipulates: "Norwegian legislation, Norwegian petroleum policy and Norwegian regulations relating to the control of such activities, safety measures and environmental protection shall apply to the activities in the area referred to in the first paragraph. The Norwegian authorities shall also be responsible for enforcement and administration in the said area." Article 6 of the agreement likewise states: "Icelandic legislation, Icelandic petroleum policy and Icelandic regulations relating to the control of such activities, safety measures and environmental protection shall apply to the activities in the area referred to in the first paragraph. The Icelandic authorities shall also be responsible for enforcement and administration in the said area."[1] It can be said that the Joint Development Case Between Iceland and Norway concerning Jan Mayen is a classic example of the joint development of transboundary offshore oil and gas resources where, with the maritime boundary between the two countries already delimited, each party applies its own domestic law.

---

[1] See Article 5 and Article 6 of Agreement on the Continental Shelf between Iceland and Jan Mayen, 22 October 1981.

As another example, in the 1974 Joint Development Case Between Japan and South Korea, Article 19 of the Agreement between Japan and the Republic of Korea concerning Joint Development of the Southern Part of the Continental Shelf adjacent to the Two Countries provides for the "application of law to matters connected with exploration or exploitation of oil and gas resources": "Except where otherwise provided in this Agreement, the laws and regulations of one Party shall apply with respect to matters relating to exploration or exploitation of natural resources in the subzones with respect to which that Party has authorized concessionaires designated and acting as operators." Article 21 of the agreement is the clause concerning "the application of law to legal actions for damages": "When damage resulting from exploration or exploitation of natural resources in the Joint Development Zone has been sustained by nationals of either Party or other persons who are resident in the territory of either Party, actions for compensation for such damage may be brought by such nationals or persons in the court of one Party (a) in the territory of which such damage has occurred, (b) in the territory of which such nationals or persons are resident, or (c) which has authorized the concessionaire designated and acting as the operator in the subzone where the incident causing such damage has occurred. The court of one Party in which actions for compensation for such damage have been brought under paragraph 1 of this article shall apply the laws and regulations of that Party."② It is evident that, in this case, Japan

② See Article 19 and Article 21 of Agreement between Japan and the Republi

and South Korea also vied to apply their own domestic laws within the joint development zone. However, the method adopted was to apply the domestic law of the operator's home country within the joint development zone, which is the most prominent feature of the Japan-South Korea Joint Development Case regarding the application of law.③

c of Korea concerning Joint Development of the Southern Part of the Continental Shelf adjacent to the Two Countries, 30 January 1974.

③ See Deng Niya, The Case of Japan-South Korea Joint Development of the East China Sea Continental Shelf and Its Implications for China, *Journal of Ocean University of China* (Social Sciences), No. 2, 2016, pp. 65-73.

Section Two: Exceptions to the Application of Law in the Joint Development of Offshore Oil and Gas Resources

As stated previously, Chapters 2 and 3 of this book have respectively elaborated on the principal types of legal application for the joint development of offshore oil and gas resources and the primary laws applicable to it. This understanding of the established patterns is derived from an analysis of the more than 30 cases of joint development of offshore oil and gas resources that have occurred in the international community to date. In other words, these represent the common features of the application of law in this field. In reality, social practice is immensely rich and multifaceted, and the practice of the joint development of offshore oil and gas resources is no exception. Broadly speaking, there are four main types of exceptions regarding the application of law to the joint development of offshore oil and gas resources.

I. A Joint Development Area Located Entirely Within One State's Exclusive Maritime Jurisdiction and Governed by its Domestic Law

As a general rule, a joint development area for offshore oil and gas resources is typically situated straddling the maritime boundary between two states or within an area of their overlapping maritime claims; it is rarely located within a maritime area under the sole jurisdiction of a single state. However, in the 1958 Joint Development of the Persian Gulf Continental Shelf by Bahrain and Saudi Arabia, the joint development area was located entirely within the jurisdictional waters of Saudi Arabia.

(I) Special Provisions of the Bahrain-Saudi Arabia Boundary Agreement

On February 22, 1958, Bahrain and Saudi Arabia concluded the Bahrain-Saudi Arabia Boundary Agreement, completing the maritime delimitation between the two states. However, pursuant to Article 2 of the Agreement, the oil resources within a hexagonal area known as Fasht bu Saafa, located under Saudi Arabian jurisdiction, were to be developed in a manner determined by Saudi Arabia. Saudi Arabia would grant the Government of Bahrain one-half of the net revenue derived from this exploitation, with the stipulation that this resource sharing would not affect the sovereignty and jurisdiction of the Government of Saudi Arabia over the area.[④]

Evidently, the Joint Development of the Persian Gulf Continental Shelf by Bahrain and Saudi Arabia does not constitute cross-border joint development of offshore oil and gas resources in the strict sense. On the one

④ See Article 2 of Bahrain-Saudi Arabia Boundary Agreement 22 February 1958.

hand, although Bahrain and Saudi Arabia had already completed their maritime delimitation, the joint development area was situated entirely within Saudi Arabia's maritime zone and was subject only to its domestic law. On the other hand, from the perspective of international law, if a maritime area is allocated to a coastal state, that state acquires full sovereign rights and jurisdiction over it. In this case, however, although Fasht bu Saafa was under Saudi Arabian jurisdiction, the revenue from its oil resources was shared with Bahrain.

(II) Reasons for the Compromise Between Bahrain and Saudi Arabia

In the case of their joint development of the Persian Gulf continental shelf, Bahrain and Saudi Arabia were able to reach a compromise for several key reasons.

1. Mutual Accommodation and Concessions. Disagreements over the sovereignty of islands and reefs had existed between Bahrain and Saudi Arabia since the late 1930s. The conclusion of the 1958 boundary treaty was made possible primarily because Bahrain relinquished its sovereign claims to the island of Lubaynah Al-Kabirah and the Fasht bu Saafa area, over which Saudi Arabia consequently gained sovereignty. In return, Saudi Arabia agreed to designate the Fasht bu Saafa area under its jurisdiction as a joint development zone, thus satisfying Bahrain's claim to the area's oil resources.[5] It is therefore evident that in order to resolve their dispute, both

⑤ See Alshaikh, Abdullatif A., Saudi Arabia and Its Gulf Cooperation Council

Bahrain and Saudi Arabia made concessions to varying degrees. In other words, the agreement was the result of a coordination of interests and mutual compromise, rather than a simple exchange of sovereignty for peace or money[6].

2. The Friendly Relationship Between the Two States. Not only were Bahrain and Saudi Arabia both formerly within the British sphere of influence, predominantly Sunni Muslim, and ruled by monarchies, but their relationship has also long been friendly and close. For instance, in 1949, when the dispute over islands and reefs became prominent again, the two kings exchanged letters, referring to each other's country as their own, to each other's people as their brothers, and expressing the hope that this fraternal relationship would last forever.[7] Furthermore, the preamble to the Bahrain-Saudi Arabia Boundary Agreement also explicitly declares: "And in view of the spirit of affection and mutual friendship and the desire of H.M. the King of Saudi Arabia to extend every possible assistance to the Government of Bahrain." This serves as further evidence of their amicable relationship.[8]

Neighbours: A Study in International Boundary Management 113, Durham These s, Durham University, 2001, available at: http://www.etheses.dur.ac.uk/1605.

⑥ See Cai Penghong, *Management Models for Joint Development in Disputed Maritime Areas: A Comparative Study*, Shanghai Academy of Social Sciences Pr ess, 1998, p. 184.

⑦ See Richard Schofield, Arabian Boundary Disputes, Vol. 12: Bahrain-Saudi Arabia, 1904-1958, Cambridge Archive Editions, 1992, pp. 305-323.

⑧ Notably, in the 1990s, Saudi Arabia significantly increased Bahrain's share o f the proceeds from the Fasht bu Saafa oilfield; in 1996, Saudi Arabia allocated the entire output of the field to Bahrain to meet the needs of its Sitra refining industry. See J. E. Peterson, "Sovereignty and Boundaries in the Gulf States,"

3. Bahrain's Practical Needs. In the case of the joint development of the Persian Gulf continental shelf, Bahrain made noticeably greater concessions, a move closely related to the significant practical difficulties it faced in the 1950s.⑨ On the one hand, Bahrain was experiencing domestic political instability, and the royal government urgently needed the oil revenue from signing the delimitation agreement with Saudi Arabia to resolve the crisis and consolidate its power. On the other hand, Bahrain also faced a threat from Iran, which had repeatedly and publicly claimed Bahrain as one of its provinces. Consequently, countering Iran's sovereign claim was considered by the Iranian side to be a significant reason for Bahrain's signing of the Bahrain-Saudi Arabia Boundary Agreement.⑩

II. Application of Law for Joint Development Being Directly Linked to the Ratio of Resource Allocation

In the 1993 Joint Development Case Between Guinea-Bissau and Senegal, Article 2 of the Agreement on Management and Cooperation

in Mehran Kamrava ed., *International Politics of the Persian Gulf*, Syracuse University Press 2011, p. 40.

⑨ See Guan Peifeng, The Delimitation of the Continental Shelf and Resource-Sharing Negotiations Between Bahrain and Saudi Arabia and Their Significance, *World History*, No. 2, 2016, p. 59; Yang Zewei (ed.), *Research on International Law Issues of Joint Maritime Development*, Social Sciences Academic Press (China), 2016, p. 132.

⑩ See Pirouz Mojtahed-Zadeh, *Security and Territoriality in the Persian Gulf: A Maritime Political Geography*, Curzon Press, 1998, p. 78.

over the territorial sea as well as to its bed and subsoil."[17] The territorial sea is under the jurisdiction of national sovereignty and is an integral part of a state's territory. Therefore, in theory, a coastal state would generally not include its territorial sea within a "block" for the joint development of offshore oil and gas resources. However, in existing international practice concerning the joint development of offshore oil and gas resources, there have been instances where coastal states have included their territorial sea within a joint development area.

For example, in the 1965 Joint Development Case Between Saudi Arabia and Kuwait, Article 1 of the Agreement Between the Kingdom of Saudi Arabia and the State of Kuwait on the Partition of the Neutral Zone, signed in 1965, provides: "The boundary line between the two sections of the Zone is to be the line which divides them into two equal parts and which begins from a point at the mid eastern shore on the low-tide line, and ends at the western boundary line of the Zone."[18] It is evident that in the Joint Development Case Between Saudi Arabia and Kuwait, a portion of the territorial sea was included within the "block" for the joint development of offshore oil and gas resources.

As another example, in the 1989 Joint Development Case Between

17 Article 2, paragraph 2 of the United Nations Convention on the Law of the Sea.

18 See "The 1965 Joint Development Case Between Saudi Arabia and Kuwait," in Yang Zewei (ed.), *International Agreements on the Joint Development of Marine Resources* (Chinese-English Bilingual Version) (Vol. I), Social Sciences Academic Press (China), 2016, pp. 28-38.

Australia and Indonesia, the Treaty Between Australia and the Republic of Indonesia on the Zone of Cooperation in an Area Between the Indonesian Province of East Timor and Northern Australia, signed in 1989, also included both Area B, located within Australia's territorial sea, and Area C, within Indonesia's territorial sea, as part of the joint development "blocks." [19] Therefore, "in special circumstances, the possibility of including parts of the territorial sea in a joint development area should not be completely excluded."[20]

In summary, in circumstances where a joint development area for offshore oil and gas resources extends into a state's territorial sea, the applicable domestic law is necessarily, and can only be, that of the coastal state.

---

19 See Yang Zewei, On the Issue of Selecting Blocks for Joint Maritime Devel opment, *Presentday Law Science*, No. 3, 2014, p. 5.

20 See Cai Penghong, *Management Models for Joint Development in Disputed Maritime Areas: A Comparative Study*, Shanghai Academy of Social Sciences Pr ess, 1998, p. 24.

and Vietnam, the Vietnamese government agreed to the exclusive application of Malaysia's petroleum law within the joint development area. This was because Vietnam not only needed to learn oil and gas exploration and development technologies and related management experience from international cooperation in joint development, but also hoped to generate revenue by accelerating these activities to promote its national economy.[28]

As another example, in the 1993 Joint Development Case Between Guinea-Bissau and Senegal, the two republics had different priorities concerning the resources within their maritime joint development area. Guinea-Bissau placed particular importance on fishery resources, while Senegal was more focused on oil and gas. Consequently, within this joint development area, they agreed to the respective application of Guinea-Bissau's fisheries law and Senegal's petroleum law.[29]

Furthermore, in the 1976 Case of Joint Development of the Frigg Gas Field by the United Kingdom and Norway, the two countries signed the Agreement between the Government of the United Kingdom of Great Britain and Northern Ireland and the Government of the Kingdom of Norway relating to the Exploitation of the Frigg Field Reservoir and the Transmission of Gas therefrom to the United Kingdom. This was aimed at

---

28 See Nguyen Hong Thao, Vietnam and Joint Development in the Gulf of Th ailand, *Asian Yearbook of International Law*, Vol. 8, 2003, p. 147.

29 See Article 24 of the Protocol to the Agreement Between the Republic of Guinea-Bissau and the Republic of Senegal Concerning the Organization and Op eration of the Management and Cooperation Agency Established by the Agreem ent of 14 October 1993.

expediting the extraction of oil and gas from the North Sea through the joint development of the Frigg Field, thereby enabling both nations to respond to and mitigate the first global energy crisis, which had erupted in 1973.[30] Similarly, in the 1979 Joint Development Case Between Thailand and Malaysia in the Gulf of Thailand, economic pragmatism, or economic factors, also played a significant role.

In conclusion, as one scholar has pointed out: "A state's urgent need for economic factors like oil and gas resources will prompt its government to seek ways to benefit from development first, thus preventing the exploitation and use of resources from being delayed by delimitation negotiations, which can sometimes even affect relations between states."[31]

III. Cultural Factors

Cultural factors are also an element that cannot be overlooked in facilitating the conclusion of joint development agreements for offshore oil and gas resources and in enabling flexible arrangements on the issue of applicable law.[32]

---

30 See Agreement Between the Government of the United Kingdom of Great Britain and Northern Ireland and the Government of the Kingdom of Norway Relating to the Exploitation of the Frigg Field Reservoir and the Transmission of Gas Therefrom to the United Kingdom, 10 May 1976.
31 See Yu Hui, Joint Development of Mineral Resources—An Asian Solution, *Asian Yearbook of International Law*, Vol. 2, 1994, p. 90.
32 See Chidinma Bernadine Okafor, Joint Development: An Alternative Legal Approach to Oil and Gas Exploitation in the Nigeria-Cameroon Maritime Boundary Dispute? *International Journal of Marine & Coastal Law*, Vol. 2, No. 4, 2006, p. 515.

area.

Generally speaking, for development taking place within a joint development area, the applicable laws include general international law, the joint development agreement, any special laws enacted by a possible joint development authority, and the domestic laws of both states party.[41] If the joint development area is divided into two parts, then in such a situation, in addition to being governed by general international law, the joint development agreement, and any possible special laws from a joint development authority, one part will be subject to the domestic law of one state party, and the other to the domestic law of the other. If the joint development area is divided into three parts, then in addition to the overall application of general international law, the joint development agreement, and any possible special laws from a joint development authority, one zone may be subject to the laws of both states party, while the other two zones are each subject to the domestic law of one of the states. The 2002 Joint Development Case Between East Timor and Australia is an example of this type.

---

41 See Dong Shijie, The Application of Law in Joint Maritime Development Z ones, *Wuhan University International Law Review*, Vol. 2, 2015, p. 74.

Chapter Summary

A survey of the historical process and international practice of the joint development of offshore oil and gas resources reveals that the application of law primarily exhibits three key characteristics: first, the international community has not established a uniform standard for the application of law in joint development; second, the law applicable to joint development is based on international law; and third, in practice, states generally tend to apply their own domestic laws.

Social practice is rich and varied, and the same holds true for the practice of joint development of offshore oil and gas resources. An analysis of the more than 30 international cases of such joint development to date reveals four main types of exceptions regarding the application of law to the joint development of offshore oil and gas resources: first, where the joint development area is located entirely within a sea area under one state's exclusive jurisdiction and is subject to that one state's domestic law; second, where the application of law is directly linked to the ratio of resource allocation between the states party; third, where the domestic law of a single state is applied exclusively; and fourth, where the joint development area extends into a state's territorial sea.

The factors influencing the application of law in the joint development of offshore oil and gas resources primarily include political will, economic considerations, cultural factors, management models, and the division of the joint development area. Among these, the political will for joint development among the relevant coastal states is the key to successful negotiations. As an act of international cooperation with a strong political dimension, every aspect of the joint development of offshore oil and gas resources—from the selection of the "blocks" to the signing and implementation of the agreement—is influenced by the strength of the parties' political will. Economic factors, such as the need for oil and gas development technology and the demand for these resources, are also a key reason why states involved in the joint development of offshore oil and gas are able to reach agreements and make concessions and compromises on the issue of applicable law. Cultural factors are also an element that cannot be overlooked in facilitating the conclusion of joint development agreements for offshore oil and gas resources and in enabling flexible arrangements on the issue of applicable law. In the international practice of joint development of offshore oil and gas resources, the application of law is relatively straightforward for transboundary resources. As a general rule, the domestic laws of the two states party apply on their respective sides of the maritime boundary. For joint development in disputed maritime areas or in zones of overlapping claims by coastal states, however, the application of law is usually more complex. In such circumstances, the applicable law is closely linked to the management model. In disputed maritime areas or in zones of overlapping claims by coastal states, the application of law for the joint development of offshore oil and gas resources is also closely linked to the division of the joint development area.

Chapter 6: The Practice of and Application of Law for the Joint Development of Offshore Oil and Gas Resources between China and Its Neighboring Countries

Section One: China's Policy Positions on the Joint Development of Offshore Oil and Gas Resources with Neighboring Countries

I. An Overview of China's Territorial Boundary Issues

China has eight countries with adjacent or opposite maritime coasts: North Korea, South Korea, Japan, the Philippines, Malaysia, Brunei, Indonesia, and Vietnam. Since the founding of the People's Republic of China, it has, in a spirit of friendly consultation, actively advanced boundary negotiations through peaceful means and prudently handled its related boundary issues. To date, China has signed boundary treaties with 12 of its neighbors, fully or largely settling its land boundary issues with these countries. They are: Myanmar (1960), Nepal (1961), North Korea (1962), Mongolia (1962), Afghanistan (1963), Pakistan (1963), Laos (1991), Russia (eastern section, 1991; western section, 1994)[①], Kazakhstan (1994), Kyrgyzstan (1996), Tajikistan (1999)[②], and Vietnam (1999).

---

① In October 2004, the foreign ministers of China and Russia signed the Supplementary Agreement between the People's Republic of China and the Russian Federation on the Eastern Section of the Sino-Russian Border in Beijing, which successfully resolved all issues concerning the China-Russia boundary.

② In May 2002, China and Tajikistan signed the Supplementary Agreement between the People's Republic of China and the Republic of Tajikistan on the China-Tajikistan Boundary, marking the complete settlement of all boundary issues historically left over between the two countries.

On October 23, 2021, the 31st Session of the Standing Committee of the 13th National People's Congress passed the *National Land Boundary Law of the People's Republic of China*, which is the country's first fundamental national law regulating land boundary affairs. In the maritime domain, China promulgated the *Law of the People's Republic of China on the Territorial Sea and the Contiguous Zone* in February 1992, issued the Statement of the Government of the People's Republic of China on the Baselines of the Territorial Sea in May 1996, ratified the United Nations Convention on the Law of the Sea in May 1996, and passed the *Law of the People's Republic of China on the Exclusive Economic Zone and the Continental Shelf* in June 1998, thereby establishing its systems for the territorial sea, contiguous zone, exclusive economic zone, and continental shelf. It is noteworthy that upon ratifying the United Nations Convention on the Law of the Sea, the Chinese government made a four-point declaration, the second point of which stated: "The People's Republic of China shall, through consultations with the states with coasts opposite or adjacent to it, delimit its maritime jurisdiction boundaries on the basis of international law and in accordance with the principle of equity."③ In the *Law of the People's Republic of China on the Exclusive Economic Zone and the Continental Shelf* promulgated in June 1998, the Chinese government

---

③ Decision of the Standing Committee of the National People's Congress on the Ratification of the United Nations Convention on the Law of the Sea (May 15, 1996), in *Collection of the Sea Laws and Regulations of the People's Republic of China*, 3rd ed., compiled by the Office of Policies, Laws, and Regulations of the State Oceanic Administration, China Ocean Press, 2001, p. 3.

reaffirmed the sovereign rights and jurisdiction over its 200-nautical-mile exclusive economic zone and continental shelf to which it is entitled under the United Nations Convention on the Law of the Sea, while also emphasizing that maritime delimitation should be effected by agreement on the basis of international law and in accordance with the equitable principle. This declaration reflects the current Chinese government's principled position on the issue of maritime delimitation.

However, China's land boundary issues have not yet been fully resolved, and its disputes over maritime delimitation and island sovereignty also face a complex and serious situation. Therefore, achieving a comprehensive and final resolution of China's boundary and maritime disputes remains a long and arduous task.[4]

II. The Evolution of China's Policy Positions on Joint Development

It is well known that China has always adhered to the "principle of peaceful settlement of international disputes" and has consistently sought to resolve international disputes through peaceful means.[5] In exploring solutions to maritime disputes, China has always actively advocated and

④ See Yang Zewei, *International Law* (4th Edition), Higher Education Press, 2022, pp. 151-152.
⑤ See Yang Zewei, Seventy Years of International Jurisprudence in New China: History, Contributions, and Future Directions, *China Legal Science*, No. 5, 2019, pp. 184-186.

upheld the policy of "sovereignty belongs to China, shelving disputes and pursuing joint development."

As early as 1972, during the negotiations for the normalization of diplomatic relations between China and Japan, the two countries reached an understanding to set aside the issue of sovereignty over the Diaoyu Islands, with both sides agreeing to "deal with it later." On October 25, 1978, when the Sino-Japanese Treaty of Peace and Friendship was signed, both sides reaffirmed this understanding. At the time, Deng Xiaoping, speaking at a press conference in Japan, pointed out that while China and Japan held different views on the Diaoyu Islands, they had agreed not to touch upon the matter, noting that it was wiser for the two governments to sidestep the issue and that a problem of this nature could be set aside. This was the embryonic form of Deng Xiaoping's concept of "sovereignty belongs to China, shelving disputes and pursuing joint development."⑥ On September 6, 1979, the Vice Premier of China's State Council, speaking at a press conference in Tokyo on the question of joint development of the Diaoyu Islands, also stated: "Considering the joint development of oil, the sovereignty issue can be temporarily shelved."⑦ In 1984, during a meeting with a delegation from the Center for Strategic and International Studies at Georgetown University, Deng Xiaoping clearly articulated the concept of

⑥ See Xiao Jianguo, *Joint Development of Petroleum on International Maritime Boundaries*, China Ocean Press, 2006, p. 204.

⑦ See *People's Daily*, September 7, 1979, p. 1.

"sovereignty belongs to China, shelving disputes and pursuing joint development." He said: "I have also conceived that for some international territorial disputes, sovereignty can be set aside for the time being to first pursue joint development. For such issues, we must proceed from a respect for reality and find a new way to resolve them."⑧ In the same year, at the Third Plenary Session of the Central Advisory Commission, Deng Xiaoping further elaborated on this idea.⑨ He pointed out: "Many international disputes, if not handled well, can become flashpoints. I have proposed that for some, perhaps the 'one country, two systems' approach could be adopted, while for others, the 'joint development' approach could be used... The Nansha Islands, on world maps, have always been demarcated as part of China; they belong to China. Now, apart from one island occupied by Taiwan, the Philippines occupies several islands, Vietnam occupies several, and Malaysia occupies several. What is to be done in the future? One way is for us to use force to reclaim all these islands; another way is to set aside the sovereignty issue and pursue joint development. This could eliminate a problem that has been accumulating for years... We Chinese are advocates of peace and hope to resolve disputes by peaceful means. What kind of peaceful means? 'One country, two systems,' 'joint development.'"⑩ At

⑧ See *Selected Works of Deng Xiaoping*, vol. 3, compiled by the Editorial Committee on Party Literature of the Central Committee of the Communist Party of China, People's Publishing House, 1993, p. 49.
⑨ See Zhang Liangfu, *China's Maritime Delimitation Disputes with its Neighbors*, China Ocean Press, 2006, p. 282.
⑩ See *Selected Works of Deng Xiaoping*, vol. 3, compiled by the Editorial Committee on Party Literature of the Central Committee of the Communist Party of China, People's Publishing House, 1993, pp. 87-88.

this point, the Chinese government's policy position of "sovereignty belongs to China, shelving disputes and pursuing joint development" was formally established.

Thereafter, Chinese state leaders and foreign ministers, on various diplomatic occasions, formally proposed the principle of "sovereignty belongs to China, shelving disputes and pursuing joint development" to the leaders of neighboring countries. For example, in April 1988, during a meeting with visiting Philippine President Corazon Aquino, Deng Xiaoping clearly stated that, for the sake of the two countries' relationship, the Nansha issue could be set aside for the time being, and the method of joint development could be adopted. In 1990, during a state visit to Indonesia, Chinese President Jiang Zemin for the first time fully articulated to the international community the proposal of "sovereignty belongs to China, shelving disputes and pursuing joint development."[11] In July 1992, at the 25th ASEAN Ministerial Meeting, the Chinese Foreign Minister elaborated on China's principled position on the Nansha issue: "We have put forward the proposal of 'shelving disputes and pursuing joint development.' We are willing to negotiate with the countries concerned to find a path toward a solution when conditions are ripe. If conditions are not ripe, the issue can be temporarily shelved without affecting our bilateral relations." In December 1992, the Chinese Premier pointed out at a press conference in

11 See Xiao Jianguo, *Joint Development of Petroleum on International Maritime Boundaries*, China Ocean Press, 2006, p. 205.

Hanoi, Vietnam: "We have proposed 'shelving disputes and pursuing joint development'; both sides have agreed to resolve the territorial dispute through peaceful means." In April 1993, when Philippine President Ramos visited China, the Chinese President, in discussing the Nansha Islands issue, reiterated the proposal of "shelving disputes and pursuing joint development." In July 1995, during a dialogue with ASEAN foreign ministers in Brunei, the Chinese Foreign Minister once again affirmed China's position and attitude on the Nansha issue, pointing out that China has always had indisputable sovereignty over the Nansha Islands and their adjacent waters, and that China's proposal of "shelving disputes and pursuing joint development" is the most realistic and feasible approach to handling the Nansha dispute at present.[12]

In the *Law of the People's Republic of China on the Exclusive Economic Zone and the Continental Shelf* promulgated in 1998, Article 2 specifically stipulates: "The People's Republic of China shall determine the delimitation of its exclusive economic zone and continental shelf in respect of the overlapping claims by agreement with the states with opposite or adjacent coasts, in accordance with the equitable principle and on the basis of international law."

In November 2002, the Declaration on the Conduct of Parties in the

12 See Xiao Jianguo, *Joint Development of Petroleum on International Maritime Boundaries*, China Ocean Press, 2006, p. 206.

South China Sea, signed by China and the 10 ASEAN nations, clearly stated: "Pending a comprehensive and durable settlement of the disputes, the Parties concerned may explore or undertake cooperative activities. These may include the following: marine environmental protection; marine scientific research; safety of navigation and communication at sea; search and rescue operation; The modalities, scope and locations, in respect of bilateral and multilateral cooperation should be agreed upon by the Parties concerned prior to their actual implementation." As can be seen, this declaration indicates the desire of the countries surrounding the South China Sea to cooperate on maritime affairs, including joint development.

It is noteworthy that President Xi Jinping has clearly pointed out the need to safeguard national maritime rights and interests, and to focus on shifting the protection of maritime rights toward a more comprehensive and balanced approach; he has also affirmed the need to uphold the policy of "sovereignty belongs to China, shelving disputes and pursuing joint development" to advance mutually beneficial and friendly cooperation, and to seek and expand the convergence of common interests.[13] Some scholars believe that President Xi Jinping's reiteration of "sovereignty belongs to China, shelving disputes and pursuing joint development" during the eighth collective study session of the Political Bureau of the CPC Central

13 See Xi Jinping, Further Care for, Understand, and Strategically Manage the Ocean to Drive New Progress in Building a Strong Maritime Nation (July 31, 2013), available at Xinhuanet, http://news.xinhuanet.com/politics/2013-07/31/c_116762285.htm.

opposition of the Chinese government, has forced the so-called Agreement Between Japan and the Republic of Korea Concerning Joint Development of the Southern Part of the Continental Shelf Adjacent to the Two Countries, which unilaterally marks off a Joint Development Zone on the East China Sea continental shelf, to gain automatic approval in the Japanese Diet by extending the Diet session. The Chinese government expresses its grave protest against this act by the Japanese government, which is a flagrant infringement of China's sovereignty." On June 26, the Chinese government again issued a statement, lodging a strong protest: "The East China Sea continental shelf is the natural prolongation of China's continental territory. The People's Republic of China has inviolable sovereignty over the East China Sea continental shelf. Those parts of the continental shelf that involve other countries should rightly be delimited through consultations between China and the countries concerned. The so-called Agreement Between Japan and the Republic of Korea Concerning Joint Development of the Southern Part of the Continental Shelf Adjacent to the Two Countries, which the Japanese government signed unilaterally with South Korea behind China's back, is completely illegal and null and void. No country or private individual may, without the consent of the Chinese government, arbitrarily undertake development activities on the East China Sea continental shelf; otherwise, they must bear full responsibility for all the consequences arising therefrom."[22]

On May 2, 1980, Japan and South Korea commenced their drilling activities in the Joint Development Zone, with a Japanese petroleum exploration company spudding the JDZ-1 well in Subzone 5.[23] On the same day, the Chinese government issued a solemn statement on the matter: "It is reported that the Japanese side has decided to begin exploratory drilling in early May on the western side of the Joint Development Zone unilaterally marked off by the so-called Agreement Between Japan and the Republic of Korea Concerning Joint Development of the Southern Part of the Continental Shelf Adjacent to the Two Countries... The Japanese government, in disregard of the Chinese government's repeated statements of its solemn position and its opposition, has insisted on taking unilateral action and has now commenced exploratory drilling and actual development. This is an act that disregards China's sovereignty and does not value the friendly relations between China and Japan, and it cannot but arouse the concern and indignation of the Chinese government and people. The Chinese government once again solemnly declares: the so-called Agreement Between Japan and the Republic of Korea Concerning Joint

---

22 See Xiao Jianguo, *Joint Development of Petroleum on International Maritime Boundaries*, China Ocean Press, 2006, p. 174.

23 It is worth noting that in May 1987, Nippon Oil Exploration Co. applied to the Japanese government for exploration rights, but by the end of the rights' va lidity period (September 1989), the South Korean side had not designated a vali dly authorized oil company. Thereafter, no further exploration or development ac tivities took place. See Yang Zewei (ed.), *Research on International Law Issues of Joint Maritime Development*, Social Sciences Academic Press (China), 2016, p. 149.

Development of the Southern Part of the Continental Shelf Adjacent to the Two Countries, which the Japanese government signed with the South Korean authorities behind China's back and without consulting China, is utterly illegal and null and void. The Chinese government will by no means turn a blind eye to acts that infringe upon China's sovereignty and major interests. Any country or private individual that arbitrarily undertakes or participates in development activities within the so-called Joint Development Zone unilaterally marked off by the said Agreement must bear responsibility for all consequences arising therefrom. The Chinese government reserves all its due rights to this zone."[24]

Furthermore, in view of the fact that Japan and South Korea had demarcated and proceeded with the joint development of a zone for offshore oil and gas resources in the East China Sea continental shelf in 1974 despite China's opposition, China began to carefully consider the possibility of joint development in disputed maritime areas. In June 1979, the Chinese side formally proposed to Japan, through diplomatic channels, the concept of jointly developing resources in the vicinity of the Diaoyu Islands. This was the first public indication that the Chinese side was willing to resolve its territorial and maritime disputes with neighboring countries through the approach of "shelving disputes and pursuing joint development."

---

24 China's Sovereignty over the East China Sea Continental Shelf Is Inviolable, *People's Daily*, May 8, 1980, p. 1, cited in Xiao Jianguo, *Joint Development of Petroleum on International Maritime Boundaries*, China Ocean Press, 2006, p p. 174-175.

In summary, pending the settlement of maritime delimitation with its neighbors, China's efforts to seek provisional arrangements, such as the joint development of offshore oil and gas resources and regional cooperation, based on a spirit of mutual understanding and cooperation, represent a proactive approach that is fully in line with international law.

Section Two: China's Exploration of and Attempts at Joint Development of Offshore Oil and Gas Resources with Neighboring Countries

As described above, the Chinese government has consistently advocated the policy of "sovereignty belongs to China, shelving disputes and pursuing joint development," and has made attempts with its neighbors to engage in the joint development of offshore oil and gas resources.

I. China and North Korea

North Korea has scarce oil and gas resources and relies entirely on imports for its oil supply. From 1965 to 1985, North Korea and China jointly conducted geophysical surveys in the eastern part of the North Yellow Sea Basin (which North Korea refers to as the West Korea Bay Basin). In the late 1970s, North Korea demarcated three blocks—A, B, and C—west of 124° east longitude for foreign bidding and subsequently collaborated on exploration with foreign oil companies from countries including Norway, Russia, Australia, Sweden, the United Kingdom, and the Netherlands. According to reports, by 1988, with the assistance of an Australian oil company, North Korea had drilled its first test well in Block C, producing 425 barrels of crude oil per day. To date, North Korea has completed the drilling of 10 wells, all of which are concentrated near the 124° east longitude line. In 2003, North Korea granted a license to Singapore's Sovereign Venture Pte Ltd, and the company claimed to have found 10 million barrels of oil reserves within its block.[25] In April 2005, North Korea signed a concession agreement with Malaysia's state oil company (Petronas) to explore and develop oil resources in maritime areas under dispute with China; later, due to objections from China, the North Korean side ultimately canceled the agreement.[26]

On December 24, 2005, China and North Korea signed the Agreement between the Government of the People's Republic of China and the Government of the Democratic People's Republic of Korea on the Joint Development of Offshore Petroleum as a provisional arrangement pending maritime delimitation.[27] It is worth noting that the sequence of events regarding North Korea's cooperation first with Malaysia and then with China leads to speculation that the cancellation of the concession agreement with Petronas may have been intended to clear the way for the subsequent joint development of offshore oil and gas between China and North Korea.

25 See Xiao Jianguo, *Joint Development of Petroleum on International Maritime Boundaries*, China Ocean Press, 2006, pp. 165-166.
26 See Selig S. Harrison, Sea-bed Petroleum in Northeast Asia: Conflict or Coo peration? in Selig S. Harrison (ed.), Sea-bed Petroleum in Northeast Asia: Confl ict or Cooperation? Woodrow Wilson International Center for Scholars, 2005, p. 13.
27 See "China and North Korea Sign Agreement to Jointly Develop Yellow Sea Oil Fields, Demonstrating Friendship Between the Two Countries" (December 2 6, 2005), on Sinopec News Net, http://www.sinopecnews.com.cn/shnews/2005-12/ 26/content_334498.shtml.

However, due to a lack of follow-up reports, the specific progress of the joint development of offshore oil and gas between China and North Korea remains unclear.

II. China and South Korea

South Korea is a country lacking in oil and gas, and is highly dependent on imports for its petroleum and natural gas. From April 1969 to September 1970, South Korea signed concession contracts with four foreign oil companies from countries such as the United States and the United Kingdom, and conducted geophysical surveys and petroleum drilling activities. China, Japan, and other countries all lodged representations on this matter through diplomatic statements or other means. In April 1970, the South Korean government promulgated the *Submarine Mineral Resources Development Act* and subsequently demarcated seven mining blocks in its surrounding maritime areas. Of these, Blocks 1-4 were in the Yellow Sea, with their western boundary running approximately along the median line with China; the southern and eastern boundaries of Blocks 5 and 7, based on the principle of natural prolongation, extended roughly to the 200-meter isobath in the East China Sea; and Block 6 was located in the Sea of Japan. In February 1973, at the invitation of the South Korean government, the American company Gulf Oil began oil and gas drilling activities in South Korea's Block 2. In March 1973, the Chinese Ministry of Foreign Affairs issued a statement, pointing out: "The South Korean authorities are now openly and unilaterally bringing in a foreign oil company to conduct drilling in the said areas. The Chinese government reserves all rights with regard to the possible consequences of this action."[28] In 1974, South Korea and Japan signed the Agreement Between Japan and the Republic of Korea Concerning Joint Development of the Southern Part of the Continental Shelf Adjacent to the Two Countries; beginning in 1979, South Korea carried out extensive exploration work in the East China Sea, and the two countries jointly drilled a total of 10 wells in the northern part of the East China Sea continental shelf.

In 1992, the China National Offshore Oil Corporation opened areas in the East China Sea for foreign bidding. In the northern Changjiang Depression, the bidding blocks offered by China were situated close to the median line claimed by South Korea and were adjacent to South Korea's mining block line and the Japan-South Korea Joint Development Zone. South Korea lodged representations with the Chinese side, arguing that some of the blocks offered by China crossed the median line, and that China's northern blocks overlapped with the line claimed by South Korea, with an overlapping area of approximately 25.66 square kilometers.[29] On August 3, 2000, China and South Korea signed the Fishery Agreement between the Government of the People's Republic of China and the

28 See Xiao Jianguo, *Joint Development of Petroleum on International Maritime Boundaries*, China Ocean Press, 2006, p. 172.
29 See Xiao Jianguo, *Joint Development of Petroleum on International Maritime Boundaries*, China Ocean Press, 2006, p. 165.

line drawn between the Diaoyu Islands and Chinese mainland. After evaluating the CNOOC blocks, several companies, including Teikoku Oil Co., Ltd. bid on three subzones that they considered to be closest to or to have crossed into the median line, and signed exploration and development contracts with CNOOC.[37]

From the interactions between China and Japan on the issue of joint development of oil and gas resources in the East China Sea, their respective basic positions can be seen. Japan's stance was that the joint development zone should be established outside the 12-nautical-mile limit of the Diaoyu Islands; and that in other maritime areas of the East China Sea, any joint development zone must straddle both sides of the median line claimed by Japan. China's position, on the other hand, was that the joint development zone should be confined to the disputed area between China and Japan in the East China Sea—that is, the area between the median line claimed by Japan and the natural prolongation of the continental shelf claimed by China—while the area west of the median line was not in dispute and thus could not be subject to joint development; and that the two sides should set aside the dispute over the Diaoyu Islands and jointly develop the oil and gas resources in their surrounding waters.[38] Evidently, major differences existed between China and Japan on the issue of joint development of oil

37 See Xiao Jianguo, *Joint Development of Petroleum on International Maritime Boundaries*, China Ocean Press, 2006, p. 164.

38 See Xiao Jianguo, *Joint Development of Petroleum on International Maritime Boundaries*, China Ocean Press, 2006, p. 177.

and gas resources in the East China Sea, which involved their respective claims regarding maritime delimitation and their positions on the Diaoyu Islands.

(II) The Sino-Japanese Principled Consensus on the East China Sea Issue

Beginning in 1998, China started developing the Chunxiao oil and gas field west of the so-called median line claimed by Japan.[39] China's oil and gas development activities in the East China Sea drew dissatisfaction from the Japanese side. From 2004 to 2007, China and Japan held 11 rounds of consultations on the issue of maritime delimitation in the East China Sea. On June 18, 2008, the two sides reached the Principled Consensus on the East China Sea Issue, the main points of which include the following: First, the two sides agreed to conduct cooperation during a transitional period pending delimitation, without prejudice to their respective legal positions. Second, a joint development block is to be selected in the East China Sea. After joint exploration, and based on the principle of mutual benefit, the two sides will choose mutually agreed-upon locations within the said block for joint development. They will strive to complete their respective domestic procedures and conclude the necessary bilateral agreements to implement the development as soon as possible, and will continue

39 See James C. Hsiung, Sea Power, the Law of the Sea, and the Sino-Japanes e East China Sea "Resource War", American Foreign Policy Interests, Vol. 27, No. 6, 2005, p. 517.

the waters of Vanguard Bank to conduct geophysical survey operations. In April 1996, Vietnam also awarded exploration rights for the two easternmost blocks of the Blue Dragon oil field to the American company ConocoPhillips. The concession area largely overlapped with the block that China had awarded to Crestone Energy of the United States.

In 2017 and 2018, Vietnam authorized the Spanish company Repsol to conduct drilling operations in Block Wanan Bei-21.[50] In 2018 and 2019, Vietnam authorized the Russian company Rosneft to conduct drilling operations in the waters northwest of Vanguard Bank. From May to July 2019, given that the Hakuryu-5 drilling rig leased by Rosneft was conducting unilateral exploration activities within the waters of the Nansha Islands, China dispatched Coast Guard vessel 35111 to conduct law enforcement operations.[51] Additionally, according to a BBC report, on June 12, 2020, the Spanish company Repsol announced its withdrawal from drilling operations in Blocks 07/03 and 135-136/03. An offshore drilling rig, which had been preparing for two months at the port of Vung Tau, Vietnam, was also told to cancel its planned operations. Vietnam's state oil company (PetroVietnam) agreed to pay Spain's Repsol and the UAE's Mubadala

---

50 See Bill Hayton, South China Sea: Vietnam Halts Drilling after "China Threats", BBC News, 24 July 2017, available at https://www.bbc.co.uk/news/world-asia-40701121; Vietnam "Scraps South China Sea Oil Drilling Project under Pressure from Beijing", South China Morning Post, 23 March 2018, available at https://www.scmp.com/news/china/diplomacy-defence/article/2138619/vietnam-scraps-south-china-sea-oil-drilling-project.

51 See China Risks Flare-Up over Malaysian, Vietnamese Gas Resources, Center for Strategic and International Studies, 16 July 2019, available at https://amti.csis.org/china-risks-flare-up-over-malaysian-vietnamese-gas-resources/.

Group payments for "contract termination" and "compensation," with the compensation amounting to at least $1 billion. In a press release, Repsol stated that it had "no intention of confirming or denying" the aforementioned payments and figures.[52]

Furthermore, on June 5, 1992, Vietnam initiated joint development with Malaysia, and this practice has been relatively successful.

(II) Attempts at and Progress in the Joint Development of Oil and Gas Resources in the South China Sea by China and Vietnam

Negotiations between China and Vietnam on maritime boundary issues began in the 1970s. In 1974 and 1977, the two countries held two rounds of talks at the vice-foreign ministerial level on the delimitation of the Beibu Gulf. Vietnam's position was that the delimitation of the Beibu Gulf had already been settled by the 1887 Convention between China and France respecting the Delimitation of the Frontier between China and Tonkin. China, however, maintained that the Gulf had never been delimited and that if the boundary were drawn according to Vietnam's claim, two-thirds of the Gulf's waters would be allocated to Vietnam, which would be unreasonable and unfair.

In September 1979, China signed agreements with several European

52 See "Vietnam's Recent Suspension of Some Oil and Gas Operations in the South China Sea and Contract Termination," BBC, July 15, 2020, https://www.bbc.com/zhongwen/simp/world-53421349.

and American oil companies for geophysical exploration in the waters west of Hainan Island. In response, Vietnam accused China of signing exploration agreements in a disputed maritime area between the two countries. In 1981, China proposed that the area between 18° and 20° North latitude and 107° and 108° East longitude be designated a "neutral zone," into which neither side would enter to conduct oil and gas exploration and development activities. China also undertook to restrict its national oil companies (including in international tenders) from crossing west of the 108° East longitude line. Although Vietnam did not explicitly accept this proposal, it did, in practice, suspend its negotiations with Western oil companies for oil and gas exploration and development in the said area.[53]

In 1992, the China National Offshore Oil Corporation authorized the American company Crestone Energy to conduct oil and gas exploration and development activities in the Vanguard Bank waters. In a tit-for-tat response, Vietnam, in 1994 and 1996, also awarded two blocks in this area to the American company Conoco for oil and gas exploration and development. In 1993, during the first round of government-level boundary negotiations between China and Vietnam, the Chinese side repeatedly expressed its willingness to "shelve disputes and pursue joint development" with Vietnam in the Nansha Sea, proposing that the Vanguard Bank Basin could serve as the first area for joint oil and gas development between the two

53 See Xiao Jianguo, *Joint Development of Petroleum on International Maritime Boundaries*, China Ocean Press, 2006, p. 184.

countries, and that each side could participate in the other's petroleum contract blocks in Vanguard Bank signed with foreign companies. [54] However, Vietnam held that the Vanguard Bank contract China had signed with the American oil company infringed upon its continental shelf rights and was unwilling to accept China's initiative. In November 1995, during the first meeting of the China-Vietnam expert group on maritime issues, the Chinese side expressed its willingness to properly resolve the Nansha dispute through bilateral negotiations and consultations, in accordance with recognized international law, including the legal principles and systems established by modern law of the sea and the United Nations Convention on the Law of the Sea. If the issue could not be resolved for the time being, the disputes could be temporarily set aside to seek joint development or various forms of cooperation.[55]

In December 2000, China and Vietnam formally signed the Agreement between the People's Republic of China and the Socialist Republic of Vietnam on the Delimitation of the Territorial Seas, Exclusive Economic Zones and Continental Shelves of the Two Countries in the Beibu Gulf. Article 7 of the agreement provides: "If any single petroleum or natural gas structure or field, or other mineral deposit of whatever character, extends across the delimitation line defined in Article 2 of this Agreement, the two

54 See Xiao Jianguo, *Joint Development of Petroleum on International Maritime Boundaries*, China Ocean Press, 2006, p. 181.
55 See Xiao Jianguo, *Joint Development of Petroleum on International Maritime Boundaries*, China Ocean Press, 2006, p. 181.

Contracting Parties shall, through friendly consultations, reach agreement as to the manner in which the structure, field or deposit will be most effectively exploited as well as on the equitable sharing of the benefits arising from such exploitation." Some scholars argue that this provision has, in effect, established a substantive legal obligation for both China and Vietnam to engage in the joint development of offshore oil and gas resources in the Beibu Gulf.[56] In October 2005, the China National Offshore Oil Corporation and the Vietnam National Petroleum Corporation signed a Framework Agreement on Oil and Gas Cooperation in the Beibu Gulf.

In 2006, China and Vietnam began discussing the joint development of oil and gas resources in the waters outside the mouth of the Beibu Gulf. In October 2011, the Agreement on Basic Principles Guiding the Settlement of Maritime Issues between the People's Republic of China and the Socialist Republic of Vietnam, concluded by the two countries, stipulated: "The two sides shall conduct periodical meetings between the Heads of Governmental delegations for border negotiations twice a year on a rotational basis and hold irregular meetings if necessary." In the view of some scholars, this agreement serves as a de facto bilateral code of conduct between the two countries.[57] In May 2012, China and Vietnam held the first round of

---

56 See Xiao Jianguo, *Joint Development of Petroleum on International Maritime Boundaries*, China Ocean Press, 2006, p. 184.

57 See Rames Amer and Li Jianwei, Recent Developments in the South China Sea, in Wu Shicun and Hong Nong (eds.), *Recent Developments in the South C hina Sea Dispute: The Prospect of Joint Development Regime*, Routledge, 2014,

consultations of the working group on the waters outside the mouth of the Beibu Gulf and exchanged views on the delimitation of these waters and the joint development of oil and gas resources.[58] In October 2013, China and Vietnam issued the Joint Statement on Deepening the China-Vietnam Comprehensive Strategic Cooperation in the New Era. The two sides agreed to actively study and discuss the issue of joint development and to establish a China-Vietnam working group on consultations for joint maritime development under the framework of the governmental border negotiation delegation. Guided by the principle of tackling easier issues before more difficult ones and making steady progress, they would steadily advance the delimitation negotiations for the waters outside the mouth of the Beibu Gulf and actively promote joint development in this area. In November 2015, the China-Vietnam Joint Statement reiterated: "The two sides will steadily advance the delimitation negotiations for the waters outside the mouth of the Beibu Gulf and actively promote joint development in this area, and have agreed to intensify the negotiations of the working group on the waters outside the mouth of the Gulf, continue to advance the work of the working group on consultations for joint maritime development, and strengthen cooperation in less sensitive fields." From December 2015 to April 2016, the two sides conducted a joint survey in the waters outside the mouth of

p. 42.

58 See "China and Vietnam Hold the First Round of Consultations of the Working Group on the Waters Outside the Mouth of the Beibu Gulf" (May 23, 2012), Xinhuanet, http://news.xinhuanet.com/world/2012-05/23/c_112019280.htm.

the Beibu Gulf.

Notably, the Joint Statement on Further Strengthening and Deepening the China-Vietnam Comprehensive Strategic Cooperative Partnership, jointly issued by the two countries in November 2022, explicitly stated: "The two sides agreed to continue to abide by the important consensus reached by the leaders of the two Parties and two countries and the Agreement on Basic Principles Guiding the Settlement of Maritime Issues between China and Vietnam... actively consult on transitional and temporary solutions that do not affect the respective positions and propositions of either side... actively advance consultations on joint maritime development and consultations on the delimitation of the waters outside the mouth of the Beibu Gulf, and work to achieve substantive progress in these two tasks at an early date; the two sides are willing to continue to actively carry out cooperation in less sensitive maritime areas."[59] As of the end of December 2022, the working group on the waters outside the mouth of the Beibu Gulf had held more than 10 rounds of consultations, and the working group on consultations for joint maritime development had also held more than 10 rounds of consultations.

59 Joint Statement on Further Strengthening and Deepening the China-Vietnam Comprehensive Strategic Cooperative Partnership (November 1, 2022), from the website of the Ministry of Foreign Affairs https://www.fmprc.gov.cn/zyxw/202211/t20221102_10795594.shtml.

V. China and the Philippines

(I) Overview of the Philippines' Cooperation with Foreign Oil Companies on Oil and Gas Exploration and Development in the South China Sea

Since the 1970s, the Philippines has signed agreements or contracts with multiple foreign oil companies regarding oil and gas exploration and development. For example, in 1974, the Philippines for the first time leased an area of approximately 26,000 square kilometers of the Reed Bank in the South China Sea to a Swedish oil company for exploration. A total of 37 wells were drilled, with about 7 of them located within China's traditional nine-dash line. In April 1976, a consortium composed of an American international oil company and a Swedish company successfully struck oil in the Reed Bank area leased to it by the Philippine government. Furthermore, the Philippine government also leased the areas of London Reefs and Tizard Bank to the Philippine National Oil Company, and the vast sea areas west of Palawan to foreign companies such as Chevron-Texaco, Phillips, and Shell. These companies all conducted extensive petroleum exploration activities within the waters of China's Nansha Islands.[60]

(II) Attempts at and Progress in the Joint Development of Oil and Gas

60 See Xiao Jianguo, *Joint Development of Petroleum on International Maritime Boundaries*, China Ocean Press, 2006, p. 169.

capital of foreign oil companies for the joint development of oil and gas resources at Reed Bank.[65] In October 2013, reports indicated that the China National Offshore Oil Corporation was in negotiations with Forum Energy (a subsidiary of Philex, which was then listed in the UK but was later delisted and taken private) on the joint exploration of oil and gas resources at Reed Bank.[66]

In 2016, after being elected President of the Philippines, Rodrigo Duterte repeatedly expressed his willingness to engage in the joint development of oil and gas resources with China in the South China Sea. In October of that year, President Duterte visited China, marking the "full recovery and development of China-Philippines relations, and the return of the South China Sea issue to the right track of bilateral dialogue and consultation for its resolution."[67] Subsequently, China and the Philippines issued the Joint Statement of the People's Republic of China and the Republic of the Philippines. This joint statement reaffirmed that "the two sides may hold regular consultations on their respective current and other concerns involving the South China Sea, and the two sides agreed to explore

65 See "Pangilinan Wants to Bring in Chinese Company for Joint Oil Exploration at Reed Bank," *World News* [Philippines], June 25, 2012, p. 2.
66 See "Energy Secretary Petilla Urges Pangilinan to Reach Agreement with Chinese Oil Company Soon," *World News* [Philippines], January 10, 2014, p. 2.
67 See "Remarks by Chinese Foreign Ministry Spokesperson Hua Chunying at a Regular Press Conference" (October 21, 2016), from the website of the Ministry of Foreign Affairs, http://www.fmprc.gov.cn/web/fyrbt_673021/jzhsl_673025/t1407728.shtml.

cooperation in other areas."[68]

On November 20, 2018, during President Xi Jinping's visit to the Philippines, the two countries signed the Memorandum of Understanding on Cooperation on Oil and Gas Development (hereinafter referred to as the MOU).[69] On July 23, 2019, the 22nd China-Philippines Foreign Ministry Consultation was held in Manila, where both sides agreed to strengthen maritime dialogue and advance maritime cooperation, including joint oil and gas development.[70] On August 29, President Xi Jinping met with President Duterte, announcing the establishment of an inter-governmental joint steering committee and an inter-enterprise working group for oil and gas cooperation, with the hope of accelerating the process of joint maritime oil and gas development and promoting substantive progress.[71] On October 28, 2019, the first meeting of the China-Philippines Inter-Governmental Joint Steering Committee on Cooperation on Oil and Gas Development was held in Beijing. The two sides confirmed the official establishment of the

68 See Article 42 of the Joint Statement of the People's Republic of China and the Republic of the Philippines (October 21, 2016), from the website of the Ministry of Foreign Affairs, http://www.fmprc.gov.cn/web/ziliao_674904/1179_674909/t1407676.shtml.

69 See Memorandum of Understanding between the Government of the People's Republic of China and the Government of the Republic of the Philippines on Cooperation on Oil and Gas Development (November 20, 2018), https://www.fmprc.gov.cn/web/ziliao_674904/tytj_674911/tyfg_674913/t1616639.shtml.

70 See "China and the Philippines Hold the 22nd Foreign Ministry Consultation," from the website of the Ministry of Foreign Affairs, https://www.fmprc.gov.cn/web/gjhdq_676201/gj_676203/yz_676205/1206_676452/xgxw_676458/t1682652.shtml.

71 See "Xi Jinping Meets with Philippine President Duterte," from the website of the Ministry of Foreign Affairs, https://www.fmprc.gov.cn/web/gjhdq_676201/gj_676203/yz_676205/1206_676452/xgxw_676458/t1693011.shtml.

committee, exchanged views on the cooperation arrangements under the MOU, and agreed to communicate and coordinate on oil and gas development cooperation and to strive for progress.[72] It has been reported that the Chinese and Philippine sides also held talks regarding cooperation on Service Contract 57 (SC 57) and Service Contract 72 (SC 72).[73]

However, the pace of cooperation has shown signs of slowing since then. The China-Philippines Bilateral Consultation Mechanism on the South China Sea was established and held its first meeting in May 2017. While it maintained a frequency of two meetings per year in 2018 and 2019, the sixth meeting was not held until May 2021—a year and a half after the fifth—and took place via video conference. Moreover, the China-Philippines Inter-Governmental Joint Steering Committee on Cooperation on Oil and Gas Development, which was established at the time of the fifth meeting, has yet to convene a second meeting, nor have there been public reports of negotiations between Chinese and Philippine enterprises.

---

72 See "First Meeting of the China-Philippines Inter-Governmental Joint Steerin g Committee on Cooperation on Oil and Gas Development Held in Beijing," fr om the website of the Ministry of Foreign Affairs, https://www.fmprc.gov.cn/web /wjbxw_673019/t1711665.shtml.

73 See Jay Batongbacal, Philippine-China Joint Development Talks Still at an I mpasse, Despite Green Light, April 13, 2018, Asia Maritime Transparency Initia tive, available at https://amti.csis.org/philippine-china-joint-development-impasse/; Yang Zewei, Joint Development in the South China Sea after the Arbitration Ca se: Opportunities, Challenges and China's Choices, *Journal of Hainan University (Humanities & Social Sciences)*, No. 6, 2017, p. 5; Kang Lin and Luo Chuan yu, Joint Development of Oil and Gas Resources in the South China Sea by C hina and the Philippines: Challenges and Directions for Efforts, *International Stu dies*, No. 5, 2018, pp. 118-120; Qi Huaigao, Bottlenecks and Countermeasures i n the Current Sino-Philippine Joint Development in the South China Sea, *Pacifi c Journal*, No. 3, 2019, pp. 2-3.

Although the COVID-19 pandemic may have been a factor affecting in-person meetings, if both sides had intended to maintain close contact, they could have easily done so via video. These signs seem to suggest that the two sides may have encountered certain obstacles in their substantive negotiations, causing the process to slow down. By the end of the Duterte administration, the Philippine side's attitude toward joint development with China had turned more negative, and in June 2022, then-Philippine Foreign Secretary Locsin announced the termination of negotiations with China on joint energy development in the South China Sea.[74]

On November 17, 2022, President Xi Jinping met with Philippine President Ferdinand Romualdez Marcos Jr. in Bangkok, Thailand. President Xi pointed out that the Chinese side has always viewed China-Philippines relations from a strategic perspective. He stated that China is willing to work with the Philippines to carry forward their friendship, continue cooperation, commit to national development and rejuvenation, and write a new chapter in China-Philippines friendship. Notably, when Philippine President Marcos visited China in January 2023, the two countries issued a Joint Statement, indicating that they would, bearing in mind the spirit of the aforementioned MOU and building on previous achievements, resume consultations on maritime oil and gas development at an early date.[75] In

74 See the website of the Chinese Ministry of Foreign Affairs, https://www.mfa.gov.cn/web/wjdt_674879/fyrbt_674889/202206/t20220624_10709637.shtml, last accessed February 23, 2023.

75 See the website of the Chinese Ministry of Foreign Affairs, https://www.mfa.gov.cn/zyxw/202301/t20230105_11001029.shtml, last accessed February 23, 2023.

response to a reporter's question, Foreign Ministry Spokesperson Mao Ning explained this by stating that the two heads of state had announced the resumption of negotiations on joint oil and gas development.[76] However, in January 2023, the Philippine Supreme Court ruled that the Tripartite Agreement for Joint Marine Scientific Research in Certain Areas in the South China Sea between China, the Philippines, and Vietnam was unconstitutional, casting a shadow over future negotiations on joint development between China and the Philippines.

VI. China and Malaysia

Malaysia's long-standing strategy in the South China Sea has been to "talk less about sovereignty and drill more for oil."[77] Consequently, Malaysia commenced its oil and gas development activities in the region as early as the 1960s. According to incomplete statistics, as of 2019, 99 of Malaysia's 142 existing offshore contract blocks, covering an area of nearly 360,000 square kilometers, fall partially or entirely within the nine-dash line. Within these areas, 3D seismic data acquisition has been carried out over 127,000 square kilometers, and 1,157 exploration and development wells have been drilled. Cumulative production has reached 1.14 billion metric

76 See the website of the Chinese Ministry of Foreign Affairs, https://www.mfa.gov.cn/web/wjdt_674879/fyrbt_674889/202301/t20230105_11001347.shtml, last acc essed February 23, 2023. Note the distinction in the relevant phrasing.
77 See Theresa Fallon, Jockeying for Position in the South China Sea: Coopera tive Strategy or Managed Conflict? in Yann-Huei Song and Keyuan Zou, eds., *Major Law and Policy Issues in the South China Sea: European and American Perspectives*, Ashgate, 2014, p. 201.

tons, making Malaysia the top producer of oil and gas from within the nine-dash line among all littoral states in the South China Sea.

Malaysia also has a successful track record of negotiating and implementing joint development of offshore oil and gas resources with Thailand, Vietnam, and Brunei. China and Malaysia have always maintained sound diplomatic relations and currently enjoy a High-Level Comprehensive Strategic Partnership. In November 2014, during a meeting with Malaysian Prime Minister Najib Razak, who was attending the 22nd APEC Economic Leaders' Meeting, Chinese President Xi Jinping stated that the two sides "should advance maritime cooperation and joint development to promote regional peace, stability, and prosperity."[78] On October 13, 2020, the two countries decided to establish the China-Malaysia High-Level Committee on Cooperation, co-chaired by their respective foreign ministers. This committee is tasked with formulating an inter-governmental cooperation framework to coordinate and advance collaboration across all sectors, thereby elevating the China-Malaysia Comprehensive Strategic Partnership to a new level.[79] However, based on publicly available literature, there have been no recorded negotiations between China and Malaysia on the joint development of oil and gas

78 Xinhua News Agency, "Xi Jinping Meets with Leaders of 5 Economies Atte nding APEC Meeting," *People's Daily* (Overseas Edition), November 11, 2014, http://news.163.com/14/1111/04/AAOCDM6500014AED.html.
79 See "Wang Yi on the Eight-Point Consensus between China and Malaysia" (October 13, 2020), China News Service, https://www.chinanews.com.cn/gn/2020/10-13/9311886.shtml.

resources in the South China Sea.

VII. China and Brunei

Since the 1970s, Brunei has strengthened its cooperation with foreign oil companies to explore and extract oil and gas resources in the Sabah and Zengmu Basins. Brunei also has practical experience in joint development with Malaysia.

The Strategic Cooperative Partnership between China and Brunei has enjoyed stable development. In November 2011, the two countries signed the Memorandum of Understanding on Cooperation in the Energy Sector; the China National Offshore Oil Corporation (CNOOC) and the Brunei National Petroleum Company signed the Memorandum of Understanding on Commercial Cooperation in the Oil and Gas Sector. In 2013, they signed a cooperation agreement and an agreement to establish a joint venture in the oilfield services sector. In October 2013, the two countries issued the Joint Statement of the People's Republic of China and Brunei Darussalam, which stated, "The Leaders agreed to support relevant enterprises of the two countries to carry out joint exploration and exploitation of maritime oil and gas resources following the principle of mutual respect, equality and mutual benefit. Such cooperation shall not be interpreted as to prejudice the position of the respective countries in relation to maritime rights and interest."[80] In November 2014, during a meeting with Sultan Hassanal Bolkiah of Brunei, who was attending the 22nd APEC Economic Leaders' Meeting, Chinese President Xi Jinping also pointed out: "The Chinese side is willing to strengthen maritime cooperation with the Bruneian side and to advance joint development in the South China Sea to achieve substantive progress at an early date."[81] In January 2020, the China-Brunei Intergovernmental Joint Steering Committee held its inaugural meeting, where the two sides agreed to establish a working group on maritime cooperation and reaffirmed their commitment to maintaining peace, stability, and security in the South China Sea.[82] In January 2021, the second meeting of the China-Brunei Intergovernmental Joint Steering Committee announced that "the two sides, under the framework of the Committee, have established an energy cooperation working group, agreed to promote the establishment of working groups in the fields of maritime cooperation, agriculture and fisheries cooperation, and tourism and cultural cooperation, and will study

80 See "Joint Statement of the People's Republic of China and Brunei Darussal am," https://baike.baidu.com/item/%E4%B8%AD%E5%8D%8E%E4%BA%BA%E6%B0%91%E5%85%B1%E5%92%8C%E5%9B%BD%E5%92%8C%E6%96%87%E8%89%BA%E8%BE%BE%E8%BE%BE%E9%92%81%E8%90%A8%E5%85%B0%E5%9B%BD%E5%9B%BD%E8%81%94%E5%90%88%E5%9B%BD%E5%A4%A7%E4%BD%BF%E5%A4%84%E6%98%8E/997969?fr=aladdin, last accessed March 2, 2023.

81 Xinhua News Agency, "Xi Jinping Meets with Leaders of 5 Economies Atte nding APEC Meeting," *People's Daily* (Overseas Edition), November 11, 2014, http://news.163.com/14/1111/04/AAOCDM6500014AED.html.

82 See "Joint Press Release of the Inaugural Meeting of the Intergovernmental Joint Steering Committee of the People's Republic of China and Brunei Darussa lam" (January 22, 2020), website of the Ministry of Foreign Affairs, https://www.mfa.gov.cn/web/.

the 'terms of reference' for the aforementioned working groups as soon as possible... Both sides reaffirmed the resolution of territorial and jurisdictional disputes through peaceful dialogue and consultation."[83]

VIII. China and Indonesia

Indonesia's primary interest in the disputed area of the South China Sea currently lies in the development of the Natuna gas field. The Indonesian government is actively cooperating with foreign companies, attracting over 40 billion USD in foreign investment to exploit and utilize the resources in this region. To date, Indonesia has signed maritime delimitation agreements with Australia, India, Malaysia, Papua New Guinea, the Philippines, Singapore, Thailand, and Vietnam in certain maritime areas.[84] However, in other more extensive maritime areas, significant disputes with its neighbors remain. Most of its exclusive economic zone in the disputed areas of the South China Sea is yet to be delimited, affecting security and cooperation in the surrounding waters.

Furthermore, Indonesia has extensive experience with joint development negotiations and cooperation models, having signed the Treaty

---

83 See "Joint Press Release of the Second Meeting of the Intergovernmental Joint Steering Committee of the People's Republic of China and Brunei Darussalam" (January 16, 2021), website of the Ministry of Foreign Affairs, https://www.mfa.gov.cn/web/ziliao_674904/zt_674979/dnzt_674981/qtzt/kjgzbdfyyq_699171/202101/t20210116_9279024.shtml.

84 For details, see the UN Division for Ocean Affairs and the Law of the Sea, available at https://www.un.org/Depts/los/LEGISLATIONANDTREATIES/STATEFILES/IDN.htm.

between Australia and the Republic of Indonesia on the Zone of Cooperation in an Area between the Indonesian Province of East Timor and Northern Australia with Australia in 1989.[85]

Indonesia has long played the role of a "mediator" in the South China Sea disputes, having hosted multiple sessions of the Workshop on Managing Potential Conflict in the South China Sea in the hope of resolving the issue properly through peaceful means. On May 8, 2000, China and Indonesia issued a joint statement agreeing to cooperate in many important fields, including minerals and fisheries. In 2011, while serving as the rotating Chair of ASEAN, Indonesia called on all parties to the South China Sea issue to maintain calm and restraint, expressing hope that the problem would be resolved through bilateral rather than multilateral negotiations.[86] The dispute between China and Indonesia is limited to maritime areas and does not involve island disputes, but publicly available literature has so far revealed no record of any negotiations between the two sides regarding joint development.

85 See "The 1989 Joint Development Case Between Australia and Indonesia," i n Yang Zewei (ed.), *International Agreements on the Joint Development of Mari ne Resources* (Chinese-English Bilingual Version) (Vol. I), Social Sciences Acad emic Press (China), 2016, pp. 272-312; Li Yawei, A Study on the Timor Sea J oint Development Case, Master's thesis, Wuhan University, 2016.

86 See Guo Jie and Zhang Hui, Five Countries Step Up Plundering of South C hina Sea Oil and Gas Resources, *Sinopec Monthly*, No. 8, 2012, p. 69.

delineate a "block" for joint development in the Gulf of Thailand[87], the initiative has yet to make any substantive progress. As another example, the national oil companies of China, the Philippines, and Vietnam signed A Tripartite Agreement for Joint Marine Scientific Research in Certain Areas in the South China Sea as early as 2005. However, its implementation was beset by highly complex issues that slowed its progress, causing them to miss the window of opportunity presented by a period of favorable China-Philippines relations. When the domestic situation in the Philippines changed, the agreement could not be carried forward and was ultimately declared void by the Philippine Supreme Court in early 2023 on the grounds that it violated the Philippine Constitution. Therefore, for future joint development of offshore oil and gas resources with its maritime neighbors, it is advisable for China to prioritize bilateral arrangements and, wherever possible, avoid tripartite or multilateral forms of cooperation.

87 See Nguyen Hong Thao, Vietnam and Joint Development in the Gulf of Th ailand, *Asian Yearbook of International Law*, Vol. 8, 2003, p. 138.

II. Establishing a Model for the Application of Law to Joint Development that Safeguards China's National Interests

(I) Further Defining Matters Open to Compromise in the Application of Law to Joint Development

As discussed above, the international community has not yet established uniform standards or common models for the application of law to the joint development of offshore oil and gas resources. Therefore, in the future application of law to joint development between China and its maritime neighbors, we should adhere to the principle of prioritizing the safeguarding of China's national interests. With regard to the application of law to low-sensitivity matters that are less associated with sovereign rights, such as marine environmental protection, appropriate compromises and concessions can be considered. Conversely, in the application of law to highly sensitive matters more closely tied to sovereign rights—such as taxation, customs, quarantine, immigration, and especially criminal jurisdiction and civil acts—any related compromises and concessions must be deliberated with great care and extreme caution. At the same time, one must not go to extremes by unrealistically and absolutely excluding the application of the other state party's corresponding domestic laws, even though "concessions by a state party in this regard are often imbued with political meaning."[88]

(II) Attention to the Conversion of Joint Development Models

While the joint development of offshore oil and gas resources initially progresses from transboundary areas to disputed sea areas or zones with overlapping claims, the latter model ceases to exist once maritime delimitation is completed. However, even after two sovereign states have finalized their maritime boundary, the possibility of a "single geological structure" (deposit clause) with a transboundary distribution cannot be ruled out. Therefore, after the delimitation of a disputed area or zone of overlapping claims, transboundary joint development remains practically significant as long as a "single geological structure" exists across the boundary.[89] In view of this, although we adhere to the easy-first principle of progressing from transboundary joint development to joint development in disputed areas, the overall trajectory of joint development will still exhibit a trend: from transboundary, to disputed-area, and then back again to transboundary joint development.

---

88 See Yusuf Mohammad Yusuf, Is Joint Development a Panacea for Maritime Boundary Disputes and for the Exploitation of Offshore Transboundary Petroleu m Deposits? *International Energy Law Review*, Vol. 4, 2009, p. 133.
89 See Dong Shijie, The Application of Law in Joint Maritime Development Z ones, *Wuhan University International Law Review*, Vol. 2, 2015, p. 85.

III. Recognizing the Positive Significance of Pre-existing Rights in Disputed Sea Areas or Zones of Overlapping Claims

A pre-existing right refers to a right acquired by a third-party oil company to which a coastal State has unilaterally granted a license for exploration and development within a specific area or block before that area is designated for joint development. The company thereby obtains certain operational and development rights over that area or a portion of the block.[90] According to Article 77 of the United Nations Convention on the Law of the Sea, "The coastal State exercises over the continental shelf sovereign rights for the purpose of exploring it and exploiting its natural resources." Therefore, a sovereign state may, in principle, only issue licenses for oil and gas exploration and development within its own internal waters, territorial sea, contiguous zone, and continental shelf; a license that exceeds this scope is invalid. However, in international practice, sovereign states often issue licenses for oil and gas exploration and development in disputed maritime areas for legal, economic, or technical reasons, as well as due to their domestic political situation, thus giving rise to the issue of pre-existing

90 See Xiao Jianguo, *Joint Development of Petroleum on International Maritime Boundaries*, China Ocean Press, 2006, p. 113; Hazel Fox et al., eds., Joint Develo pment of Offshore Oil and Gas: A Model Agreement for States for Joint Develop ment with Explanatory Commentary, British Institute of International and Comparat ive Law, 1989, p. 214.

rights.[91]

In the international practice of joint offshore oil and gas development to date, the states party to such arrangements generally recognize pre-existing rights within the joint development area.

For example, in the 1965 Joint Development Case Between Saudi Arabia and Kuwait, Article 11 of the Agreement between the Kingdom of Saudi Arabia and the State of Kuwait on the Partition of the Neutral Zone, signed by the two countries, explicitly provides: "The existing oil concession agreements shall continue to be valid, and the two contracting parties shall, in their respective partitioned zones, respect the terms of the existing oil concession agreements and their revised texts. Both contracting parties shall also, through the necessary legislative and legal measures, ensure that the concessionaire companies continue to exercise their rights and fulfill their obligations." As can be seen, in this case, both Saudi Arabia and Kuwait recognized the pre-existing rights within the joint development area for offshore oil and gas resources.[92]

As another example, in the 1979 Joint Development Case Between Thailand and Malaysia in the Gulf of Thailand, Thailand, prior to negotiating with Malaysia to resolve their maritime dispute, had already

91 See Yang Zewei, A Study on the Issue of Pre-existing Rights in Joint Marit ime Development, *Law Review*, No. 1, 2017, pp. 121-122.
92 See Article 11 of Agreement between the Kingdom of Saudi Arabia and the State of Kuwait on the Partition of the Neutral Zone, 7 July 1965.

issued licenses for oil and gas exploration and development to two American oil companies in accordance with its domestic petroleum laws. These two companies thereby obtained exclusive operating rights to the respective offshore blocks, which were situated in the area of overlapping continental shelf claims by Thailand and Malaysia. Malaysia, however, had not unilaterally authorized any foreign oil companies to develop the oil and gas resources in the area.[93] Nevertheless, the 1979 Memorandum of Understanding Between Malaysia and the Kingdom of Thailand on the Establishment of the Joint Authority for the Exploitation of the Resources of the Sea Bed in a Defined Area of the Continental Shelf of the Two Countries in the Gulf of Thailand explicitly recognized that any "concessions, licenses issued, or agreements or arrangements made" that had already been granted within the joint development area would be unaffected by the bilateral joint development arrangement and would remain in effect.[94]

Furthermore, in the 1992 Joint Development Case Between Malaysia and Vietnam, as early as the mid-1980s, Malaysia had begun to engage in oil and gas exploration and development activities in the maritime area of overlapping claims with Vietnam. It subsequently granted concessions to

93 See He Hairong, *A Study on the Legal Issues of Joint Maritime Development in the Gulf of Thailand*, Wuhan University Press, 2020, p. 94.
94 See Article 3(2) of the Memorandum of Understanding between Malaysia and the Kingdom of Thailand on the Establishment of the Joint Authority for the Exploitation of the Resources of the Sea Bed in a Defined Area of the Continental Shelf of the Two Countries in the Gulf of Thailand, 21 February 1979.

three foreign oil companies to explore and exploit the petroleum resources of this area. In 1991, Hamilton Oil Corporation, a Malaysian concessionaire, discovered an oil field with a daily output of 4,400 barrels.[95] Nevertheless, the 1992 Memorandum of Understanding between Malaysia and the Socialist Republic of Vietnam for the Exploration and Exploitation of Petroleum in a Defined Area of the Continental Shelf involving the Two Countries also explicitly provided that the exploitation rights previously granted by Malaysia to foreign oil companies within the joint development area would remain in effect.[96]

In fact, China has also previously taken similar actions regarding pre-existing rights in the South China Sea, authorizing foreign oil companies to conduct oil and gas exploration and development or issuing public tender announcements for relevant maritime areas. For example, in 1992, China granted a concession to the American company Crestone Energy to conduct commercial development in the maritime area near Vanguard Bank in the South China Sea.[97] In addition, on June 23, 2012, the China National Offshore Oil Corporation publicly issued its Announcement of Blocks in Chinese Waters Open for Foreign Cooperation in 2012. Of the nine offshore

---

95 See He Hairong, *A Study on the Legal Issues of Joint Maritime Development in the Gulf of Thailand*, Wuhan University Press, 2020, p. 95.

96 See Article 3(c) of the Memorandum of Understanding between Malaysia and the Socialist Republic of Vietnam for the Exploration and Exploitation of Petroleum in a Defined Area of the Continental Shelf Involving the Two Countries, 5 June 1992.

97 See Zou Keyuan, China's U-Shaped Line in the South China Sea Revisited, *Ocean Development & International Law*, Vol. 43, No. 1, 2012, p. 22.

blocks offered for joint exploration and development with foreign companies, seven were located in the Zhongjiannan Basin, and two were in parts of the Wan'an and Nanweixi Basins in the South China Sea.[98] Although these actions were met with strong opposition from the Vietnamese side[99], we should fully recognize the positive impact and importance of such pre-existing rights. If the Chinese government issues licenses to foreign oil companies for oil and gas exploration and development in relevant maritime areas of the South China Sea, thus giving rise to the issue of pre-existing rights, then the possibility that both sides would explicitly recognize these rights in future joint development between China and its maritime neighbors cannot be excluded.

IV. Paying Attention to the Influence of the Distance Factor on the Application of Law in Joint Development

The proximity of an offshore oil and gas joint development zone to Chinese mainland may also influence the applicability of Chinese law within such a zone.

---

98 See "Announcement of Blocks in Chinese Waters Open for Foreign Coopera tion in 2012," on the website of the China National Offshore Oil Corporation, http://www.cnooc.com.cn/data/html/news/2012-06-23/chinese/322013.htm.

99 See Huang Wei, A Study on the Legal Issues of CNOOC's 2012 Announce ment of Tenders for South China Sea Oil and Gas, *Law Science Magazine*, No. 10, 2012, p. 17; Zhang Sheng, New Developments in Vietnam's Infringing Oil and Gas Activities in the South China Sea and China's Legal Response, *Journa l of Boundary and Ocean Studies*, No. 1, 2020, p. 121.

It is universally acknowledged that the importance of legal enforcement is self-evident. The ancient Chinese sage Xu Gan pointed out long ago in his *Zhong Lun*: “The effectiveness of rewards and punishments lies not in their severity, but in their certainty. If they are consistently enforced, the people will be compliant even if the measures are not severe. If they are not, the people will grow indifferent even if the measures are harsh.”[100] The American sociological jurist Roscoe Pound also held that “the life of the law is in its enforcement.”[101] Likewise, the fundamental issue for the application of law in an offshore oil and gas joint development zone is its effective enforcement.

In fact, the implementation of certain laws in an offshore oil and gas joint development zone does not depend on on-site enforcement by public officials from the states concerned. For example, with respect to customs and tax law, enforcement personnel are not required to conduct on-site enforcement within the joint development zone, as the enterprises engaged in the exploration and development of offshore oil and gas resources typically establish offices within the territory of the state party. However, the implementation of other laws does require on-site enforcement by public officials from the states party to the joint development. For instance, should a marine environmental pollution incident or a criminal case arise within the joint development zone, the state concerned must dispatch its

100 See Shen Zongling (ed.), *Jurisprudence*, Higher Education Press, 1994, p. 341.
101 See Roscoe Pound, *Jurisprudence*, Vol. 1, West Publishing Co., 1959, p. 353.

personnel to the zone to investigate the cause of the incident, take protective measures, or arrest the criminal suspects. It is clear, therefore, that for laws requiring on-site enforcement, their effective implementation within an offshore oil and gas joint development zone is most susceptible to the influence of distance.[102]

Therefore, in future offshore oil and gas joint development activities between China and its maritime neighbors, the potential blocks that are most susceptible to the influence of distance are concentrated primarily in the southern region of the South China Sea. If, in the coming years, China and other states bordering the South China Sea were to engage in joint development in the southern sea area, a flexible and adaptive approach could be adopted due to the great distance from Chinese mainland. For instance, in matters with fewer implications for sovereignty, enforcement could be conducted in accordance with the joint development agreement. For matters with stronger implications for sovereignty, however, such as those concerning criminal jurisdiction, China should insist on the application of its laws. Nevertheless, it is gratifying to note that as China's achievements in island and reef construction in the South China Sea continue to expand, the influence of the distance factor on the application of law in joint development between China and other neighboring states will be reduced.

---

102 See Dong Shijie, The Application of Law in Joint Maritime Development Zones, *Wuhan University International Law Review*, Vol. 2, 2015, p. 86.

saw no further progress.

As China and Vietnam have already delimited their boundary in the Beibu Gulf, the joint development of oil and gas resources conducted in this region constitutes transboundary joint development. The applicable law includes: the joint development agreement for oil and gas resources in the Beibu Gulf signed by the governments of China and Vietnam; the domestic laws of each country, applied in their respective jurisdictional waters; and the relevant unitization agreements for exploration and development signed by the national oil companies of China and Vietnam.

(II) The Application of Law to Joint Development of Offshore Oil and Gas Resources in Disputed Sea Areas of the South China Sea Between China and Vietnam

Southward from the delimited point at the mouth of the Beibu Gulf, China and Vietnam have not yet established a maritime boundary in the vast sea areas of the South China Sea. Consequently, the joint development of oil and gas resources in these waters constitutes joint development in an area of overlapping maritime claims.

1. The Area Outside the Mouth of the Beibu Gulf

Since the area outside the mouth of the Beibu Gulf is not far from the mainland of either party, and both sides have conducted oil and gas exploration and development in the relevant sea areas, any joint development in this region would likely still be undertaken by China National Offshore Oil Corporation and the PetroVietnam. A management model similar to the Malaysia-Vietnam Joint Development Case could therefore be adopted, whereby a joint authority established by the two national oil companies would formulate specific rules for exploration and development. With respect to matters such as criminal and civil jurisdiction, customs, quarantine, and taxation, the domestic laws of China and Vietnam would apply respectively, as agreed upon by the two sides. Considering the pressure of domestic public opinion in both China and Vietnam, the room for concession and compromise on both sides is limited.

2. The Central and Southern Sea Areas of the South China Sea

Should China decide to pursue the joint development of oil and gas resources with Vietnam in the central and southern areas of the South China Sea, it would be best to select a sea area where the dispute involves only one other country; the waters near Vanguard Bank could be considered a potential block.[105] Vanguard Bank is located in the western part of the Nansha Islands, approximately 35 nautical miles southwest of Grainger Bank. It extends 63 kilometers from east to west and has an average width of 11 kilometers. The sea area near Vanguard Bank possesses abundant oil and gas resources, and its vicinity is arguably the region with the most

105 See Robert Beckman et al., eds., *Beyond Territorial Disputes in the South China Sea: Legal Framework for the Joint Development of Hydrocarbon Resources*, Edward Elgar Publishing Limited, 2013, p. 326.

favorable petroleum geological structures in the southern sea area. Vietnam operates several oil wells at Vanguard Bank, and the oil and natural gas produced there account for a significant portion of Vietnam's GDP. In recent years, Vietnam has intensified its exploration and development of oil and gas resources in the waters near Vanguard Bank, making it one of the hotspots for investment by international oil companies. If China were able to jointly develop oil and gas resources with Vietnam in the waters near Vanguard Bank, it could also, to a certain extent, curb Vietnam's infringing activities against China in the southern South China Sea. In fact, China has also long sought to take action in these waters. As early as May 1992, China signed a contract with the American company Crestone Energy for the exploration and development of oil and gas resources at Vanguard Bank. In 1994, Crestone Energy began exploration activities in the Block Wanan Bei-21. However, due to obstruction from Vietnam, the petroleum contract has never been performed. Although the contractual rights to the Block Wanan Bei-21 have changed hands several times, they remain valid.[106] Reportedly, the contractual rights for Block Wanan Bei-21 were acquired in 2014 by a private company wholly owned by Mr. Xue Guanglin, the chairman of Brightoil Petroleum, through a purchase from another company.[107]

---

106 See Zou Keyuan, China's U-Shaped Line in the South China Sea Revisited, *Ocean Development and International Law*, Vol. 43, No. 1, 2012, p. 22; Li G uoqiang, Policy Adjustments for the Exploration and Development of Oil and G as Resources in the South China Sea, *International Studies*, No. 6, 2014, p. 11 0.

107 See "Clarification Statement from Brightoil Petroleum (Holdings) Limited"

Furthermore, on June 23, 2012, China National Offshore Oil Corporation officially released the Announcement of Blocks in Chinese Waters Open for Foreign Cooperation in 2012.[108] From July to October 2019, China's survey vessel Haiyang Dizhi 8 also conducted operations in the relevant blocks,[109] and the related sea areas could also be considered for joint development negotiations with the Vietnamese side.

The central and southern sea areas of the South China Sea constitute disputed waters between China and Vietnam where no maritime boundary has been delimited, and are geographically closer to Vietnam. Although China has made significant achievements in its island and reef construction in the South China Sea since 2014, challenges in law enforcement and

(July 6, 2017), on the Brightoil Petroleum (Holdings) Limited website, http://www.bwoil.com/attachment/2017112318152217823869 17_sc.pdf; "Brightoil Petroleum's Clarification on the Exploitation Rights to the Wanan Bei-21 Sea Area," ACN Newswire, July 6, 2017, http://ch.acnnewswire.com/press-release/simplifiedchinese/37398/. It is worth noting that there is a discrepancy between the clarification statement published on the Brightoil Petroleum website and the one reported by ACN Newswire. The news report states that "the contractual rights for Wanan Bei-21 were acquired in 2014 by a private company wholly owned by the company's chairman, Mr. Xue Guanglin, through a purchase from another company," but this detail is absent from the clarification on the Brightoil Petroleum website. Although both statements are dated July 6, 2017, Brightoil Petroleum did not publish its version on its website until September 6, 2017, whereas ACN Newswire released the information on July 6, 2017.

108 See "CNOOC Announces Geographical Coordinates of 9 Open Bidding Blocks in the South China Sea" (June 27, 2012), on China News Service, http://finance.chinanews.com/ny/2012/06-27/3989795.shtml.

109 See China Risks Flare-Up over Malaysian, Vietnamese Gas Resources, Center for Strategic and International Studies, 16 July 2019, available at https://amti.csis.org/china-risks-flare-up-over-malaysian-vietnamese-gas-resources/; Laura Zhou, Chinese survey ship involved in South China Sea stand-off with Vietnam back home, tracker says, *South China Morning Post*, 10 November 2019, available at https://www.scmp.com/news/china/diplomacy/article/3034645/chinese-survey-ship-involved-south-china-sea-stand-vietnam.

participated from the outset"; Article 7 further states: "After a find has been declared commercial, each of the Parties shall carry its costs in the further development of the field in proportion to its share under the contract concerned." Therefore, the oil companies of China and Vietnam can draw on this practice in the joint development of oil and gas resources in the southern South China Sea to push forward substantive joint exploration operations.

II. The China-Philippines Joint Development Zone and the Application of Law

(I) The China-Philippines Joint Development Zone for Offshore Oil and Gas Resources

The South China Sea dispute involves numerous factors, including disputes over territorial sovereignty and maritime rights and interests, differing interpretations of historic rights, and divergent understandings of the United Nations Convention on the Law of the Sea as well as the fundamental principles of international law. In recent years, the adverse consequences of the so-called "South China Sea arbitration case" have persisted, leading neighboring countries to raise numerous questions about China's nine-dash line and its claims to lawful maritime rights and interests in the South China Sea. Determining whether a legitimate area of overlapping claims exists between China and the countries concerned, and where the boundaries of such an area lie, has become problematic.[115] Some scholars argue that joint development in the South China Sea is impossible to achieve until the maritime claims of the relevant claimant states are accurately defined and justified.[116] This issue is particularly prominent in the case of the Philippines. Especially with the early 2023 ruling by the Philippine Supreme Court that the tripartite joint exploration agreement between China, the Philippines, and Vietnam violated the Philippine Constitution and that the relevant sea area is state property of the Philippines, the acknowledgement by the Philippines that the proposed blocks for oil and gas cooperation lie within an area of overlapping claims or a disputed sea area has become a foundational—and difficult—issue for launching joint development negotiations between China and the Philippines.

(II) The Application of Law to the Joint Development of Offshore Oil and Gas Resources between China and the Philippines

1. A Flexible Approach to the Application of Law

Considering that the sea areas for potential joint development between China and the Philippines are distant from Chinese mainland, and despite the significant achievements in China's island and reef construction in the

115 See Robert Beckman et al., eds., *Beyond Territorial Disputes in the South China Sea: Legal Framework for the Joint Development of Hydrocarbon Resources*, Edward Elgar Publishing Limited, 2013, pp. 301-306.

116 See Robert Beckman et al., eds., *Beyond Territorial Disputes in the South China Sea: Legal Framework for the Joint Development of Hydrocarbon Resources*, Edward Elgar Publishing Limited, 2013, p. 306.

pre-existing rights in the region are first acknowledged, and then, during the course of joint development, the joint development management authority enters into new contracts with the relevant oil and gas companies.

3. Fully Leveraging the Role of the Joint Authority

As discussed above, recognizing pre-existing rights in the joint development between China and Malaysia in the Zengmu Basin means that previous petroleum contracts must continue to be honored. This may affect the uniformity of legal application within the joint development zone. Therefore, a China-Malaysia joint authority for oil and gas development could be established and empowered to formulate the legal regime for the zone. This would diminish the influence of the petroleum contracts previously signed unilaterally by Malaysia with foreign oil companies on the application of law, thereby preserving the integrity of legal application within the joint development zone.

IV. The China-Brunei Joint Development Zone and the Application of Law

In March 2009, Brunei and Malaysia successfully resolved their maritime dispute[120] through an exchange of letters[121]. Consequently, the

120 See Jeffrey J. Smith, Brunei and Malaysia Resolve Outstanding Maritime Boundary Issues, American Society of International Law Law of the Sea Reports, Vol. 1, 2010, pp. 1-4.

121 See The Exchange of Letters Between Malaysia and Brunei, 16 March 2009, available at http://www.thestar.com.my/story/?file=%2f2010%2f5%2f3%2fnation%

only maritime boundary Brunei has yet to delimit is with China. Because Brunei's territory is relatively small, the area of disputed waters between the two countries is also comparatively small. This facilitates the joint development of oil and gas resources between China and Brunei in the Sabah Basin.

The issue of the application of law in the China-Brunei joint oil and gas development zone can be approached from the following two aspects: First, by respecting Brunei's pre-existing rights in the Sabah Basin joint development zone. An approach similar to Brunei's own can be adopted by entering into new petroleum exploration and development contracts with foreign oil companies[122]. This would reduce obstacles to joint development and ensure the integrity of the application of law within the zone. Second, considering that the relevant joint development zone is distant from Chinese mainland, the implementation of Chinese domestic law in the zone faces numerous difficulties. Therefore, for matters within the zone that do not have significant sovereign implications, Brunei's domestic law could be applied exclusively.[123]

2f20100503123605&sec=nation.

122 See Robert Beckman et al., eds., *Beyond Territorial Disputes in the South China Sea: Legal Framework for the Joint Development of Hydrocarbon Resources*, Edward Elgar Publishing Limited, 2013, pp. 207-209.

123 See Yang Zewei (ed.), *Research on International Law Issues of Joint Maritime Development*, Social Sciences Academic Press (China), 2016, p. 80.

V. The Sino-Indonesian Joint Development Zone in the Natuna Sea and the Application of Law

(I) The Sino-Indonesian Joint Development Zone for Offshore Oil and Gas Resources in the Natuna Sea

China and Indonesia have an area of overlapping maritime claims spanning 50,000 square kilometers in the southern South China Sea. The Natuna gas field, located within this overlapping area, has estimated recoverable reserves of approximately 1.31 trillion cubic meters. [124] Therefore, the Natuna Sea area is also a potential "block" for the joint development of offshore oil and gas resources by the two countries.

(II) Applicable Law for the Joint Development of Offshore Oil and Gas Resources by China and Indonesia in the Natuna Sea

1. Drawing Lessons from the Joint Development Case between Australia and Indonesia

In December 1989, Indonesia and Australia signed the Treaty between Australia and the Republic of Indonesia on the Zone of Cooperation in an Area between the Indonesian Province of East Timor and Northern

124 See Liang Jinzhe, Some Thoughts on the Development of Disputed Areas in the South China Sea, in Zhong Tianxiang et al. (eds.), Proceedings of the Symposium on the South China Sea Issue, Hainan South China Sea Research Center, 2002, p. 113; An Yingmin, On the Choice of Models for the Joint Development of Oil and Gas Resources in the Disputed Areas of the South China Sea, *Journal of Contemporary Asia-Pacific Studies*, No. 6, 2011, pp. 130-131.

Australia. This treaty is regarded as "the most detailed treaty on joint development yet concluded in terms of its textual provisions."[125] Its institutional design for the joint development of offshore oil and gas resources is not only highly detailed but also scientific. Furthermore, the joint development area for oil and gas between Indonesia and Australia covers approximately 60,000 square kilometers, while the disputed area in the Natuna Sea is also extensive, measuring 50,000 square kilometers; both are very large regions.[126] Therefore, Joint Development Case between Australia and Indonesia serves as a valuable reference for the joint development of oil and gas resources by China and Indonesia in the Natuna Sea in at least the following three respects.

First, the joint development agreement between China and Indonesia concerning oil and gas resources in the Natuna Sea can also contain detailed provisions. Second, in terms of delimiting the joint development zone, China and Indonesia could also divide it into three blocks: one block, serving as the core development area, would be jointly managed by both countries with revenues shared equally; in addition to the joint development agreement and the rules set by the managing authority, the laws of both China and Indonesia would be applicable. Another block would be under Chinese jurisdiction, subject to Chinese law, but with a portion of the

---

125 Xiao Jianguo, *Joint Development of Petroleum on International Maritime B oundaries*, China Ocean Press, 2006, p. 10.
126 See Stuart Kaye, The Timor Gap Treaty: Creative Solutions and Internation al Conflict, *Sydney Law Review*, Vol. 16, No. 1, 1994, p. 79.

revenues to be shared with Indonesia. A third block would be under Indonesian jurisdiction, subject to Indonesian law, but with a portion of the revenues to be shared with China. Third, China and Indonesia could also grant the management body for the joint development—the Joint Authority—extensive powers.[127]

2. Applying Indonesian Domestic Law and Using Indonesia as the Logistical Support Base for the Joint Development Zone

The Natuna Islands are approximately 1,900 kilometers from Chinese mainland. Indonesia has already constructed natural gas pipelines from the West Natuna Islands to Singapore and Malaysia.[128] Therefore, Indonesia's Natuna Islands could serve as the logistical support base for the two countries' joint development zone in the Natuna Sea, with Indonesian domestic law applied specifically for this purpose. This approach would not only facilitate joint development by leveraging Indonesia's existing infrastructure, such as for oil and gas processing, but is also economically feasible. The proximity allows for swift and convenient logistical support, potentially yielding maximum economic benefits.

In summary, for China, the issue of applicable law can be handled with

127 See Yang Zewei, On the Legal Basis, Development Trends, and China's Im plementation Path for Joint Maritime Development, in *Chinese Yearbook of Inter national Law* (2015), Law Press China, 2016, p. 137.

128 In the 2002 Joint Development Case Between East Timor and Australia, A ustralia constructed a natural gas pipeline to Darwin. See Robert Beckman et a l., eds., *Beyond Territorial Disputes in the South China Sea: Legal Framework for the Joint Development of Hydrocarbon Resources*, Edward Elgar Publishing Limited, 2013, p. 266.

a flexible approach when pursuing the joint development of offshore oil and gas resources with its neighbors in the South China Sea. Based on the principle of proximity, it is entirely feasible to apply the domestic law of the neighboring country to numerous matters. However, the bottom line that must be upheld is that the designated block must be explicitly defined as an "area of overlapping claims" where a sovereignty dispute exists between the two parties, and the chosen model of cooperation must be "joint development" that reflects shared ownership and jurisdiction over the oil and gas resources.

Chapter Summary

China has yet to fully resolve its land boundary issues with neighboring countries, and its disputes over maritime delimitation and island sovereignty also face a complex and serious situation. Therefore, a comprehensive and complete resolution of China's border and maritime disputes remains a long and arduous task.

China has always adhered to the "principle of peaceful settlement of international disputes," insisting on resolving international disputes through peaceful means. In exploring paths to resolving maritime disputes, China has always actively advocated and adhered to the principle of "sovereignty belongs to China, shelving disputes and pursuing joint development." As early as 1972, when the two countries were negotiating the normalization of diplomatic relations, China and Japan reached an understanding to shelve the issue of sovereignty over the Diaoyu Islands. In 1984, during a meeting with a delegation from the Center for Strategic and International Studies at Georgetown University, Deng Xiaoping clearly articulated the concept of "sovereignty belongs to China, shelving disputes and pursuing joint development." Subsequently, Chinese state leaders, foreign ministers, and other officials have, on various diplomatic occasions, formally put forward the proposal of "sovereignty belongs to China, shelving disputes and pursuing joint development" to the leaders of neighboring countries.

In 1974, Japan and South Korea signed the Agreement between Japan and the Republic of Korea concerning Joint Development of the Southern Part of the Continental Shelf Adjacent to the Two Countries. The Chinese Ministry of Foreign Affairs protested this and issued a statement declaring that the act by the Japanese government and the South Korean authorities of unilaterally establishing a so-called Japan-ROK joint development zone on the East China Sea continental shelf, without China's involvement, was an infringement of China's sovereignty.

The Chinese government has consistently advocated the principle of "sovereignty belongs to China, shelving disputes and pursuing joint development," and has pursued attempts and explorations in the joint development of offshore oil and gas resources with neighboring countries such as North Korea, Japan, Vietnam, the Philippines, Malaysia, and Brunei.

The existing international practice in the application of law for the joint development of offshore oil and gas resources offers the following four lessons and points of reference for China's future application of law in joint development with its maritime neighbors. First, adhering to the principle of tackling easier issues before more difficult ones, starting with transboundary and bilateral joint development. Second, establishing a model for applicable law in maritime joint development that is conducive to safeguarding China's national interests. Third, recognizing the positive significance of pre-existing rights in disputed maritime areas or areas of overlapping claims. Fourth, paying attention to the influence of proximity on the application of law in the joint development of offshore oil and gas resources.

In the future, when China and its South China Sea neighbors, such as Vietnam, the Philippines, Malaysia, Brunei, and Indonesia, engage in the joint development of offshore oil and gas resources in potential cooperation zones, the application of law will generally involve several components. In addition to the bilateral joint development agreement for oil and gas resources, the respective domestic laws of each country in the areas under their jurisdiction, relevant exploration and development agreements signed by their oil companies, and any special laws, attention must also be paid to the handling of pre-existing rights and the special circumstances of individual national systems. The Chinese side can adopt a flexible attitude in handling the issue of applicable law, but the bottom line that must be upheld is that the designated block must be explicitly defined as an "area of overlapping claims" where a sovereignty dispute exists between the two parties, and the chosen model of cooperation must be "joint development" that reflects shared ownership and jurisdiction over the oil and gas resources.

Conclusion and Outlook

I. The Main Conclusions of This Book

A clear definition of property rights is of paramount importance in oil and gas development. Due to the fluid nature of oil and gas resources, determining ownership is critical in situations where a single underground reservoir underlies surface lands belonging to different owners. The rule of capture became the cornerstone for determining the ownership of oil and gas resources and for the legal framework of the oil and gas industry. While this rule promoted the rapid development of the industry, it also brought about significant negative consequences. With the emergence and development of the doctrine of correlative rights, the unitization of a single reservoir became both a practical option and a legal requirement. As modern industry developed, nations placed increasing importance on acquiring oil and gas resources, leading to the rise of the concept of permanent sovereignty over natural resources. The ownership of oil and gas resources is, of course, encompassed within this principle. Given the distinct legal regimes for land and sea in international law, coastal States, in accordance with international legal rules including the United Nations Convention on the Law of the Sea (UNCLOS), exercise varying degrees of sovereignty and sovereign rights over offshore oil and gas resources located in their territorial sea, contiguous zone, exclusive economic zone, and continental shelf. For transboundary oil and gas resources and those in areas of overlapping maritime claims, the relevant coastal States hold "common" ownership. Although the rule of capture laid the legal foundation for the development of the oil and gas industry, it does not apply within the international legal framework governing the exploration and development of offshore oil and gas resources. It is precisely because the shortcomings of the rule of capture are recognized—and particularly under the norms of international law requiring due regard for the interests of other parties and the principle of good neighbourliness—that joint development has become a realistic, viable, and inevitable choice for coastal States when developing oil and gas resources in transboundary areas and areas of overlapping claims.

Joint development of offshore oil and gas resources refers to the joint exploration and exploitation of oil and gas resources in transboundary or disputed maritime areas by two or more States, based on a joint development agreement concluded between them. The application of law to the joint development of offshore oil and gas resources is the specialized activity in state practice whereby sovereign states, the designated management institution or legal persons for the joint development, based on the relevant provisions of a joint development agreement, apply specific legal rules to handle matters related to the joint development activities, such as taxation, revenue distribution, and civil or criminal cases. The primary subjects in the application of law to the joint development of offshore oil and gas resources include sovereign states, joint authorities, legal persons, international judicial institutions, arbitral tribunals, and domestic courts. The object of the application of law in this context refers to the matters or issues that arise during the joint development process and require regulation under different legal systems, such as international or domestic law.

A review of the 60-plus-year evolution of the joint development of offshore oil and gas resources reveals four distinct stages. First, the emergence stage (1958-1969), which saw a total of six cases of joint development in the Persian Gulf and Western Europe. Second, the development stage (1970-1993), featuring a total of 16 cases that involved 27 countries: 11 in Asia, 5 in Europe, 7 in Africa, 3 in the Americas, and Australia in Oceania. Third, the decline stage (1994-1999), with only one such case: the Joint Declaration on Cooperation over Offshore Activities in the South West Atlantic, signed by the United Kingdom and Argentina in September 1995. Fourth, the stabilization stage (2000-present); since the beginning of the 21st century, joint development activities have gradually increased once more, resulting in 15 instances of state practice.

The application of law to the joint development of offshore oil and gas resources primarily involves the following five scenarios: first, the Application of Law to Joint Development in Disputed Maritime Areas; second, the Application of Law to Joint Development in Transboundary Maritime Areas; third, the Application of Law to Joint Development within a State's Exclusive Jurisdiction; fourth, the Application of Law to Joint Development on the Continental Shelf Beyond 200 Nautical Miles; and fifth, the Application of Law to Joint Development Beyond National

Jurisdiction.

The application of law to the joint development of offshore oil and gas resources can be categorized into three main types: separate, joint, and comprehensive application. Among these, the separate application of joint development law can be further divided into absolute and relative forms. Joint application of joint development law refers to the application of a single legal framework, mutually agreed upon by the parties, to the entire joint development area. The comprehensive application of joint development law incorporates elements of both separate and joint application.

The laws applicable to the joint development of offshore oil and gas resources mainly include international law, domestic law, special law, and international petroleum development contracts. The international law applicable to the joint development of offshore oil and gas resources primarily includes the fundamental principles of international law, the United Nations Convention on the Law of the Sea, joint development agreements, international legal regimes related to navigation, fishing activities, and environmental protection, customary international law, general principles of law, and international judicial precedents. International petroleum development contracts primarily refer to agreements concerning exploration, development, and production activities signed between a joint development institution (which can be either a host state government or a joint authority) and foreign oil companies serving as contractors. From the perspective of ownership, these contracts are mainly divided into concession systems and contractual systems, which include types such as early and modern concessions, as well as production sharing contracts and service contracts. The special law applicable to the joint development of offshore oil and gas resources mainly involves matters such as fiscal and tax administration and the management of oil and gas exploration. The application of law to the joint development of transboundary offshore oil and gas resources is relatively straightforward: each state party generally applies its domestic law to the area within the joint development zone that falls on its side of the boundary line. In disputed maritime areas or areas of overlapping claims, the application of domestic law is more complex, with different arrangements such as the joint application of the domestic laws of both states parties, the separate application of the domestic laws of both states parties, the application of one state's domestic law to specific matters, and cases where the applicable domestic law is not explicitly stipulated.

The application of law to the joint development of offshore oil and gas resources is characterized by three main features: first, the international community has not established a uniform standard for the application of law in joint development; second, the law applicable to joint development is based on international law; and third, in practice, states generally tend to apply their own domestic laws. The application of law to the joint development of offshore oil and gas resources is subject to the following four main exceptions: first, where the joint development area is located entirely within a sea area under one state's exclusive jurisdiction and is subject to that one state's domestic law; second, where the application of law is directly linked to the ratio of resource allocation between the states party; third, where the domestic law of a single state is applied exclusively; and fourth, where the joint development area extends into a state's territorial sea. The factors influencing the application of law in the joint development of offshore oil and gas resources primarily include political will, economic considerations, cultural factors, management models, and the division of the joint development area.

The existing international practice in the application of law for the joint development of offshore oil and gas resources offers the following four lessons and points of reference for China's future application of law in joint development with its maritime neighbors. First, adhering to the principle of tackling easier issues before more difficult ones, starting with transboundary and bilateral joint development. Second, establishing a model for applicable law in maritime joint development that is conducive to safeguarding China's national interests. Third, recognizing the positive significance of pre-existing rights in disputed maritime areas or areas of overlapping claims. Fourth, paying attention to the influence of proximity on the application of law in the joint development of offshore oil and gas resources.

China has always actively advocated and adhered to the principle of "sovereignty belongs to China, shelving disputes and pursuing joint development," and has pursued attempts and explorations in the joint development of offshore oil and gas resources with neighboring countries such as North Korea, Japan, Vietnam, the Philippines, Malaysia, and Brunei. In the future, when China and its South China Sea neighbors, such as Vietnam, the Philippines, Malaysia, Brunei, and Indonesia, engage in the joint development of offshore oil and gas resources in potential cooperation zones, the application of law will generally involve several components. In addition to the bilateral joint development agreement for oil and gas resources, the respective domestic laws of each country in the areas under their jurisdiction, relevant exploration and development agreements signed by their oil companies, and any special laws, attention must also be paid to the handling of pre-existing rights and the special circumstances of individual national systems. The Chinese side can adopt a flexible attitude in handling the issue of applicable law, but the bottom line that must be upheld is that the designated block must be explicitly defined as an "area of overlapping claims" where a sovereignty dispute exists between the two parties, and the chosen model of cooperation must be "joint development" that reflects shared ownership and jurisdiction over the oil and gas resources.

II. Outlook

(I) Cultivating Political Will as an Urgent Priority

Political will is the decisive factor in the success or failure of joint development negotiations.[①] The research in this book finds that the greatest challenge to joint development between China and its neighboring countries currently stems from the political will of those neighbors.

Take the Philippines as an example. Although the Philippine side has repeatedly expressed its willingness in recent years to pursue joint development of offshore oil and gas resources with China, this has amounted to little more than lip service. The underlying reason is that the necessary political will in the Philippines has yet to coalesce. For the Philippines, such political will depends to a great extent on a foundation of domestic public support, or on the ability of its governing administration to shape public opinion. Ever since the ruling in the so-called "South China Sea Arbitration" was rendered, the overall climate of public opinion in the Philippines has been unfavorable to the joint development of offshore oil and gas resources with China. Even former President Duterte, who was relatively friendly toward China, could not, for the sake of cooperation, risk facing domestic accusations of "unconstitutionality" and the threat of impeachment.

American scholar Stacie E. Goddard argues that whether a territory constitutes an "indivisible part" of a country is not determined by the

① See Robert Beckman et al., eds., *Beyond Territorial Disputes in the South China Sea: Legal Framework for the Joint Development of Hydrocarbon Resources*, Edward Elgar Publishing Limited, 2013, pp. 309-310, 315-316.

of the Malaysia-Thailand Joint Authority.[7] Malaysia also remained deeply concerned that the Malaysia-Thailand Joint Authority could, in some sense, become a "government within a government."

Coastal states sign agreements for the joint development of offshore oil and gas resources primarily out of considerations for their national interests.[8] When coastal states undertake such development, it is neither to apply a new international legal regime in the joint development zone, nor to alter the rights they enjoy and the obligations they bear in the relevant maritime areas. Therefore, the joint development of offshore oil and gas resources is merely a legal method that is more suited to practical needs, one driven by economic interests rather than law, aimed at setting aside disputes to jointly develop oil and gas resources for economic gain. Consequently, from the perspective of the legal characteristics of joint development, establishing a simple, convenient, and efficient model is undoubtedly the best choice for coastal states. For this reason, the comprehensive application of the laws of the states parties has become the more pragmatic choice in reality. Taking into account the current legal and

---

⑦ See "The 1979 Joint Development Case Between Thailand and Malaysia in t he Gulf of Thailand," in Yang Zewei (ed.), *International Agreements on the Joi nt Development of Marine Resources* (Chinese-English Bilingual Version) (Vol. I), Social Sciences Academic Press (China), 2016, pp. 177-262; Wang Xiaomei, A Study on the Joint Development Case between Thailand and Malaysia, Mast er's thesis, Wuhan University, 2015.

⑧ See Vasco Becker-Weinberg, Theory and Practice of Joint Development in In ternational Law, in Gao Zhiguo et al., eds., *Cooperation and Development in th e South China Sea*, China Democracy and Legal System Publishing House, 201 3, p. 99.

political systems of China and its neighboring countries, I believe that if China is to pursue the joint development of offshore oil and gas resources with its neighbors in the future, the best choice would be to directly allocate the produced oil and gas in terms of benefit sharing, adopt a joint operation model for management, and maintain a flexible attitude toward the law applicable to daily petroleum operations.

As mentioned previously, there are two methods for benefit sharing in the joint development of offshore oil and gas resources: one is for the produced oil and gas to first be allocated between the states parties (acting directly or through a joint authority) and the oil companies according to the terms of their agreement, with the resulting state revenue then being distributed between the states parties; the other is for the produced oil and gas to be allocated directly between the states parties, after which each state party distributes its share with the oil companies in accordance with its own domestic laws. For the states parties, the legal rationale for the second method is clear (as the two parties distribute the developed resources based on their shared ownership of them), the method is simple (the output can be allocated at the wellhead as soon as the proportions are agreed upon), and each state party can then distribute its allotted share of the oil and gas production with the oil companies according to its own domestic fiscal and tax system. This resolves both the issues of fairness and balance in benefit sharing and the problem of applying separate laws for fiscal and tax

Bibliography

I. International Law Cases

(I) Judgments of the International Court of Justice

1. North Sea Continental Shelf Cases (Federal Republic of Germany/Denmark; Federal Republic of Germany/Netherlands), Judgment, I.C.J. Reports 1969.

2. Aegean Sea Continental Shelf, Judgment, I.C.J. Reports 1978.

3. Continental Shelf case (Tunisia/Libyan Arab Jamahiriya), Judgment, I.C.J. Reports 1982.

4. Delimitation of the Maritime Boundary in the Gulf of Maine Area, Judgment, I.C.J. Reports 1984.

5. Continental Shelf case (Libyan Arab Jamahiriya/Malta), Judgment, I.C.J. Reports 1985.

6. Maritime Delimitation in the Area between Greenland and Jan Mayen, Judgment, I.C.J. Reports 1993.

7. East Timor (Portugal v. Australia), Judgment, I.C.J. Reports 1995.

8. Maritime Delimitation and Territorial Questions between Qatar and Bahrain (Qatar v. Bahrain), Merits, Judgment, I.C.J. Reports 2001.

9. Land and Maritime Boundary between Cameroon and Nigeria (Cameroon v. Nigeria: Equatorial Guinea intervening), Judgment, I. C.J. Reports 2002.

10. Territorial and Maritime Dispute between Nicaragua and Ho nduras in the Caribbean Sea (Nicaragua v. Honduras), Judgment, I.C. J. Reports 2007.

11. Case Concerning Maritime Delimitation in the Black Sea (R omania v. Ukraine), Judgment, I.C.J. Reports 2009.

12. Territorial and Maritime Dispute (Nicaragua v. Colombia), J udgment, I.C.J. Reports 2012.

(II) Judgments of the International Tribunal for the Law of the Sea

Dispute concerning Delimitation of the Maritime Boundary betw een Bangladesh and Myanmar in the Bay of Bengal, Judgment of 1 4 March 2012, Case No. 16.

(III) International Arbitral Awards

1. Anglo-French Continental Shelf Arbitration, 1977-1978.

2. Arbitration between the United Kingdom of Great Britain an d Northern Ireland and the French Republic on the Delimitation of t he Continental Shelf, Decision of the Court of Arbitration dated 30

June 1977.

3. Case concerning the delimitation of the maritime boundary between Guinea and Guinea-Bissau, Arbitral Award of 14 February 1985.

4. The Eritrea-Yemen Arbitration, Award of the Arbitral Tribunal in the Second Stage of the Proceedings (Maritime Delimitation), 17 December 1999.

5. Arbitration between Barbados and the Republic of Trinidad and Tobago, Award of the Arbitral Tribunal, 11 April 2006.

6. Arbitration between Guyana and Suriname (Guyana/Suriname), Award of the Arbitral Tribunal, 17 September 2007.

7. Bay of Bengal Maritime Boundary Arbitration between Bangladesh and India (Bangladesh v. India), P.C.A. Award, 7 July 2014.

II. Cases of Joint Development of Offshore Oil and Gas Resources

(I) The 1958 Joint Development of the Persian Gulf Continental Shelf by Bahrain and Saudi Arabia

Bahrain-Saudi Arabia boundary agreement, 22 February 1958 (available at http://www.un.org/Depts/los/LEGISLATIONANDTREATIES/PDFFILES/TREATIES/BHR-SAU1958BA.PDF).

(II) The 1960 Joint Development Case between Czechoslovakia and Austria[①]

Agreement between the Government of the Czechoslovakia Republic and the Austrian Federal Government Concerning the Working of Common Deposits of Natural Gas and Petroleum, 23 January 1960, CZECHOSLOVAKIA-AUSTRIA, U.N.T.S. vol. 495, pp. 134-140 (available at https://treaties.un.org/doc/Publication/UNTS/Volume%20495/volume-495-I-7241-English.pdf).

(III) The 1962 Case of Joint Development of Resources in the Ems Estuary between the Netherlands and the Federal Republic of Germany

Supplementary Agreement to the Treaty Concerning Arrangements for Cooperation in the Ems Estuary (Ems-Dollard Treaty), Signed between the Kingdom of the Netherlands and the Federal Republic of Germany, the United Nations, Treaty Series, vol. 508, footnote 1, p. 20.

(IV) The 1965 Joint Development Case between Saudi Arabia and Kuwait

① The joint development implemented under the Agreement between the Czechoslovakia Republic and the Austrian Federal Government Concerning the Working of Common Deposits of Natural Gas and Petroleum of January 23, 1960, also became a case of joint development in this period. Although the agreement concerned the development of land-based resources, it set a precedent for addressing the development of transboundary offshore oil and gas resources.

1. Agreement between the Kingdom of Saudi Arabia and the State of Kuwait on the Partition of the Neutral Zone, 7 July 1965 (U.N. Treaty Series, Vol. 1750, I-30549).

2. Agreement between the Kingdom of Saudi Arabia and the State of Kuwait concerning the Submerged Area Adjacent to the Divided Zone, 2 July 2000 (available at http://www.un.org/Depts/los/LEGISLATIONANDTREATIES/PDFFILES/TREATIES/SAU-KWT2000SA.PDF).

(V) The 1967 Joint Development Case between Iran and Iraq

In January 1967, Iran and Iraq signed the Agreement on the Joint Development of the Khanaqin-Kana-Naft-i-Shah Oilfield.

(VI) The 1969 Joint Development Case between Qatar and Abu Dhabi

1. Agreement between Qatar and Abu Dhabi on the settlement of maritime boundary and ownership of islands, 20 March 1969 (available at http://www.un.org/Depts/los/LEGISLATIONANDTREATIES/PDFFILES/TREATIES/QAT-ARE1969MB.PDF).

2. Agreement on Settlement of Maritime Boundary Lines and Sovereignty Rights over Islands between Qatar and Abu Dhabi, 30 March 1969, ST/LEG/SER.B/16, p. 403.

3. Agreement between the Government of the State of Qatar an

d the Government of the United Arab Emirates Relating to the Transmission of Gas by Pipeline Between the State of Qatar and the United Arab Emirates, 26 September 2004 (available at http://www.almeezan.qa/AgreementsPage.aspx?id=1483&language=en).

(VII) The 1971 Joint Development Case between Iran and the United Arab Emirates

Memorandum of Understanding between Iran and Sharjah, November 1971 (Middle East Economic Survey, Vol. 15, No. 28, 1972, Supplement).

(VIII) The 1974 Delimitation and Joint Development Case between France and Spain

1. Convention between France and Spain on the Delimitation of the Territorial Sea and the Contiguous Zone in the Bay of Biscay, 29 January 1974 (available at http://www.un.org/Depts/los/LEGISLATIONANDTREATIES/PDFFILES/TREATIES/FRA-ESP1974VZ.PDF).

2. Convention between the Government of the French Republic and the Government of the Spanish State on the Delimitation of the Continental Shelves of the two States in the Bay of Biscay, 29 January 1974 (available at http://www.un.org/Depts/los/LEGISLATIONANDTREATIES/PDFFILES/TREATIES/FRA-ESP1974CS.PDF).

(IX) The 1974 Joint Development Case between Japan and South

Korea

Agreement between Japan and the Republic of Korea Concerning Joint Development of the Southern Part of the Continental Shelf Adjacent to the Two Countries, 30 January 1974 (available at http://cil.nus.edu.sg/rp/il/pdf/1974%20Agreement%20between%20Japan%20and%20Korea%20Concerning%20JD%20of%20the%20Southern%20Part%20of%20Continental%20Shelf-pdf.pdf).

(X) The 1974 Joint Development Case between Sudan and Saudi Arabia

Agreement between Sudan and Saudi Arabia relating to the Joint Exploitation of the Natural Resources of the Sea-Bed and Sub-soil of the Red Sea in the Common Zone, 16 May 1974 (ST/LEG/SER.B/18, pp. 452-455).

(XI) The 1975 Joint Development Case between Iran and Iraq

1. The Algiers Accord, 6 March 1975 (available at http://mideastweb.org/algiersaccord.htm).

2. Treaty concerning the Frontier and Neighbourly Relations between Iran and Iraq, 13 June 1975 (available at http://www.parstimes.com/history/iran_iraq_1975.html).

3. Agreement Between Iran and Iraq concerning the Use of Frontier Watercourses, 26 December 1975 (available at http://www.ucdp.

uu.se/gpdatabase/peace/Iran-Iraq%2019751226b.pdf).

(XII) The 1975 Joint Development Case between Rwanda and Zaire

On May 3, 1975, Rwanda and Zaire signed the Agreement between the Republic of Rwanda and the Republic of Zaire Concerning the Exploration, Development, and Commercialization of the Natural Gas of Lake Kivu.

(XIII) The 1976 Case of Joint Development of the Frigg Gas Field by the United Kingdom and Norway

1. Agreement between the Government of the United Kingdom of Great Britain and Northern Ireland and the Government of the Kingdom of Norway Relating to the Exploitation of the Frigg Field Reservoir and the Transmission of Gas therefrom to the United Kingdom, 10 May 1976 (Vol. 1098, I-16878).

2. Agreement Relating to the Exploitation of the Murchison Field Reservoir and the Offtake of Petroleum Therefrom, 16 October 1979.

3. Agreement Relating to the Exploitation of the Statfjord Field Reservoirs and the Offtake of Petroleum Therefrom, 16 October 1979.

(XIV) The 1979 Joint Development Case Between Thailand and

Malaysia in the Gulf of Thailand

1. Memorandum of Understanding between Malaysia and the Kingdom of Thailand on the Establishment of the Joint Authority for the Exploitation of the Resources of the Sea Bed in a Defined Area of the Continental Shelf of the Two Countries in the Gulf of Thailand, 21 February 1979 (available at http://cil.nus.edu.sg/rp/il/pdf/1979%20MOU%20between%20Malaysia%20and%20Thailand-pdf.pdf).

2. 1990 Agreement between Thailand and Malaysia on the Constitution and Other Matters Relating to the Joint Authority, 30 May 1990 (available at http://cil.nus.edu.sg/rp/il/pdf/1990%20Agreement%20between%20Malaysia%20and%20Thailand%20on%20the%20MTJA-pdf.pdf).

3. Malaysia-Thailand Joint Authority (Standards of Petroleum Operations) Regulations 1997 (available at http://www.mtja.org/GIF/rules/regulations.pdf).

4. Malaysia-Thailand Joint Authority Procedures for Drilling Operations 2009 (available at http://www.mtja.org/pdf/rules/MTJA_procedures_for_drilling_operations_rev1_14dec09_bw.pdf).

5. Malaysia-Thailand Joint Authority Procedures for Production Operations 2009 (available at http://www.mtja.org/pdf/rules/MTJA_procedures_for_production_operations_rev1_14dec09_bw.pdf).

(XV) The 1981 Joint Development Case in the Gulf of Maine between the United States and Canada

1. Treaty to Submit to Binding Dispute Settlement the Delimitation of the Maritime Boundary in the Gulf of Maine Area, 29 March 1979 (available at http://www.un.org/Depts/los/LEGISLATIONANDTREATIES/PDFFILES/TREATIES/CAN-USA1979GM.PDF).

2. Delimitation of the Maritime Boundary in the Gulf of Maine Area, Judgment, I.C.J. Reports 1984 (available at http://www.icj-cij.org/docket/files/67/6369.pdf).

(XVI) The 1981 Joint Development Case Between Iceland and Norway concerning Jan Mayen

1. Agreement on the Continental Shelf between Iceland and Jan Mayen, 22 October 1981 (available at http://www.un.org/Depts/los/LEGISLATIONANDTREATIES/PDFFILES/TREATIES/ISL-NOR1981CS.PDF).

2. Maritime Delimitation in the Area between Greenland and Jan Mayen, Judgment, I.C.J. Reports 1993 (available at http://www.icj-cij.org/docket/files/78/6743.pdf).

(XVII) The 1988 Joint Development Case between Tunisia and Libya

1. In August 1988, Tunisia and Libya signed the Agreement on

the Delimitation of the Continental Shelf and Joint Development be tween Libya and Tunisia.

2. Continental Shelf (Tunisia/Libyan Arab Jamahiriya), Judgment, I.C.J. Reports 1982 (available at http://www.icj-cij.org/docket/files/63 /6267.pdf).

(XVIII) The 1989 Joint Development Case between Australia an d Indonesia

Treaty between Australia and the Republic of Indonesia on the Zone of Cooperation in an Area between the Indonesian Province of East Timor and Northern Australia, 11 December 1989 (available at http://www.austlii.edu.au/au/other/dfat/treaties/1991/9.html).

(XIX) The 1988 Joint Development Case between the Yemen A rab Republic and the People's Democratic Republic of Yemen

On November 19, 1988, the Yemen Arab Republic and the Peo ple's Democratic Republic of Yemen signed the Aden Agreement bet ween the Yemen Arab Republic and the People's Democratic Republ ic of Yemen.

(XX) The 1992 Joint Development Case between Malaysia and Vietnam

Memorandum of Understanding between Malaysia and the Socia list Republic of Vietnam for the Exploration and Exploitation of Pet roleum in A Defined Area of the Continental Shelf Involving the Two Countries, 5 June 1992 (available at http://cil.nus.edu.sg/rp/il/pdf/1992%20MOU%20between%20Malaysia%20and%20Vietnam%20for%20the%20Exploration%20and%20Exploitation%20of%20Petroleum-pdf.pdf).

(XXI) The 1993 Joint Development Case between Guinea-Bissau and Senegal

Agreement on Management and Cooperation between the Republic of Guinea-Bissau and the Republic of Senegal, 14 October 1993 (available at http://www.un.org/Depts/los/LEGISLATIONANDTREATIES/PDFFILES/TREATIES/SEN-GNB1993MC.PDF).

(XXII) The 1993 Joint Development Case between Jamaica and Colombia

Maritime Delimitation Treaty between Jamaica and the Republic of Colombia, 12 November 1993 (available at http://www.un.org/depts/los/LEGISLATIONANDTREATIES/PDFFILES/TREATIES/JAM-COL1993MD.PDF).

(XXIII) The 1995 Joint Development Case between the United Kingdom and Argentina

1. Joint Statement of 15 February 1990 Re-establishing Diplomatic Relations between Britain and Argentina (available at http://www.

fiassociation.com/shopimages/pdfs/5.%201990%20Joint%20British-Argentine%20Statement%20on%20the%20Reestablishment%20of%20Diplomatic%20Relations.pdf).

2. UK-Argentina Joint Statement on the Conservation of Fisheries (David Freestone, UK/Argentina Co-operation on Fisheries Conservation, *International Journal of Estuarine and Coastal Law*, Vol. 145, No. 6, 1991, pp. 146-148).

3. Joint Declaration of 27 September 1995 on Cooperation Over Offshore Activities in the South West Atlantic (available at http://www.fiassociation.com/shopimages/pdfs/7.%201995%20Joint%20Declaration%20on%20Cooperation%20Over%20Offshore%20Activities%20in%20the%20South%20West%20Atlantic..pdf; T. W. Wälde & Andrew Mc Hardy, Argentina-United Kingdom: Joint Declaration on Cooperation over Offshore Activities in the Southwest Atlantic, International Legal Materials, Vol. 35, No. 2, 1996, p. 302).

4. Declaration of the British Government with regard to the Joint Declaration signed by the British and Argentine Foreign Ministers on Cooperation over Offshore Activities in the South West Atlantic (available at http://www.fiassociation.com/shopimages/pdfs/7.%201995%20Joint%20Declaration%20on%20Cooperation%20Over%20Offshore%20Activities%20in%20the%20South%20West%20Atlantic..pdf).

5. Statement by the Argentine Government with regard to the J

oint Declaration signed by the Foreign Ministers of Argentina and the United Kingdom on Exploration and Exploitation of Hydrocarbons (available at http://www.fiassociation.com/shopimages/pdfs/7.%201995%20Joint%20Declaration%20on%20Cooperation%20Over%20Offshore%20Activities%20in%20the%20South%20West%20Atlantic..pdf).

(XXIV) The 2000 Joint Development Case between China and Vietnam in the Beibu Gulf

1. On December 25, 2000, China and Vietnam signed the Agreement between the People's Republic of China and the Socialist Republic of Vietnam on the Delimitation of the Territorial Seas, Exclusive Economic Zones and Continental Shelves of the Two Countries in the Beibu Gulf (available at http://www.npc.gov.cn/wxzl/gongbao/2004-08/04/content_5332197.htm).

2. On December 25, 2000, China and Vietnam signed the Agreement between the Government of the People's Republic of China and the Government of the Socialist Republic of Vietnam on Fishery Cooperation in Beibu Gulf.

(XXV) The 2001 Joint Development Case between Nigeria and São Tomé and Príncipe

Treaty between The Federal Republic of Nigeria and The Democratic Republic of São Tomé e Príncipe on the Joint Development o f Petroleum and other Resources, in respect of Areas of the Exclusive Economic Zone of the Two States, 21 February 2001 (available at http://www.un.org/Depts/los/LEGISLATIONANDTREATIES/PDFFILES/TREATIES/STP-NGA2001.PDF).

(XXVI) The 2001 Joint Development Case between Thailand and Cambodia

1. Memorandum of Understanding between the Royal Thai Government and the Royal Government of Cambodia regarding the Area of their Overlapping Maritime Claims to the Continental Shelf, 18 June 2001.

2. Termination of the Memorandum of Understanding between the Royal Thai Government and the Royal Government of Cambodia regarding the Area of their Overlapping Maritime Claims to the Continental Shelf (available at http://www.ryt9.com/es/mfa/88839).

(XXVII) The 2002 Joint Development Case between East Timor and Australia

1. Timor Sea Treaty between the Government of East Timor and the Government of Australia, 20 May 2002, Australian Treaty Series 2003 No. 13 (available at http://www.un.org/Depts/los/LEGISLATIONANDTREATIES/PDFFILES/TREATIES/AUS-TLS2002TST.PDF).

2. Exchange of Notes Constituting an Agreement between the G

overnment of Australia and the Government of the Democratic Repu blic of Timor-Leste concerning Arrangements for Exploration and Ex ploitation of Petroleum in an Area of the Timor Sea between Austra lia and East Timor, 20 May 2002 (available at http://www.un.org/De pts/los/LEGISLATIONANDTREATIES/PDFFILES/TREATIES/AUS-TL S2002EX.PDF).

3. Petroleum Mining Code for the Joint Petroleum Development Area (available at http://www.anp-tl.org/webs/anptlweb.nsf/vwAll/Res ource-Petroleum%20Mining%20Code/$File/PMCtoCoM0602.pdf?openel ement).

4. Product Sharing Contract for the Joint Petroleum Developmen t Area (available at http://www.laohamutuk.org/Oil/PetRegime/JPDA% 20PSC%208-05.pdf).

5. Memorandum of Understanding between the Government of t he Democratic Republic of East Timor and the Government of Austr alia concerning an International Unitization Agreement for the Greate r Sunrise field, 20 May 2002.

6. Agreement between the Government of Australia and The Go vernment of the Democratic Republic of Timor-Leste relating to the Unitisation of the Sunrise and Troubadour Fields, 6 March 2003, Au stralian Treaty Series 2007, No. 11 (available at http://www.un.org/D epts/los/LEGISLATIONANDTREATIES/PDFFILES/TREATIES/AUS-T

LS2002SUN.PDF).

7. Treaty between Australia and the Democratic Republic of Ti mor-Leste on Certain Maritime Arrangements in the Timor Sea, 12 J anuary 2006 (Australian Treaty Series 2007, No. 12).

(XXVIII) The 2002 Joint Development Case between the Repub lic of the Congo and Angola

On November 27, 2002, the Republic of the Congo and Angola signed the Agreement on the Development of Oil Fields in the Ma ritime Border Zone.

(XXIX) The 2003 Joint Development Case between Barbados a nd Guyana

Exclusive Economic Zone Cooperation Treaty between the Repu blic of Guyana and the State of Barbados Concerning the Exercise of Jurisdiction in Their Exclusive Economic Zones in the Area of B ilateral Overlap Within Each of Their Outer Limits and Beyond the Outer Limits of the Exclusive Economic Zones of Outer States, 2 D ecember 2003 (The Law of the Sea Bulletins, No. 55, p. 36).

(XXX) The 2005 Joint Development Case between China and North Korea

On December 24, 2005, China and North Korea signed the Agr eement between the Governments of China and North Korea on the

Joint Offshore Development of Petroleum.

(XXXI) The 2006 Joint Development Case between Micronesia and the Marshall Islands

Treaty between the Federated States of Micronesia and the Republic of the Marshall Islands concerning Maritime Boundaries and Cooperation on Related Matters, 5 July 2006 (Federated States of Micronesia - the Republic of the Marshall Islands, U.N.T.S. Registration No. I-54649, pp. 1-6, available at https://treaties.un.org/doc/Publication/UNTS/No%20Volume/54649/Part/I-54649-08000002804c6ee9.pdf).

(XXXII) The 2006 Joint Development Case between Micronesia and Palau

Treaty between the Federated States of Micronesia and the Republic of Palau concerning Maritime Boundaries and Cooperation on Related Matters (available at http://www.un.org/Depts/los/LEGISLATIONANDTREATIES/PDFFILES/FSM-PALAU.pdf).

(XXXIII) The 2007 Joint Development Case between Trinidad and Tobago and the Bolivarian Republic of Venezuela

Framework Treaty Relating to the Unitisation of Hydrocarbon Reservoirs That Extend Across the Delimitation Line between the Republic of Trinidad and Tobago and the Bolivarian Republic of Venezuela, 20 March 2007 (Republic of Trinidad and Tobago - the Bolivari an Republic of Venezuela, U.N.T.S. Vol. 2876, pp. 1-24, available at https://treaties.un.org/doc/Publication/UNTS/No%20Volume/50196/Part/I-50196-08000002802bb3a7.pdf).

(XXXIV) The 2008 Joint Development Case between China and Japan

On June 18, 2008, China and Japan reached the Principled Consensus on the East China Sea Issue (available at http://www.gov.cn/jrzg/2008-06/18/content_1020543.htm).

(XXXV) The 2009 Joint Development Case between Malaysia and Brunei

The Exchange of Letters between Malaysia and Brunei, 16 March 2009 (available at http://www.thestar.com.my/story/?file=%2f2010%2f5%2f3%2fnation%2f20100503123605&sec=nation).

(XXXVI) The 2010 Joint Development Case between Russia and Norway

Treaty between the Kingdom of Norway and the Russian Federation concerning Maritime Delimitation and Cooperation in the Barents Sea and the Arctic Ocean, 15 September 2010 (available at http://www.un.org/Depts/los/LEGISLATIONANDTREATIES/PDFFILES/TREATIES/NOR-RUS2010.PDF).

(XXXVII) The 2012 Joint Development Case between the Unite

d States and Mexico

1. Treaty between the Government of the United States of America and the Government of the United Mexican States on the Delimitation of the Continental Shelf in the Western Gulf of Mexico beyond 200 Nautical Miles, 9 June 2000 (available at http://www.un.org/Depts/los/LEGISLATIONANDTREATIES/PDFFILES/TREATIES/USA-MEX2000CS.PDF).

2. Agreement between the United States of America and the United Mexican States Concerning Transboundary Hydrocarbon Reservoirs in the Gulf of Mexico, 20 February 2012 (available at http://www.state.gov/documents/organization/185467.pdf).

(XXXVIII) The 2012 Joint Development Case between Seychelles and Mauritius

1. Treaty Concerning the Joint Management of the Continental Shelf in the Mascarene Plateau Region, 13 March 2012.

2. Treaty Concerning the Joint Exercise of Sovereign Rights over the Continental Shelf in the Mascarene Plateau Region, 13 March 2012.

III. Books in English

1. Kamal Hossain, Law and Policy in Petroleum Development: Changing Relations between Transnationals and Governments, France

s Pinter Ltd, 1979.

2. Mark J. Valencia, The South China Sea: Hydrocarbon Potenti al and Possible Joint Development, Pergamon Press, 1981.

3. Raymond F. Mikesell, Petroleum Company Operations and A greements in the Developing Countries, Washington, D.C., 1984.

4. Keith W. Blinn, Claude Duval, International Petroleum Explo ration and Exploitation Agreements: Legal, Economic and Policy As pects, Euromoney Publications, 1986.

5. Hazel Fox, et al., ed., Joint Development of Offshore Oil an d Gas: A Model Agreement for States for Joint Development with Explanatory Commentary, British Institute of International and Comp arative Law, 1989.

6. Hazel Fox, ed., Joint Development of Offshore Oil and Gas, Vol. II, British Institute of International and Comparative Law, 199 0.

7. J. F. O'Connor, Good Faith in International Law, Dartmouth: Dartmouth Publishing Company Limited, 1991.

8. Nico Schrijver, Sovereignty over Natural Resources: Balancin g Rights and Duties, Cambridge University Press, 1997.

9. Mark J. Valencia, Jon M. Van Dyke, Noel A. Ludwig, Shari

ng the Resources of the South China Sea, Martinus Nijhoff Publishers, 1997.

10. R. R. Churchill, A. V. Lowe, The Law of the Sea, Juris Publishing, 1999.

11. Selig S. Harrison, Seabed Petroleum in Northeast Asia: Conflict or Cooperation?, Woodrow Wilson International Center for Scholars, Asia Program, 2005.

12. Victor Prescott, Clive Schofield, The Maritime Political Boundaries of the World, 2nd Edition, Martinus Nijhoff Publishers, 2005.

13. Zou Keyuan, Law of the Sea in East Asia, Routledge, 2005.

14. Sam Bateman, Ralf Emmers, Security and International Politics in the South China Sea: Towards a Cooperative Management Regime, Routledge, 2009.

15. Stacie E. Goddard, Indivisible Territory and the Politics of Legitimacy: Jerusalem and Northern Ireland, Cambridge University Press, 2009.

16. Terence Daintith, Finders Keepers? How the Law of Capture Shaped the World Oil Industry, Routledge, 2010.

17. Robert Beckman et al., eds., Beyond Territorial Disputes in

the South China Sea: Legal Frameworks for the Joint Development of Hydrocarbon Resources, Edward Elgar Publishing Limited, 2013.

18. Stefan Talmon and Bing Bing Jia, eds., The South China Sea Arbitration: A Chinese Perspective, Hart Publishing, 2014.

19. Vasco Becker-Weinberg, Joint Development of Hydrocarbon Deposits in the Law of the Sea, Springer-Verlag Berlin Heidelberg, 2014.

20. Tran Truong Thuy and Le Thuy Trang, eds., Power, Law, and Maritime Order in the South China Sea, Lexington Books, 2015.

21. David Jay Green, The Third Option for the South China Sea: The Political Economy of Regional Conflict and Cooperation, Palgrave Macmillan, 2016.

22. William E. Hughes, Fundamentals of International Oil and Gas Law, PennWell Corporation, 2016.

23. Gerald Blake, ed., Maritime Boundaries and Ocean Resources, Routledge, 2018.

24. Alexander Orakhelashvili, Akehurst's Modern Introduction to International Law, 8th edition, Routledge, 2019.

25. James Crawford, Brownlie's Principles of Public International Law, 9th edition, Oxford University Press, 2019.

26. Malcolm N. Shaw, International Law, 9th edition, Cambridg e University Press, 2021.

IV. Papers in English

1. Joseph W. Morris, The North Sea Continental Shelf: Oil and Gas Legal Problems, International Lawyer, Vol. 2, 1967.

2. William T. Onorato, Apportionment of an International Petrol eum Deposit, International and Comparative Law Quarterly, Vol. 17, 1968.

3. William T. Onorato, Apportion of an International Common Petroleum Deposit, International and Comparative Law Quarterly, Vo l. 26, No. 2, 1977.

4. J. C. Woodliffe, International Unitisation of an Offshore Gas Field, International and Comparative Law Quarterly, Vol. 26, No. 2, 1977.

5. Rainer Lagoni, Interim Measures Pending Maritime Delimitati on Agreements, American Journal of International Law, Vol. 78, No. 2, 1984.

6. Joseph P. Tomain, The Rule of Capture: Government and the Oil Industry, Journal of Energy Law and Policy, Vol. 5, 1984.

7. Alberto Székely, Transboundary Resources: A View from Me

xico, Natural Resources Journal, Vol. 26, No. 4, Fall 1986.

8. Mark J. Valencia and Masahiro Miyoshi, Southeast Asian Sea s: Joint Development of Hydrocarbons in Overlapping Claim Areas? Ocean Development and International Law, Vol. 16, No. 3, 1986.

9. Mark J. Valencia, Taming Troubled Waters: Joint Developme nt of Oil and Mineral Resources in Overlapping Claim Areas, San Diego Law Review, Vol. 23, No. 3, 1986.

10. Ian Townsend Gault, Joint Development of Offshore Mineral Resources — Progress and Prospects for the Future, Natural Resour ces Forum, Vol. 12, No. 3, 1988.

11. Masahiro Miyoshi, The Basic Concept of Joint Development of Hydrocarbon Resources on the Continental Shelf: With Special Reference to the Discussions at the East-West Centre Workshops on the South-East Asian Seas, International Journal of Estuarine and Co astal Law, Vol. 3, No. 1, 1988.

12. Ernst Willheim, Australia-Indonesia Sea-Bed Boundary Nego tiations: Proposals for a Joint Development Zone in the Timor Gap, Natural Resources Journal, Vol. 29, No. 3, 1989.

13. Mochtar Kusuma-Atmadja, Indonesia's National Policy on O ffshore Mineral Resources: Some Legal Issues, Ocean Yearbook, Vol. 9, 1991.

14. Peter B. Payoyo, Legal Framework for the Development and Management of Non-Living Marine Resources: Philippine Concerns, Philippine Law Journal, Vol. 66, No. 2, 1991.

15. Yu Hui, Joint Development of Mineral Resources — An Asian Solution, Asian Yearbook of International Law, Vol. 2, 1992.

16. Gao Zhiguo, Legal Concept and Aspects of Joint Development in International Law, Ocean Yearbook, Vol. 13, 1998.

17. Nguyen Hong Thao, Vietnam and Joint Development in the Gulf of Thailand, Asian Yearbook of International Law, Vol. 8, 1998.

18. David M. Ong, Joint Development of Common Offshore Oil and Gas Deposits: 'Mere' State Practice or Customary International Law? American Journal of International Law, Vol. 93, No. 4, 1999.

19. David M. Ong, The 1979 and 1990 Malaysia-Thailand Joint Development Agreements: A Model for International Legal Cooperation in Common Offshore Petroleum Deposits, International Journal of Marine and Coastal Law, Vol. 114, No. 2, 1999.

20. David M. Ong, The New Timor Sea Arrangement 2001: Is Joint Development of Common Offshore Oil and Gas Deposits Mandated under International Law? International Journal of Marine and Coastal Law, Vol. 17, No. 1, 2002.

21. John Holmes, End the Moratorium: The Timor Gap Treaty as a Model for the Complete Resolution of the Western Gap in the Gulf of Mexico, Vanderbilt Journal of Transnational Law, Vol. 35, No. 3, 2002.

22. Jason S. Johnston, The Rule of Capture and the Economic Dynamics of Natural Resource Use and Survival under Open Access Management Regimes, Environmental Law, Vol. 35, 2005.

23. Bruce M. Kramer and Owen L. Anderson, The Rule of Capture — An Oil and Gas Perspective, Environmental Law, Vol. 35, 2005.

24. Yucel Acer, A Proposal for a Joint Maritime Development Regime in the Aegean Sea, Journal of Maritime Law and Commerce, Vol. 37, No. 1, 2006.

25. Christopher C. Joyner and Kelly Zack Walters, The Caspian Conundrum: Reflections on the Interplay between Law, the Environment and Geopolitics, International Journal of Marine and Coastal Law, Vol. 21, No. 2, 2006.

26. Chidinma Bernadine Okafor, Joint Development: An Alternative Legal Approach to Oil and Gas Exploitation in the Nigeria-Cameroon Maritime Boundary Dispute, International Journal of Marine and Coastal Law, Vol. 21, No. 4, 2006.

27. Chidinma Bernadine Okafor, Model Agreements for Joint D evelopment: A Case Study, Journal of Energy & Natural Resources Law, Vol. 25, No. 1, 2007.

28. Leszek Buszynski and Iskandar Sazlan, Maritime Claims an d Energy Cooperation in the South China Sea, Contemporary Southe ast Asia, Vol. 29, 2007.

29. Mark J. Valencia, The East China Sea Dispute: Context, Cl aims, Issues, and Possible Solutions, Asian Perspective, Vol. 31, No. 1, 2007.

30. Dominic Roughton, Rights (and Wrongs) of Capture: Interna tional Law and the Implications of the Guyana/Suriname Arbitration, Journal of Energy & Natural Resources Law, Vol. 26, No. 3, 2008.

31. Luis E. Rodriguez-Rivera, Joint Development Zones and Ot her Cooperative Management Efforts Related to Transboundary Marit ime Resources: A Caribbean and Latin American Model for Peaceful Resolution of Maritime Boundary Disputes, in Symposium: Frontier Issues in Ocean Law: Marine Resources, Maritime Boundaries, and t he Law of the Sea, 2008.

32. Luis E. Rodriguez-Rivera, Joint Development Zones and Ot her Cooperative Management Efforts Related to Transboundary Marit ime Resources: A Caribbean and Latin American Model for Peaceful

Resolution of Maritime Boundary Disputes, Issues in Legal Scholar ship, Vol. 7, No. 1, 2008.

33. Gao Jianjun, A Note on the 2008 Cooperation Consensus B etween China and Japan in the East China Sea, Ocean Development and International Law, Vol. 40, No. 3, 2009.

34. Cecilia A. Low, The Rule of Capture: Its Current Status an d Some Issues to Consider, Alberta Law Review, Vol. 46, No. 3, 20 09.

35. Masahiro Miyoshi, The North Sea Continental Shelf Cases Revisited: Implications for the Boundaries in the Northeast Asian Se as, Asian Yearbook of International Law, Vol. 15, 2009.

36. Lowell B. Bautista, The Legal Status of the Philippine Trea ty Limits in International Law, Aegean Review of the Law of the S ea and Maritime Law, No. 1, 2010.

37. Karla Urdaneta, Transboundary Petroleum Reservoirs: A Rec ommended Approach for the United States and Mexico in the Deep waters of the Gulf of Mexico, Houston Journal of International Law, Vol. 32, No. 2, 2010.

38. Chijioke S. Ugwuanyi, Does the Use of Joint Development Agreements Bar International Maritime Boundaries Delimitation? Dub lin Legal Review Quarterly, No. 1, 2011.

39. Jorge A. Vargas, The 2012 U.S.-Mexico Agreement on Transboundary Hydrocarbon Reservoirs in the Gulf of Mexico: A Blueprint for Progress or a Recipe for Conflict, San Diego International Law Journal, Vol. 14, No. 1, 2012.

40. Jose Luis Herrera Vaca, The New Legal Framework for Oil and Gas Activities near the Maritime Boundaries between Mexico and the U.S.: Comments on the Agreement between the United Mexican States and the United States of America Concerning Transboundary Hydrocarbon Reservoirs in the Gulf of Mexico, Journal of World Energy Law and Business, Vol. 5, No. 3, 2012.

41. Robert Beckman, The UN Convention on the Law of the Sea and the Maritime Disputes in the South China Sea, American Journal of International Law, Vol. 107, 2013.

42. Shih-Ming Kao, Nathaniel S. Pearre, Potential Alternatives to the Disputes in the South China Sea: An Analysis, China Oceans Law Review, Vol. 2013, No. 17, 2013.

43. Timothy H. Baker, Aloise Bozell Vasant, United States and Mexico Open Offshore Transboundary Hydrocarbon Reservoirs to Development, Natural Resources & Environment, Vol. 29, No. 1, 2014.

44. Nigel Bankes, Recent Framework Agreements for the Recognition and Development of Transboundary Hydrocarbon Resources, I

nternational Journal of Marine and Coastal Law, Vol. 29, No. 4, 2014.

45. Melissa H. Loja, Is the Rule of Capture Countenanced in the South China Sea? The Policy and Practice of China, the Philippines and Vietnam, Journal of Energy & Natural Resources Law, Vol. 32, No. 4, 2014.

46. N. Elias Blood-Patterson, Smoke on the Water: The Role of International Agreements in the Philippine-Chinese Dispute over the South China Sea, New York University Journal of International Law and Politics, Vol. 46, No. 4, 2014.

47. Youri van Logchem, Exploration and Exploitation of Oil and Gas Resources in Maritime Areas of Overlap under International Law: The Falklands (Malvinas), Hague Yearbook of International Law, Vol. 28, 2015.

48. Guillermo J. Garcia Sanchez, Richard J. McLaughlin, The 2012 Agreement on the Exploitation of Transboundary Hydrocarbon Resources in the Gulf of Mexico: Confirmation of the Rule or Emergence of a New Practice, Houston Journal of International Law, Vol. 37, No. 3, 2015.

49. Constantinos Yiallourides, Oil and Gas Development in Disputed Waters under UNCLOS, UCL Journal of Law and Jurisprudenc

e, Vol. 5, No. 1, 2016.

50. Danae Azaria, The Scope and Content of Sovereign Rights in Relation to Non-Living Resources in the Continental Shelf and the Exclusive Economic Zone, Journal of Territorial and Maritime Studies, Vol. 3, No. 2, 2016.

51. Guo Ran, Sino-Vietnam Dispute over Hydrocarbon Resources Exploration in Nansha Waters after the South China Sea Arbitration, Hong Kong Law Journal, Vol. 47, No. 3, 2017.

52. Youri van Logchem, The Status of a Rule of Capture Under International Law of the Sea with regard to Offshore Oil and Gas Resource Related Activities, Michigan State International Law Review, Vol. 26, No. 2, 2018.

53. Constantinos Yiallourides, Joint Development of Seabed Resources in Areas of Overlapping Maritime Claims: An Analysis of Precedents in State Practice, University of San Francisco Maritime Law Journal, Vol. 31, No. 2, 2018.

54. Anita L. Parlow, Toward Distributive Justice in Offshore Natural Resources Development: Iceland and Norway in the Jan Mayen, Ocean and Coastal Law Journal, Vol. 23, No. 1, 2018.

55. Andrew Belack, A Big Fracking Deal: Pennsylvania's Departure from Traditional Rule of Capture Interpretation Paves Way for

Fracking Trespass Claims, Washington Journal of Environmental Law & Policy, Vol. 10, Issue 1, 2020.

56. Guillermo J. Garcia Sanchez, The Footprint of the Chinese Petro-Dragon: The Future of Investment Law in Transboundary Reso urces, Tulane Law Review, Vol. 94, No. 2, 2020.

57. Helmut Tuerk, Questions Relating to the Continental Shelf beyond 200 Nautical Miles: Delimitation, Delineation, and Revenue Sharing, International Law Studies Series, US Naval War College, V ol. 97, 2021.

V. Books in Chinese

1. Zhou Zhonghai, *International Law of the Sea*, China Universi ty of Political Science and Law Press, 1987.

2. Li Haopei, *Concepts and Sources of International Law*, Guiz hou People's Publishing House, 1994.

3. Cai Penghong, *Management Models for Joint Development in Disputed Maritime Areas: A Comparative Study*, Shanghai Academy of Social Sciences Press, 1998.

4. Yu Mincai, *Legal Issues in Marine Petroleum Exploration an d Development,* China Renmin University Press, 2001.

5. China Petroleum and Petrochemical Engineering Institute (ed.),

A Primer on Contemporary Technology in the Petroleum and Petrochemical Industries: Exploration (Second Edition), China Petrochemical Press, 2005.

6. Fu Kuncheng (ed.), *Relevant Conventions on the Law of the Sea and Chinese-English Index*, Xiamen University Press, 2005.

7. Zhang Haiwen (ed.), *Collected Interpretations of the United Nations Convention on the Law of the Sea*, China Ocean Press, 2006.

8. Zhang Liangfu, *China's Maritime Delimitation Disputes with its Neighbors*, China Ocean Press, 2006.

9. Xiao Jianguo, *Joint Development of Petroleum on International Maritime Boundaries*, China Ocean Press, 2006.

10. Gao Zhiguo, Jia Yu, and Zhang Haiwen (eds.), *Theory and Practice of International Law of the Sea*, China Ocean Press, 2006.

11. Gao Zhiguo, Zhang Haiwen, and Jia Yu (eds.). *Research on the Developing Trends of International Law of the Sea*, China Ocean Press, 2007.

12. Gao Zhiguo and Zhang Haiwen (eds.), *Collected Essays on the Study of National Maritime Policy*, China Ocean Press, 2007.

13. Wang Nianping, *A Comparative Study of International Petro*

leum Contract Models—With a Discussion on Their Implications for China's Petroleum and Energy Legal System, Law Press China, 2009.

14. Zhang Haiwen and Li Yunhong (eds.), *A Compilation of Maritime Legislation of Countries Worldwide: Volume on African, Latin American, and Caribbean Countries*, Law Press China, 2012.

15. Zhang Haiwen and Li Yunhong (eds.), *A Compilation of Maritime Legislation of Countries Worldwide: Volume on Asian and Oceanian Countries*, Law Press China, 2012.

16. Zhang Haiwen, *The South China Sea and Its Islands*, China Intercontinental Press, 2014.

17. Yang Zewei (ed.), *Research on International Law Issues of Joint Maritime Development*, Social Sciences Academic Press (China), 2016.

18. Yang Zewei (ed.), *International Agreements on the Joint Development of Marine Resources* (Chinese-English Bilingual Version), Social Sciences Academic Press (China), 2016.

19. Yang Zewei (ed.), *A Sequel to International Agreements on the Joint Development of Marine Resources*, Wuhan University Press, 2018.

20. Yang Zewei (ed.), *A Study on the Theory and Practice of International Law on Joint Maritime Development*, Wuhan University

Press, 2018.

21. Yang Zewei (ed.), *A Study on the Evaluation and Implementation of Certain Regimes of the United Nations Convention on the Law of the Sea*, Wuhan University Press, 2018.

22. Deng Niya, *A Study on the Legal Issues of Management Models for Joint Maritime Development*, Wuhan University Press, 2019.

23. Dong Shijie, *A Study on the Legal Issues of Existing Petroleum Contracts in Disputed Maritime Areas*, Wuhan University Press, 2019.

24. Sun Chuanxiang, *A Study on International Law Issues of the Sino-Japanese Continental Shelf Delimitation in the East China Sea*, Wuhan University Press, 2019.

25. He Hairong, *A Study on the Legal Issues of Joint Maritime Development in the Gulf of Thailand*, Wuhan University Press, 2020.

26. Liu Liang, *A Study on the Nature of the Recommendations of the Commission on the Limits of the Continental Shelf*, Wuhan University Press, 2020.

27. Yang Zewei, *International Law* (4th ed.), Higher Education Press, 2022.

21. Yang Zewei, On the Developing Trends of Joint Maritime Development, *Oriental Law*, No. 3, 2014.

22. Li Guoqiang, Policy Adjustment for the Exploration and De velopment of Oil and Gas Resources in the South China Sea, *Intern ational Studies*, No. 6, 2014.

23. Yang Zewei, On the Issue of Applicable Law in Joint Mari time Development Zones, *Journal of Guangxi University (Philosophy and Social Sciences)*, No. 4, 2015.

24. Dong Shijie, Application of Law in Joint Maritime Develop ment, *Wuhan University International Law Review*, No. 2, 2015.

25. Dong Shijie, A Study on the Unilateral Exploitation of Oil and Gas Resources in Disputed Maritime Areas, *Northeast Asia For um*, No. 5, 2015.

26. Liu Caiyong, The Development Status, Problems, and New Trends of Vietnam's Oil and Gas Industry, *Southeast Asian Affairs*, No. 1, 2015.

27. Xie Xiaojun, Zhang Gongcheng et al, Geological Conditions, Distribution Characteristics, and Favorable Exploration Directions fo r Oil and Gas in the Zengmu Basin, *China Offshore Oil and Gas*, No. 1, 2015.

28. Yan Shuangwu, Li Guoxuan, American Transnational Oil Co

mpanies in the South China Sea Issue, *Pacific Journal*, No. 3, 2015.

29. Deng Niya, On the Critical Date and Its Application to the Sovereignty Dispute over the Nansha Islands and Reefs, *Journal of Guangxi University* (Social Sciences Edition), No. 4, 2015.

30. Li Jinming, An Analysis of the Prospects for Joint Develop ment of Oil and Gas Resources in the Reed Bank between China a nd the Philippines, *Pacific Journal*, No. 5, 2015.

31. Yang Zewei, On the Impact of the Construction of the 21st Century Maritime Silk Road on the Resolution of the South China Sea Dispute, *Journal of Boundary and Ocean Studies*, No. 1, 2016.

32. Dong Shijie, On the Application of Law in Potential Joint Development Zones in the South China Sea, *Journal of Guangxi Un iversity (Philosophy and Social Sciences)*, No. 2, 2016.

33. Sun Chuanxiang, The Three-Stage Theory of International Maritime Delimitation: Formation, Practice, and Review, *Law Review*, No. 6, 2016.

34. Yang Zewei, On the Construction of the 21st Century Marit ime Silk Road and the Transformation of the International Maritime Legal Order, *Oriental Law*, No. 5, 2016.

35. Yang Zhenhua, An Analysis of the Basis for the UK's Sov ereignty Claims in the Falkland Islands (Malvinas) Dispute, *Internati*

62. Ma Zhongfa, On Improving the Legal System for China's Marine Development and Utilization, *Guangxi Social Sciences*, No. 1, 2022.

63. Ni Ran, Xie Qingxia, A Study on the "Separation of Three Powers" Development System for Resources in the International Sea bed Area, *Journal of Zhejiang Ocean University (Humanities Editio n)*, No. 1, 2022.

64. Qin Guanwen, Feng Jinlong, The Legal Dilemmas and Goo d Governance Path for Resource Development in the International S eabed Area: A Perspective of a Maritime Community with a Shared Future, *Journal of Southwest Petroleum University (Social Science E dition)*, No. 1, 2022.

65. Zhang Xinjun, The U.S. Imagination of International Comm onization and the South China Sea Order: Sovereignty, Maritime Are as, and Mechanisms, *Oriental Law*, No. 1, 2022.

66. He Hairong, Fundamental Legal Issues to be Resolved for J oint Development in the South China Sea, *Journal of Hainan Unive rsity (Humanities & Social Sciences)*, No. 2, 2022.

67. Sun Chuanxiang, An Analysis of the Proactive Role of Non -Geographical Factors in the Practice of International Maritime Deli mitation, *Wuhan University International Law Review*, No. 2, 2022.

68. Zhang Hua, Judicial Activism in the Development of the UN Convention on the Law of the Sea: An Examination Based on Maritime Delimitation, *Chinese Journal of Maritime Law*, No. 2, 2022.

69. Zhou Jiang, Xu Ruosi, The Evolution of the Marine Environmental Governance Rules System under the UN Convention on the Law of the Sea and China's Response, *Chinese Journal of Maritime Law*, No. 2, 2022.

70. Zhu Junyu, Paths to Improve the Dispute Resolution Mechanism for Resource Development in the International Seabed Area, *Qiusuo*, No. 3, 2022.

71. Yang Zewei, China and the UN Convention on the Law of the Sea for 40 Years: Journey, Impact, and Future Prospects, *Contemporary Law Review*, No. 4, 2022.

72. Jia Yu, China's Contribution to Shaping the International Maritime Legal Order: Commemorating the 40th Anniversary of the Opening for Signature of the UN Convention on the Law of the Sea, *Asia-Pacific Security and Maritime Affairs*, No. 5, 2022.

73. Zhu Lijiang, Wu Junsong, The UN Convention on the Law of the Sea in the Context of Global Climate Change: Rights Challenges, Rule Reconstruction, and Litigation Prospects, *Pacific Journal*, No. 9, 2022.

Acknowledgements